SALMAN
KHAN

Also by Mohar Basu

Shah Rukh Khan

SALMAN KHAN

THE SULTAN OF BOLLYWOOD

MOHAR BASU

PHOTOGRAPHS BY
PRADEEP BANDEKAR

HARPER
NON-FICTION

First published in India by Harper Non-Fiction 2026
An imprint of HarperCollins *Publishers* India
HarperCollins *Publishers* India, Cyber City, Building 10-A, Gurugram,
Haryana-122002, India
www.harpercollins.co.in

2 4 6 8 10 9 7 5 3 1

Copyright © Mohar Basu 2026

HB-P-ISBN: 978-93-7307-614-0
PB-P-ISBN: 978-93-7307-010-0
E-ISBN: 978-93-7307-074-2

Typeset in 11.5/15 Adobe Garamond Pro at
HarperCollins *Publishers* India

Printed and bound at
Replika Press Pvt. Ltd.

HarperCollins *Publishers*, Macken House, 39/40 Mayor Street Upper, Dublin 1,
D01 C9W8, Ireland

To the crowds that still believe in the impossible, who gather every Friday to lose themselves in another story; and to those who build those worlds for them. This book is for everyone out there who believes Salman Khan when he says that the purpose of a movie is to simply make you walk out of the theatre a better person.

The detailed notes pertaining to this book are available on the HarperCollins *Publishers* India website. Scan this QR code to access the same.

Contents

" Mere baare mein itna mat sochna ... Main dil mein aata hoon, samajh mein nahi. "

Kick, 2014

Prologue

RIGHT before the interval of *Bajrangi Bhaijaan*, the hall itself seems to tremble as the surround sound swells. Salman Khan looks at the audience with teary, bloodshot eyes brimming with rage. He has, until now, been calm and gentle, almost naive. But now the storm bottled inside him threatens to let loose.

The audience goes still, which is unusual for a theatre like Gaiety Galaxy, which prides itself on hosting viewers who dance, rejoice and celebrate the experience of cinema. But during this scene, there is silence. You can feel the energy in the air throbbing.

A mute Pakistani girl runs towards Salman and, instinctively, he hugs her.

He then wipes his tears. And it begins.

Salman starts to pummel the goons one after another, a solo war with fury in his fists. The crowd inside Mumbai's iconic single-screen Gaiety Galaxy cinema hall erupts into cheers so loud they almost drown out the Dolby sound system. But through it all one can hear the steady chants of the Hanuman Chalisa rising from the speakers.

Jai Hanuman gyaan gun saagar … Jai kapees tihu lok ujagar ...

Today is Eid. Inside this temple of cinema, men in skullcaps are on their feet, rooting for this devotee of Hanuman, in awe of the man who plays Bajrangi Bhaijaan on-screen. Boys and girls with mehendi still drying on their palms are whistling like they have seen God. An uncle in front of me yells, '*Jeeyo, Bhaijaan!*', as Salman tackles yet another adversary.

And throughout, the chants continue.

You do not sit through moments such as these. You rise with them. You become part of something bigger, collective and unusual.

This is what real cinema feels like. When Salman is at his most sincere, he delivers something that cuts through the slapstick and the swagger, revealing just how much heart he can bring to a film.

Over the years, we have seen Salman's walk morph from boyish and casual to intense, bull-like. We've seen him become a myth. And like all myths, he means different things to different people. And we don't know which version really exists. Or which we will find when we walk into the cinema hall.

That day, standing in that dark hall surrounded by strangers who felt like kin, the myth of Salman could so easily be deconstructed. He stands for pure, unadulterated, joyous cinema, whatever it means for every generation, every era, every audience member from every social strata. It's the kind of cinema that invites everyone in.

When Salman is on-screen, he does not care if you are Hindu or Muslim, rich or poor, left or right. You are a believer in this medium of cinema and it is his purpose to give you what you came for. Entertainment. Togetherness. Paisa vasool, or bang for your buck.

Through the entire five-minute sequence before the interval, the Hanuman Chalisa permeates the hall as Salman demolishes the bad guys.

Two scenes later, standing outside a Hanuman temple, he vows: '*Ab toh hum khud Munni ko uske ghar chhod karke aayenge* [Now I will drop Munni home myself].'

Just a man, a girl and a man-made border that's illegal to cross, so what if a child needs to be united with her parents. He is dissuaded by everyone around him, but Salman says, '*Sab sukh lahe tumhari sarna, tum rakshak kahu ko darna* [All happiness comes from taking refuge in You. You are the protector, so why should anyone fear anything]?.'

I remember the crowd at Gaiety dancing as Bajrangi decides to take Munni back to Pakistan.

Salman's critics are right when they say that his cinema has no logic. That is because it reposes itself on faith. I've been to temples where the Hanuman Chalisa is played on loop, blaring from speakers non-stop through the day. But here, in this single-screen theatre on Eid is when I saw the chalisa come alive. The walls shook. People roared. Nobody flinched at the impossibility of the idea. Because it all seemed possible.

And who better to solidify this belief than Salman Khan? Bhaijaan himself.

What struck me amid all that cheering that evening was the make-up of the audience. This was a Muslim-majority crowd, people who had just come from their Eid prayers. And they were watching India's biggest Muslim superstar chant a Hindu prayer while protecting a Pakistani child and guiding her back to her parents in Pakistan.

There was no discomfort among anyone in the crowd about this. They were united in their love for Salman and what his cinema pulled off. There was no concept too far-fetched, no storyline too absurd.

Salman's brand of cinema erases the lines that reality draws in our lives. It builds bridges where others draw borders. It makes you love those you are conditioned to hate. It is not interested in subtlety. It believes in gestures so loud that they drown out everything else. At a time when the world urges you to take sides, Salman tells you to take a lost child back home against all odds.

There is a reason why Salman is worshipped by middle-aged uncles and college kids, by aunties and neighbourhood dadas, by autowallahs and doctors alike. You do not aspire to be him, but you are inspired by him. He helps people escape their realities into glorious worlds where they can do what's right, what everyone says is impossible, all within the confines of a dark cinema hall.

Like most of you readers, I, too, cried through the film. A lump sat in my chest for days after. I went into the cinema hall a sceptic, ready to laugh at the impossibility and foolishness of Bajrangi's courage, but somewhere along the way, ended up rooting for everything he stood for.

In the last scene, hordes of people from Pakistan break open the gates for Bajrangi to return home to India. He turns around one last time and sends a salaam as goodbye. But as he turns to go back to his homeland, the little girl finally speaks her only words in the entire film: '*Mama, Jai Shri Ram!*' Her voice, loud and clear, goes all the way to the other side of the gate, where Bajrangi stands—and all the way into the hearts of the people sitting in the cinema hall.

Salman made me believe that day that goodness still exists and that we are all capable of it. It can cross borders, it can fight wrong and it can reinforce our faith in humanity again.

This is what makes him the global star he is. He talks a universal language. Cinema at its worst is just escapism and at its best the simplest way to bring people together, kindling faith and hope when everything around is rendered hopeless by unkindness and evil. And Salman is capable of both.

I walked out of Gaiety in a haze that day. More of Salman's fans were queued up with their families for the next show. Somewhere in the distance firecrackers burst in the air. People wished each other 'Eid Mubarak' between hugs, but also 'Jai Sri Ram' as they came out of the cinema.

It's been a decade since that day, and that was perhaps the last time I saw people celebrate each other with such warmth. Every morning in 2025 I have opened my phone to news of violence and hate—loud, cheap, despicable. It seems easy to slide into this endless, exhausting narrative of hatred.

Love, on the other hand, takes courage. Which is something I have rarely seen on-screen since that day at Gaiety. I have never experienced that feeling again.

That day outside the hall, as a group of boys danced near the auto stand while a cheap speaker hoarsely blasted 'Selfie Le Le Re', I stood rooted to the spot, soaking in the magic of the movie I had just watched. I do not call myself a Salman fan, but something in me shifted that day.

I smiled.

We were all versions of our fractured selves, trying our best to be our best in a world that seems all too ready to give in to hate. But I realized that day that our souls still held on to a deep springwell of love.

And that people would always, given a chance, choose to be human.

"Swagat nahi karoge aap humara?"

Dabangg, 2010

1

Beginnings

'EVERYTHING about Salman begins with his father. His story is pure cinema if you think of it. He is a boy who was dismissed as lost, drifting in the shadow of a brilliant man, branded a rebel without a cause. But somewhere along the way, he outran the myth he was meant to follow,' a veteran journalist once told me while describing what makes Salman who he is.

To me, this sentence felt like a map to understanding the actor. To understand Salman, you have to understand the khandaan (family) and its patriarch, Salim Khan. For India, he is the architect of modern Hindi cinema. A disruptor, who, along with his writing partner Javed Akhtar, constructed the DNA of present-day Bollywood. He is the man Salman hero-worships.[1]

Salim Khan is a complex man to understand. A boy who lost his mother at eight and his father at fifteen, his life was shaped by loss and loneliness. Perhaps that is why he learnt early on to be stoic, and to wrap his pain up in stories. His hardships would eventually become Hindi cinema's most iconic dialogue: *Mere paas Maa hai* [I have my mother] …'

Salim is a man born to be seen. Slightly arrogant, with an acerbic sense of humour, he is a charmer who always commands your attention.

And his life has been full of experiences. Some that hardened him, some that made him brave enough to believe that no matter how tough the going gets, it is going to pass. Two months after his father's death, Salim appeared for his board exams and passed with flying colours. Even at that young age, he didn't let life beat him.

Becoming a trained pilot, with a hundred hours of flying under his belt, also made Salim a favourite with women. Peers remember Salim as a stud—broodingly handsome and someone who had a way with words. He was great at cricket, like his elder brother Abdul Hafeez Khan, who even played in the Ranji Trophy. His college mates said his coming to college felt like a 'hero ki entry scene'. He rode into the driveway perched on his Royal Enfield, crisp white shirt and tailored khaki trousers perfectly pressed, and sandals. It is obvious that Salman has inherited the effortless swagger and unmissable devil-may-care attitude of his father.

In 1958, Salim moved to Bombay (now Mumbai) in a bid to try his luck in tinseltown. That's what good-looking boys in the 1950s felt drawn to—Mayanagri. It took him two years to land a film, and he debuted in 1960's *Baraat* as an actor. Between then and 1963, he appeared in *Police Detective, Ramu Dada, Professor, Raaka, Kabli Khan* and *Bachpan*. But not everyone is cut out for the big screen, and while he got roles, he knew acting would reduce him to mediocrity—and he wasn't one to be content being mediocre.

In 1966, Salim met his writing partner, Javed Akhtar. They were two people who elevated each other's talents and brought out the best in each other. The duo went on to dominate the next two decades in Bollywood with twenty-two blockbusters in a row, starting with *Haathi Mere Saathi* in 1971. Together, Salim–Javed defined an entire generation, giving voice to the angst and ambition of the youth and turning the idea of a Hindi film hero on its head. With their writing, Bollywood saw the birth of the iconic new-age version of the hero with a vigilante streak that marked the 1970s. Their signature was that they changed affable men to brooding, invariably played by Amitabh Bachchan, starring as the rebellious protagonist who fought social injustice on his own terms. Their films, such as *Zanjeer* and *Deewaar*, gave birth to Bachchan's 'Angry Young Man', a figure who embodied the collective frustrations and aspirations of a restless nation.

Salman's mother, Salma Khan, entered Salim's life in 1958, when he moved to the city. Born Susheela Charak, she was the daughter of a Dogra Rajput dentist. Despite coming from different socio-religious backgrounds, they fell in love after courting for five years. Her father wasn't happy. When Salim went to meet Salma's father to persuade him for their alliance, her father said, 'Every parent wants a good spouse for their children. This relation is not plausible, though you are educated, belong to a good family and your future is promising. You are a Muslim, and this difference cannot be bridged.'[2]

There is a reason Salim went on to become one of sharpest screenwriters India has ever seen. The sting of a lonely childhood and the scars of early loss gave his stories an edge and likely fuelled his art. That same weight bled into his words too. He told Dr Charak, 'There might be innumerable differences between me and your daughter, but religion would never be one of them.' In 1964, he married Susheela, who then changed her name to Salma. The Charaks didn't meet the Khans for ten years, until their youngest son, Sohail, was born.

Their eldest and inarguably their brightest, Salman was born on 27 December 1965 at 10.45 a.m. in Kalyanmal Nursing Home in Indore. Salim was still struggling at that time. It is said that Salman opened his eyes immediately after birth, unlike many infants who take days, even weeks, to do so. While newborns keep their fists clenched and eyes shut, Salman seemed eager to see the world.

Salman grew up witnessing his father's rise. It was also understandable that Salim had limited time to give him in his early years. Javed remembers Salman as a quiet and reserved child, contrary to his present-day 'Dabangg' image.

Salman was raised in the shadow of Salim. The silent, temperamental, explosive parent is a large part of who he is. The search for that elusive approval became a quiet undercurrent in Salman's life.

Much of what we think we know about Salman has been written in bold strokes—the bad boy, the generous mentor, the unpredictable star.

But very little has been said about the little boy who perhaps never stopped looking for approval from the man who raised him.

In that sense, maybe we don't truly know the man so vilified—and deified—by the world.

A lot of Salman's home life was dictated by his father's temperament. Hot-headed and mercurial, Salim's rage impacted his children. In his book *Hall of Fame: Salman Khan*, Biswadeep Ghosh writes, 'One day, Salman and his brother Arbaaz watched a martial arts film for the first time. Excited, they started imitating the moves at home. Their feet hit the walls, leaving marks. When their father saw the stains, he was furious. The boys ran into the bathroom and locked the door. Their father ordered them to come out, but they refused. Angry, he began banging on the door and even smashed the glass panes with a hockey stick. Terrified, the boys had no choice but to step out. What followed was the worst beating they had ever received.'[3]

Salman's childhood was particularly tough. As the eldest sibling, he had to be a shield for his younger brothers as he saw his parents slowly become estranged.

He and his brother Arbaaz (just a year and a half younger) often witnessed fights at home, which only got more intense with time. The turmoil made Salman grow protective of his mother as well.

Salman and Arbaaz became a unit unto themselves. As her firstborn, Salman shared a special bond with Salma. Growing up as an introverted child of few words, he soon became his mother's quiet confidante. His quiet nature was often mistaken for arrogance, pushing him further into his shell. In those moments of solitude, Salma became his safe place—the one person he could truly open up to.

It didn't help that Salim was unbelievably harsh with his eldest son. 'I wanted Salman to excel so that he could set an example for his brothers and sister. I just couldn't accept anything less than perfection from him. I admit I was hard on him, behaved more like a coach or a tutor than a father. She [Salma] has always played a buffer's role when I was angry with him. He shares a closer rapport with her than with me. He can tell her things he'd never dream of confiding in me, he can show his emotions in front of her,' Salim said in an interview.[4]

As a kid, every time Salma would get ready, Salman would hold on to her pallu and run behind her, crying. 'I had another habit. My mom used to feed me yellow dal and chawal. I stopped eating that the day she stopped feeding me with her own hands,' Salman said in an old interview.[5]

Salim often jokes that Salma is the reason Salman is still single. 'He starts dating an actress and a few years later, he starts to look for his mother in these women, which he is unable to find. This is such a contradiction in him. *Pasand aati hai heroine, usme ghuserne ki koshish kartey hai apni mother ko* [He likes a heroine and then tries to find his mother in them]...'[6] Even today, Salma doesn't go to bed until Salman has slept. Her other sons tease her for being Salman's watchman.

So much of who we are comes from how we grow up. The way we were spoken to, the love we got (or didn't), how safe we felt ... All of it quietly builds who we become. Many times, we are all just trying to get back to that one person or place that made us feel okay.

For Salman, it was Salma. Her love didn't have to be earned. She saw him when the world didn't, heard him when he barely spoke. And maybe that's why he has always been so close to her.

At the heart of Salman's bond with his father is reverence—fear, admiration and attachment, all rolled into one. Salman has always believed his father loved him the most. 'That's why I got beaten up the most! I was also the one who messed up the most. I once set 750 rupees on fire! But it's a fact that if there's anyone I hero-worship, it's my father,' Salman said in his first press interview.[7]

Growing up, he idolized his father for being an honest man. No matter what professional slump Salim went through, he always ensured his family's lifestyle remained the same. Undoubtedly, Salim's story is inspiring. He came to the city with Rs 60 in his pocket and became one of the most revered men in the movie business.

It was the early 1980s when Salim and Javed found themselves on the brink of a split after their golden run of twenty-two blockbusters. And it was around the same time that Salim became besotted with the Indo-Burmese actress Helen. Salim calls their love affair an emotional accident. On Arbaaz Khan's chat show *The Invincibles*, Salim revealed, 'First came respect, then came love. She was young, I was young. I didn't mean for it to happen.'[8]

While it is all in the past now, it was speculated upon by tabloid reporters that jar, joru and zameen (wealth, woman and property) caused the Salim–Javed split. Javed had started seeing Shabana Azmi and Helen was in a relationship with Salim. *Amar Ujala* journalist Inder Mohan Pannu said in an interview that the writers had the power to decide the cast for their films. Salim and Javed jointly wrote *Main Azaad Hoon* and pitched it to a producer. Javed suggested Shabana's name as the female lead opposite Amitabh Bachchan, but Salim objected, saying her art-film image wouldn't suit the role, and preferred Parveen Babi or Zeenat Aman instead. The disagreement led the producer to drop the project. The rift intensified with the casting of *Immaan Dharam*. 'When it came to Amitabh to choose a heroine for the film *Imaan Dharam [sic]*, he immediately put forward Helen's name,' Pannu wrote. 'Javed Akhtar had objected to this. But then Salim Khan's dominance showed its effect and Helen came into the film much to Javed's displeasure.' Being almost a decade older than Javed, Salim often had his way. Pannu even narrates the story of the day their friendship broke. After finishing a film's story session, Salim was at the wheel, driving Javed Akhtar home. As Javed stepped out, he quietly told Salim, 'This journey ends here.' Not long after, Javed began talks with Yash Chopra to pen the lyrics for *Silsila*, and with that ended an era that defined the movie industry of India.[9]

The end of the partnership was devastating for the Khan family. Salman, in Namrata Rao's docuseries *Angry Young Men*, described the moment his father came home and announced the news to them. 'I remember when the partnership broke up ... he came home, he was disturbed ... and he said, "Javed and my partnership ... he wants to break off."'

It is almost as if it was etched in his memory. Javed's children, Zoya and Farhan, were relatively young to register the heaviness of what this would mean for them in the years to come. Salman recalled his father telling his mother, 'It wasn't that I was walking to his house, and Javed was standing in the balcony, and he didn't like my walk. Or the track pants I was wearing, he didn't like them. He must have his reasons. If he wants to go, he wants to go. So that's all he said.'[10]

After the split, Salim went through a low of sorts, triggered more by the grief of losing a friend than the mere end of a work partnership. Salman gets emotional and says, 'Dad used to really love Javed saab. And he was dad's closest friend.'[11]

The end put into motion other simmering issues that went beyond merely a professional void. It unleashed a wave of pain that would ripple through everything else, even cracking the foundation of Salim's marriage with Salma.

While everyone had hoped it would be a fleeting affair between Salim and Helen, it ended up becoming more. In an interview with Arbaaz Khan for *The Invincibles*, Helen said she never wanted the family to split up. 'In the beginning [of the relationship], when I would pass Bandstand, I would duck because I knew Mummy [Salma] would be standing at the balcony so she wouldn't see me,' she said.[12]

Salman was taken aback when his father decided to take a second wife. 'It was very difficult in the beginning, when everybody was talking about it. My mother just couldn't take it. It hurt her terribly. She used to worry all the time, go into depression frequently. When she cried, we children used to cry with her,' Salman recalled in an interview to *Stardust*.[13]

She would stay up for her husband to return at night. 'Then gradually she started accepting it. Dad explained to us that he still loved Mom and that he would always be around. I was about ten when it started. It took us some time to accept Helen Aunty. But today, she's part of the family,' Salman said in a *Filmfare* interview in 1990.[14]

Over the years, Helen has grown to be a mother to them. When she was given the Filmfare Lifetime Achievement Award in 1998, Salman, with his brothers Sohail and Arbaaz, went up on stage with her. Salman quipped, 'She is tongue-tied but her sons are not. This is Filmfare's way of saying "Chill out, Helen Aunty. Sit at home, relax and take care of your children!" We are so fortunate we have two mothers, and we love that feeling.'[15]

Earlier this year, the paps spotted Salman giving his mother and Helen a peck each at the launch of his nephew Ayaan Agnihotri's music video in Dubai. A fan wrote, '*Isliye itna bada superstar hai; parents ki dua uske saath hai* [This is why he is such a huge star. His parents' blessings are always with him]…'[16]

On Mother's Day 2025, Salman posted a picture on Instagram with both Helen and Salma, and wrote, 'Thank u dad for the best mothers in the world. To the most beautiful women in my world. Happy Mother's …'[17]

For anyone who has grown up in a typical desi household, love often feels tied to the numbers on a report card. Salman's life wasn't very different. Arbaaz was a star student, but their parents were sceptical about Salman's academic abilities. He struggled with mathematics and often avoided homework. He studied at St. Stanislaus in Bandra. He was an average student but had a flair for creative things. Very early on, he started sketching and painting, and did both portraits and landscapes. Salman was brilliant at sports. He had a natural knack for cricket and was a left-handed batsman and a right-handed bowler.

His teachers remember him as a kid who stood out on his own merit. Despite the tumultuous situation at home, he was well behaved, respectful and popular among peers. Salman was never a troublemaker or a bully. No matter how well he behaved or how admired he was, his growing lack of interest in studies became the most defining concern for his parents.

He was in his early teens when Salim took the tough call of sending him to the Scindia boarding school in Gwalior. It was one of the country's top institutions, originally meant only for royals. 'I always wanted the best for him and sent him to good schools. Since I'm from Indore, I decided to send him to Gwalior. Unfortunately, he didn't like it there. A good education is bound to stand you in good stead, it's something to fall back upon. I'm glad he's made it, God forbid if he hadn't,' said Salim in a 1990 *Filmfare* interview.[18]

Some people are not cut out for scoring top marks in physics and maths. Their interests lie elsewhere. Even the best school in the country couldn't ignite Salman's interest in academics. Within two years, he returned to Mumbai to go back to St. Stanislaus High School.

In hindsight, Gwalior opened Salman up in ways that city life could never have. His father's home in Indore is where he spent every summer vacation. He would ride his bicycle for hours, play with a slingshot and even learnt to steer a horse cart. Evenings often ended at sugarcane juice parlours that were called 'madhushala' (presumably inspired by Harivansh Rai Bachchan's poem of the same name). This childhood home had a large compound, where he and other kids would gather every evening, climb trees and pluck fresh fruit.

Salman was a child of the wild, drawn to the woods and the open skies. He found solace in long walks through dense forests and spending his nights under the stars. His love for the rustic life pulled him to remote villages, where he rode bullock carts, milked cows and drank raw milk. His thirst for adventure was reckless. In his teenage years, he would roar through the dirt roads and the rugged terrain in his Jeep. The visual of him tearing through the countryside, leaving clouds of dust in his wake, was common during their summer visits.

Salman's interest in fitness goes back to his childhood days in Indore. He was a skinny kid, but watching older relatives train sparked something in him. Whenever he returned to Indore, he made it a point to work out at the Christian College gym. The cousins had a ritual—intense workouts followed by indulgent stops at the Aggarwal sweet shop near Nasiha Chowk, where they'd snack on milk and jalebis.

Summer vacation was when cousins and friends got together. It was also the time Salman got to meet his childhood friend, Dalla. They bonded over his ability to impeccably hurl a stone across the river. Salman still checks in on Dalla, who now works as a farm labourer in Bardari village, through his cousin. Dalla recalled in Jasim Khan's *Being Salman* that their childhood was filled with swims in rivers, horse rides and driving tractors through the lush forests in the area. 'We were inseparable,' he told Jasim, clearly moved that Salman continued to remember him with affection. Dalla learnt that Salman had asked a relative to bring him over for a reunion. 'It meant so much to me. I'm planning to meet him this summer,' he was quoted as saying.[19]

In *Being Salman*, the author also quoted Salman's cousin Mubin Khan, who said that he could not count the number of times they had fallen while attempting stunts. They would often break the bicycle altogether. But the bruises would never deter them from taking risks again. Mubin said, 'We would go to faraway places on Jeeps and motorcycles. We often chose mud roads. Sometimes the vehicles would be stuck in the mud. We enjoyed pulling them out of it. The whole gang would jump into the well and swim together. This was the kind of family enjoyment we had.' By the time Salman became a teenager, he was all about rush and rebellion. From an early age, he developed a penchant for stunts. He would fearlessly perform wheel hops and balance his bicycle on staircases.

The streak continued in Mumbai. His teachers remember a major accident Salman had in the tenth standard while driving a Jeep with his brothers Arbaaz and Sohail. Salman broke his leg and was admitted in Bhatia Hospital on Tardeo Road for a month. Everyone was worried about his board exams. But despite the setback, he appeared for the exams and performed reasonably well, scoring an 80 in mathematics.

Aided by the scores, soon he found himself in St. Xavier's College, but by then his heart was already set on the silver screen. His interest and fate lay not in classrooms and books, but in the spotlight. Salman's early experiences now

Salman was a child of the wild, drawn to the woods and the open skies. He found solace in long walks through dense forests and spending his nights under the stars. His love for the rustic life pulled him to remote villages, where he rode bullock carts, milked cows and drank raw milk. His thirst for adventure was reckless. In his teenage years, he would roar through the dirt roads and the rugged terrain in his Jeep. The visual of him tearing through the countryside, leaving clouds of dust in his wake, was common during their summer visits.

seem like an audition for the action hero he would one day become. While others his age were shuffling between classrooms, tuitions and textbooks, he was learning how to take risks, to live life on the edge.

It's in these years that he developed his sense of fearlessness. The reckless abandon with which he threw himself into life mirrored the roles he would later pick up—a man who charges into danger and saves everyone. Through all the chaos, the bruises and the brushes with injury, Salman was showing the world how it would be impossible to tame him.

When kids go through difficult times together, they often form a bond unlike any other. That is what happened with Salman and his siblings. When their parents were going through their rough patch, they knew that whatever was happening at home could only be fixed with time. But they never pretended to have it all together. All of them went through the same ache and the same uncertainty. And somewhere over the decades, that understanding stayed with them—that they didn't have all the answers, but they had each other.

Everyone who is part of the film industry knows that Salman and his siblings are inseparable. But the first time I noticed it was at the Mumbai sessions court in 2015, when public prosecutor Pradeep Gharat, after wrapping up his arguments in Salman's 2002 hit-and-run case, walked over to Alvira and said, 'Salman is really lucky to have a sister like you.'[20]

Anyone who has covered the case can tell you that Alvira showed up week after week, at every hearing, even when Salman couldn't. She was always in the same seat in the courtroom.

And it is not just Alvira. The family has stood by each other through the madness of the world, through all the highs and lows—from Salman's court cases, his spats with colleagues and friends, when his comments on Yakub Memon attracted the ire of people, to Arbaaz's divorce and Sohail's separation—weathering both public scrutiny and personal trials together as a team. The Khan siblings are a close-knit tribe, with Salman leading the pack.

In his son Arhaan's podcast *Dumb Biryani*, Arbaaz opened up about his siblings. 'We are together when there is a crisis. That's when people actually run away from each other. Like Salman and I do not meet that often or communicate that often but if he realizes that I am in some kind of strife, that man is not going to hesitate, whether it is Sohail, me or anybody else. It's not about financial help. I can't help Salman financially because he has enough, but it's not always that—you need emotional support, you need to be there, be there as a listener or guide them ... That's what people lose out on. Sometimes just being there is enough. When people stand by you when you are [at] rock bottom, you've earned people.'[21]

Sohail, who is the youngest of the brothers, sees Salman as a father figure. 'If Salman Bhai walks into the room, I stand up. It is just a gesture of respect,' he says.[22] Arbaaz, Alvira and Salman are more of equals, given that they are almost the same age. Sohail is a bit more pampered and shielded.

Every time he is asked, Salman only has funny anecdotes to tell about his brothers. From how Sohail can sleep through intense air turbulence for forty-five minutes to how he and Arbaaz once threw three stones at him and left him bleeding, he has an array of wacky stories to share from their growing-up years. He skims past the rough bits.

On his chat show *10 Ka Dum*, Salman narrated how Sohail's expression of love makes him laugh even today. 'Sohail sometimes calls me at 2–2.30 in the night and cries, saying, "Salman Bhai ..." I ask him, "What happened? Something wrong? Are you okay? Did you get in trouble? Are mom and dad okay?" And he says, "I just called to tell you I love you." I told him you could do this when I am there also.'[23]

But the family would not have survived the tough times had Arpita not entered their lives. She came to them at a time when they were in dire need of hope. And she was the ray of sunshine they needed.

In the late 1980s, Salim used to see a homeless woman every morning when he went for his morning walks. Occasionally he would give the woman and her daughter some food. One day during his walk, he saw the woman lying dead on the footpath near Bandstand. The little girl was weeping next to the lifeless body. He informed the authorities about the body, but realized that over the years he had come to love the kid. Seeing that she had no parent to shield her from the world any more, he brought her home and, within days, decided to legally adopt her.

The child filled everyone's life with joy at a time when they were grappling with turbulent emotions following Salim's and Helen's marriage, Salim's career lull after his split with Javed and Salman's own inability to land a Bollywood break. Arpita's arrival wasn't just a new lease of life for her—it became a turning point for the Khans as well. They were drowning, and she saved them. It's true when they say that kids can help families find their way back to love again. Arpita did just that.

No wonder she is everyone's favourite!

At Arpita's wedding in 2014, she wrote a heartfelt note for her family. She had every intention of reading it out herself, but when the time came, standing under the weight of all that emotion, she broke down. Tears came before the words.

She walked over to her dear friend, actress Priyanka Chopra, handed her the folded piece of paper and asked her to read it. Priyanka took the mic and addressed the crowd, saying, 'Arpita is afraid she might break down, so I'm going to read out what she has to say.' And then came Arpita's words, simple and heavy with love: 'I am the luckiest girl to be brought up in a family like mine. My brothers are my pillars of strength. Sohail bhai and I shared the same room until he got married. He is like a friend to me. Arbaaz bhai is like my guide, he always told me what's good and what's bad. Salman bhai, though, has the biggest heart. For him, I can do no wrong. Everything I did, he was there to support me.' That night, the famously stoic Salman sat misty-eyed, watching his youngest sibling begin a new life.[24]

Every time you pass Galaxy Apartments in Bandra, Salman's home, you'll see throngs of fans gazing at it. Shoma Chaudhury, in her 2011 interview with Salman, described his home as a typical Pathan household. 'Everything is open and big-hearted in the Khans' household: the hugs are big, the coffee is big, the table is always laden with food.'[25]

Just as Shah Rukh Khan's home is a reminder that dreams can come true, Salman's plain abode stands as the story of a man who, despite making it big, never forgets where he comes from. Salman defeats the idea that fame changes people.

I remember my first time seeing the house in 2014. The autorickshaw stopped outside an obscure building in Bandra and said, '*Yeh raha Galaxy Apartments. Utro* [Here's Galaxy Apartments. Get off].'

Having arrived from Kolkata just a year ago, I was still adjusting to Mumbai's ways. But the one thing I knew about the city was that this was where the country's demigods lived.

But as I stood on the wide road in front of Galaxy Apartments, I blinked at the plain structure, a bit thrown off. The name painted on the building was fading, and it needed a fresh coat of paint.

Rishi Kapoor had once famously said in an interview, 'If you want to know what stardom is, stand outside Galaxy.'[26] But this was nothing like I had imagined a superstar's home to be. It was charming, yes, but in a simple, old-school sort of way. Yes, it overlooked the sea, but it didn't have the tall walls and gilded gates that celebrity houses did.

What I couldn't wrap my head around was why one of the biggest superstars in the world would choose to live here.

Salman is much like where he comes from—uncomplicated, no-frills, a man who refuses to let go of his past. He has come to be loved for not having any pretences. This is a man who can have anything but chooses to stay tethered to his roots. Galaxy Apartments, more than any of his films or interviews, tells you who Salman Khan really is.

There is a story that Salim narrated in an interview, which attests to why Salman never moved to a different home. 'He has no ambition to own a fancy bungalow or building. He still lives in the same flat, just below mine. You should see how small that flat is. Half of it is a gym. There's not even proper space for a wardrobe. Some years ago, we bought him a duplex-terrace apartment at Carter Road. I called him to say, "Now you've got a house that befits your status as a star. Tell me when you wish to move there." He wondered whether his mother and I will join him. When we refused, saying that we're too comfortable in this house, he was upset and said he won't go either. We had to sell that property eventually. That's how he is.'[27]

Whether he admits it or not, Salman is one of the most loved superstars India has ever seen. Yes, he hates being called that. Yes, he loves living in his unassuming 1 BHK apartment, which he used to share with his siblings as a ten-year-old. And yes, in interview after interview he goes out of his way to bust myths about himself. 'I am not a superstar. The way I dress, the way I interact, I don't think I am a superstar. A superstar is a person who thinks he is a superstar in his mind. But I don't have that misconception. I am a normal, average Bandra boy,' he said in a 2023 interview.[28]

But is he really just another boy from Bandra?

A fan, Ashish Mirchandani, who runs a well-known Salman Khan fan club called the Salman Khan Army, decoded this aam-aadmi talk. 'When I was younger, we'd see him on Carter Road. He is the only superstar to treat his fans like they are the same as him. There's no power equation or hierarchy. If you meet Bhai, you'll see how he treats you. He is one of us. He was always this person. I knew one of his schoolteachers, who told me that even though he was Salim Khan's son, he was always down to earth. His father was a big name when he was in school. And yet, he would play with everyone in school. He came from money and luxury. A lot of famous people's children in the school were snobs, but not Bhai. I never forgot that story. I am a Bandra boy, just like Bhai, and I want to be a kind-hearted, warm man, just like him. Every time I cross Bhai's house, I stop and stare at it for a bit. This man could own all the penthouses in Bandra, and yet this is where he lives. If you ask him why, he will say that staying here reminds him that he can go hug his parents whenever he wants. Or he can whistle and call people. He hates tall buildings with intercoms. He just wants to climb a floor and sit with his parents after a long day at work. It is such a simple thing. No matter how far you go, it is always the small things that will make you who you are. No one should be surprised by the fact that Bhai is as loved as he is. Pay attention—it's the small moments that make him big.'

Salman has a rather uncomplicated explanation for why he never moved from his family home. His siblings Arbaaz, Sohail, Alvira and Arpita have married and moved on, but he has stayed. In a 2017 interview he said, 'Ever since I was a child I have taken the same left turn or right turn, and I would not have it any other way.'[29] As kids, the siblings would go to their neighbours' homes and collect in the complex's lawns for their evening games. 'The entire building is like one big family. When we were little, all the kids of the building would play together in the garden below and sometimes even sleep there. Back then, there weren't different houses, all the houses were treated as our own and we would go into anyone's house to eat food. I still stay in the same flat because I have countless memories attached to that house,' he added.

On a December morning, if you walk down Bandstand, you can see the charm that Salman finds irreplaceable. There is an old-world feel to it. Narrow lanes lined with quaint cottages whose chipped pastel walls are draped in bougainvillea. The area surrounding Salman's house is a time capsule. Ashish tells me that the scent of fresh pav from the local bakeries mixed with the briny air hasn't changed. Having lived a few years in Indore and Gwalior, Salman loved the unhurried pace and idyllic charm of his lane.

'I am not a superstar. The way I dress, the way I interact, I don't think I am a superstar. A superstar is a person who thinks he is a superstar in his mind. But I don't have that misconception. I am a normal, average Bandra boy.'

Pockets of Bandra remain oblivious to the frenzied lives of the superstars who live there. Bandra is home to three of the world's biggest stars—Shah Rukh, Salman and Aamir—who live only a few blocks from each other. And each of them couldn't be more different from the other.

Salman's friends come from all walks of life. If one is a farmer from Madhya Pradesh, another is the designer-producer Shabina Khan. Shabina, in a column she once wrote about him, said, 'Salman and I have known each other since our school days. He was in the all-boys' school opposite mine. I still remember him as the kid who had a silver "BMX" cycle in the late '70s, which was a pretty cool thing those days. We would always cross each other's paths while going to school, but we finally got talking only during the SSC exams. We bonded over the infamous exam paper leaks that happened at night (of course we realized soon enough that the examination papers were fake and didn't help us at all!). After class X, we ended up going to the same college. I still remember those lazy, hazy days when we used to sit in front of each other in class during the exams since our initials were both "S.K." and Salman would be asleep in the first hour during the exams because he had to wait for me to finish writing my supplement of eight pages—which he would take from me ...'[30]

Shabina let us in on a Bandra secret too. 'Salman used to have an old, red, open dilapidated car that he would drive around Bandstand to impress the girls. And the funniest thing was that whenever a pretty young thing would walk past, his car would break down. During those days there was a very cool club called the Playmate Club at the Sea Rock Hotel, which we were all members of. Rekhaji, who was a superstar then, would conduct aerobic *[sic]* classes at the Mind and Body Temple at that club. Salman would come to class only to check Rekhaji out in her leotards and leg warmers! It was also at this club that Salman taught me how to swim, even though I was petrified of water! Every Sunday was spent swimming, followed by the buffet brunch.'[31]

Ashish says Bandra boys crushing on Rekhaji feels a bit too familiar. It's a rite of passage. He tops it off with another nugget of Bandra lore. In the 1980s, Salman would spend most of his evenings at a park near an old bungalow in the neighbourhood. That was one of his haunts. About a decade later, this building would become a city landmark. We know it as Mannat today. It's well known that Salman was offered Mannat before Shah Rukh bought it. At that time, Salim had said, '*Itne bade ghar ka kya karoge* [What will you do with such a big house]?'

And thus Salman stayed where he felt at peace. For a man who has a 150-acre farmhouse in Panvel (which is named after his sister Arpita), a beach house in Gorai, an apartment in Burj Pacific, Dubai, other than several other real estate investments, he returns home every night to his 350 sq. ft home, exactly a floor below his parents'.

Films were always Salman's destiny. He may cringe at talk of his stardom, but even he admits that everything good in his life has come from cinema. It saved him. His life panned out in the public eye in extremes, but acting anchored him.

It was clear by the time he passed out of school that studies weren't his forte. Bitten by the acting bug, he dropped out of St. Xavier's College after his second year. 'After all, does a fish have to be taught how to swim? He was destined to join the industry,' said Salim Khan in Jasim Khan's biography of Salman.

At eighteen, Salman had already written a few scripts while also modelling. By the time he turned twenty-three, Salman was a well-known model and caught everyone's attention when he became the face of Campa Cola with Aarti Gupta, who later married the leading ad film-maker Kailash Surendranath. How Campa Cola came about is also a story in itself, a typical Salman one at that. While speaking on *The Tara Sharma Show*, Salman recalled that one day he was swimming at the Sea Rock Club (where he was a regular) when he spotted a beautiful woman in a red sari. Attempting to impress her, he swam the entire length underwater, only to surface and find her gone.

The next day, he received a call out of the blue from Far Productions (now Far Commercials) for a Campa Cola commercial. He hadn't auditioned for it. Curious about how they had got his number, he later learnt that the woman he had tried to impress was the girlfriend of Kailash, the ad director. It was an outstation shoot and Salman was a bundle of nerves. He almost fled from the airport while on his way to the shoot. He felt out of place when he saw Jackie Shroff and a few other actors. It was Aarti who saw him peeking from behind a pillar and convinced him to board the flight.[32]

But he got his first taste of fame in one of Limca's earliest campaigns. The drink was being introduced to a market that was already dominated by Coca-Cola. In the ad, a young Salman, face flushed and glistening with sweat after a spirited football match, held up a bottle of Limca to the camera. Both the beverage and the boy were being positioned as fresh, exciting contenders. Soon after, he appeared in commercials for Double Bull shirts and Hero Honda's CD 100 bike. In the latter, Salman was seen riding through open roads with an easy swagger, as the ad promoted the bike's strength, stamina and fun factor.

Kailash Surendranath has a role to play in Salman heading towards the big screen. In her book *Salman Khan: The Man, The Actor, The Legend*, Devapriya Sanyal quotes Kailash as saying, 'What used to happen in those days was I used to live in Breach Candy. Salman used to come to Elphinstone College and use my house as a base ... We used to hang out at this club called Studio 29 and I made sure that we were all having a good time. We would hang out at night in our house, even if we had early morning shoots ... This went on for a few nights and Salman used to enjoy this quite a bit ... One day I told him, "Salman, why are you wasting your time and your father's money?", to tell him that he should be doing more. But I had said that casually, rather like a joke. He said that it hit him and he never took money from home again. He lived off whatever he made through his modelling and other projects. In that sense, I must have been an example, as I was working from an early age. To Salman, family has always been very important and he is working selflessly and tirelessly to support them.'[33]

His modelling acts caught the attention of Bollywood bigwigs. Leading star Jackie Shroff recalls noticing a seventeen-year-old Salman. 'Salman was just 17 years old and he was getting to know the world of showbiz at that time. Me and Sanjay baba (Sanjay Dutt) used to see this kid and how he used to style, and slowly, he also started modelling. I saw his photos while working with his father and I showed them to my directors and he started getting roles,' he said.[34]

Salman's journey in films began behind the scenes. He was an assistant director on *Falak* (1988), which starred Jackie Shroff and was directed by Shashilal K. Nair. The film was written by Salim Khan. It bombed at the box office. After that Salman went from producer to producer asking for a gig. While he wasn't exactly a fresh face—he was a well-known model by then—to producers he wasn't established enough to get budgets rolling. Unlike 2025, when nepotism is reason enough for studios such as Netflix to bankroll a film such as *Nadaaniyan*, producers back then expected debutants to bring in the X factor on-screen and do their fair share of hard work.

Being an outsider himself, Salim strictly advised Salman to not use his name to secure work in the industry. While Sunil Dutt and Rajendra Kumar were producing major films to launch their sons, Salman was struggling to find an opportunity on his own. Salim clearly told Salman he could not afford to lose money on a home production.

Salim, headstrong in his beliefs and an industry veteran by then, didn't think recommendations would help in the long run. As a man who had seen the highs and lows of the industry business, he knew that one would have to stand on their own to make it big. 'I have neither recommended my son to anybody nor ever planned to make a launch movie for them. I felt if they have the talent, people will take notice.'[35]

Salim felt there were many examples where parents made movies to launch their children, but nothing came of them. 'Only those with talent excel and the rest go nowhere. How many times can you make a movie to support your progeny? Nothing helps if the public does not accept you. One cannot give any explanations for the public's preferences. We have seen many times one of two siblings becoming a star and another failing, despite both of them being equally talented. For example, Ashok Kumar and Kishore Kumar were superstars, but Anoop Kumar could not make it big,' Salim said.[36]

So struggle was the only way forward for Salman. Salim would joke with Salman, 'I haven't even put money on horses after coming to Mumbai—how can I invest in a donkey like you?'[37]

But then, there is this famous insider theory in Bollywood: If the camera likes you, you'll invariably end up in front of it. Choreographer-turned-film-maker Ahmed Khan, too, believed this about Salman. 'You put him in the frame and he lights up the scene,' he had told me once. Salman's most-loved collaborator, Sooraj Barjatya, agrees. But his first director, J.K. Bihari, didn't have the same feelings about the young actor then. His casting for *Biwi Ho To Aisi* was a stroke of luck.

In a 2014 interview, Salman narrated the story of his first break. 'He [Bihari] was desperate as nobody was coming for an audition for the film. His office was more like a garage. Bihari said he would sign anybody who would enter the building and ask for a role. "Don't think I am impressed by anything in you, you are not getting this role because you are Salim's son. I had decided whosoever would be the next entrant would be my man," he said. I could only say "Thank you, sir" in reply.'[38]

Biwi Ho To Aisi hit theatres on 22 August 1988. Salman, then only twenty-two years old, watched it at a trial with Arbaaz and hated every minute of his performance. The film ran for five weeks, but he was convinced he had failed as an actor. 'The more people see it, the faster they'll forget me,' he thought.

For a young Salman, it felt like the curtains had dropped before the show had even begun. He even asked his father to write him a script.

Salim refused.

Whether we admit it or not, most of us carry our parents inside us. Sometimes in how we speak or walk, and often in the way we see the world. Even our politics, our sense of right and wrong, whom we empathize with, begins at home. But in most South Asian families, the father–son bond has fewer words and more silences. Fathers are providers and mothers are the ones who nurse our emotional lives.

For Salman, Salim's silence was initially a gap but later became a gift.

In a candid interview, Salim gave his perspective on parenting Bollywood's most wild child and how he tried to keep him grounded. 'In our culture, or at least the culture I come from, fathers don't praise their children openly. There's a sense of pride when somebody else says good things about them. So, if you are expecting to hear something flattering about Salman, let me warn that you've come to the wrong person. I'm not the sort of dad to say, "My son is a genius."'[39]

Salim in the same interview talks about Govinda being far more versatile than Salman. He discusses criticism of Salman, speaking of the times he felt his son's behaviour was wrong. It was refreshingly candid, especially in an industry where veterans talk up their children. Salim left the fate of Salman to the public. Because he believed that hardships were character-building in nature.

Salim spoke of the similarities between him and Salman. 'I've been Salman's role model. A father is his son's first hero. He is an important influence, especially in the son's personal development, his habits and social behaviour. Salman used to hear tales of my Indore days, how I rode a motorcycle, wore clothes, walked and talked. In his twenties, Salman was exactly like me. At that age, I lived an adventurous life, full of thrill and excitement. When you are young, you're wild and reckless. Not that we harmed others. Salman, in some ways, was living my life.'[40]

Over the years, as Salman's stardom grew, Salim began to feel more connected with his son because of their experiences and mistakes. He began to feel a sense of empathy and forgiveness towards Salman. 'I was one of those fathers who threw his children into the water. I wanted them all, especially Salman, being the eldest, to grow up on their own,' Salim added.[41]

Salman, despite being an industry kid, didn't have a godfather. Salim, despite being an auteur in his field, never involved himself in the script narrations of Salman's films. From the very beginning, he encouraged Salman to make his own decisions. Salman made his share of mistakes and missteps, fell hard and rose big, but Salim allowing him that autonomy was crucial in helping him become his own person. Salim believes he has learnt from each of his falls, and that's where the stardom of Salman comes from. 'There's a difference between climbing and growing. Climbing is instant, whereas the process of growth is slow. Salman has grown, not climbed, into this position. It has been slow going ... Compared to the other Khans, Aamir and Shah Rukh, his track record has been somewhat inconsistent. Though all the Khans are highly appreciated and command huge fan followings, Salman is loved. That's the difference between him and the other Khans. There's an extra something that he has. Honestly, I don't know what that extra something is. Maybe people find him kind-hearted. Or, it could be his simplicity.'[42]

Salman's story of becoming a star begins with a son negotiating what it means to be his father's son and doing right by him! Living up to Salim's legacy without an ounce of support from him was meant to be his trajectory. But who would have thought that without even realizing it, he was going to outshine his hero?

Salman is Bollywood's ultimate wild card. Just when you think he has run out of steam, he bounces back, leaving everyone surprised. Before every release, distributors wait with bated breath, hoping that this industry Superman will rescue them.

When critics wrote him off after a series of flops—*Marigold* (2007), *Yuvvraaj* and *God Tussi Great Ho* (2008)—he bounced back with

Wanted (2009). When they said his films were critic-proof, he left them weeping with *Bajrangi Bhaijaan* (2015). In fact, Salman might just be the most frequently written-off superstar of our times, but the very fact that he perseveres feels like a magic trick in itself.

Earlier in 2025, when *Sikandar* underperformed at the box office, the trade was quick to whisper that perhaps Salman needed to take a break and rethink his choices like Shah Rukh did after *Zero* (2018). Bollywood can be unforgiving. Even to those who have given it decades of hard work. At every blip, the biggest stars are told it's the end of the road for them.

And yet Salman endures.

This began as early as 1988, long before his superstardom. Salman's friend Mohnish Bahl bluntly told him he wouldn't make it in the industry. The attrition rate, even for industry kids, wasn't great—and as veteran actor Nutan's son, Mohnish knew that. Mohnish's first few films were washouts and he was disillusioned by the industry. Salman's film, *Biwi Ho To Aisi*, had done well, but Salman was dejected.

Mohnish told Salman that he was short, looked like Sanjay Dutt so producers wouldn't find anything novel about him and even that his own family didn't think he would go anywhere. 'I thought *Biwi Ho To Aisi* would be my first and last film,' Salman admitted in an interview.[43]

At that time, Aamir Khan, another Bandra boy, had become a sensation with his romantic drama *Qayamat Se Qayamat Tak (QSQT)*, which was written and mounted by his uncle Nasir Hussain, director of iconic films such as *Yaadon Ki Baaraat* and *Teesri Manzil*. The film served as a launchpad for two people: Aamir and Nasir's son Mansoor, who directed the film. A few lanes away, Salman would tell himself it would never happen for him! 'It was a big bojh on my chaati [burden on my chest]. I felt if I didn't do well, I would be screwed. I was like *Bandra main toh koi nahi puchega toh Bhayandar main jaake rehna padega* [No one will ask for me in Bandra, so I'll have to live in Bhayandar].'[44]

All Salman wanted back then was to earn Rs 10,000 a month, just enough to stash in the bank and return to writing or modelling. His first salary? Rs 75, for dancing at the Taj Hotel, a gig a friend dragged him into. The numbers feel laughable today, especially considering that even his biggest flops limp their way to Rs 200 crore.

Fame of mythic proportions was never the plan. Salman stumbled into the industry with no plan, no blueprint, no manic hunger for fame, no long-term strategy. As he once said at the launch of Sania Mirza's autobiography, *Ace against Odds*, 'Stardom was in my destiny.'[45]

Perhaps he is right. How else can we explain that the very film he was desperate to escape ended up changing his life? In the movies, destiny has a way of making you the hero you never planned to be. In 1989, Sooraj Barjatya's *Maine Pyar Kiya* launched him as the leading man and introduced us to his most affable and unforgettable avatar, Prem.

"Agar tum mujhe yun hi dekhti rahi, toh tumhe mujhse pyaar ho jayega. "

Hum Dil De Chuke Sanam, 1999

2

Prem

'WHY would Salim saab's son work with me?' was director Sooraj Barjatya's first thought when Salman's name was suggested to him for *Maine Pyar Kiya*. Shabana Dutt, a model who had worked with Salman in a Lakhani footwear commercial, had floated the idea to Sooraj. Shabana had auditioned to play the female lead in the film, which didn't work out for various reasons, but she played a crucial part in the creation of one of the most iconic director–actor partnerships in Hindi cinema.

To understand how Salman became the iconic Rajshri hero Prem, one needs to know the man who served as the inspiration behind the character. It might surprise you, but the real Prem is perhaps Sooraj himself. When you meet Sooraj, you quickly realize that he embodies the quiet calm and simple charm of Prem. There is something serene about him, and that is beautifully adapted and translated by Salman in his many avatars that Sooraj sketched for him after their first hit together.

Though Sooraj's family came from the movie business, no one had yet attempted film-making. 'We [the Barjatya family] operate from

31

the idea that money needs to be multiplied. Film-making, in that sense, is a gamble,' Sooraj told me.

But very early on, Sooraj knew movies were his calling. His family was one of the biggest distributors in the industry, and in 1962 they set up a production studio, Rajshri Productions. Having grown up listening to stories, Sooraj pleaded with his family to let him make a film.

It turns out that the family business of producing and distributing films was on a decline when Sooraj was spinning these elaborate dreams. 'My directorial debut was made to launch me as a last resort to resurrect Rajshri,' he said. It was a do-or-die situation.

His father, Rajkumar Barjatya—or Raj Babu, as the industry remembers him as—gave him the chance to make one film.

Raj Babu was of the belief that love stories should be made by young people. 'So he told me, "Do it your way … We are there to guide and correct the screenplay, but you put your thoughts into it." He didn't allow any other writer. He said I should write in Hindi. He allowed me to do the movie and allotted us a budget,' Sooraj said.

And that was how Prem was born.

Salman went for that audition knowing he would decline the film. There was already a presumption about the film in his mind. The palette of piousness the production house was known for didn't appeal to him—he didn't want to wear a dhoti for any film. It would take away from his cool-boy status.

When Sooraj first saw Salman, he was shocked. 'He was too short to make the cut for a Hindi-film hero!' Sooraj laughed. Salman had carried his portfolio pictures. Sooraj recalls looking at the pictures in his hand and then looking up at Salman again. 'They say there are faces that the camera loves. Salman's face is one of those. It comes alive in front of the camera,' he told me.

Sooraj didn't know what to make of the narration initially. Salman was nearly sinking into the chair, clearly not too interested. As the scenes moved, Salman started sitting more and more upright.

'"Kabootar Ja Ja Ja" had him,' Sooraj says. It was one of the points in the script when the love story came alive. It was a dream sequence for any young actor. That scene had iconic written all over it.

And by the time the interval point of the narration came, Salman was convinced he wanted to do it.

But now Sooraj wasn't sure if this was the hero he wanted. The quality of Salman's voice wasn't that good. His dialogue delivery was feeble and had no throw. The film initially had elaborate dance sequences. Salman brought in his friend Farah Khan to help him with the screen test. 'I put on "Hum Toh Tere Aashiq Hai Sadiyo Purane" to see if Salman could dance, and Farah showed him the steps. But even after multiple tries, Salman got the footwork all wrong. Farah got exasperated and left,' Sooraj says, laughing.

Sooraj was convinced he would have to let Salman go. In a last-ditch attempt, he tried a scene. He handed Salman a guitar and played Kishore Kumar's 'O Hansini' in the background. Lost in the moment, Salman strummed and hummed with the guitar in his hand. Sooraj glanced at the footage and saw glimpses of Prem. 'I have rarely seen a nod that perfect. That face is designed for romance,' he said.

But soon Sooraj found out that Salman already had a debut film, *Biwi Ho To Aisi*, lined up for release, in which he was playing the second lead. That was a deal breaker. *Maine Pyar Kiya* needed a fresh face. And so Salman couldn't be Prem. There would be no partnership.

Salman realized he would destroy Sooraj's debut too if he tried piggybacking on him. By then, he had watched the rushes of *Biwi Ho To Aisi*. He decided to come clean to Sooraj on his acting chops. But Sooraj was undeterred by the bad acting. His main concern was that this wasn't the fresh face he was seeking.

'For six months after that day, Salman kept sending other actors. "*Mere se better yeh hai, isko le lo* [He is better than me. Cast him]." And one day I decided to go and meet him to tell him that we would not be able to do the film with him. But even there, he had two people lined up for me to audition. I was pleasantly surprised by the genuineness of this man. He was so truthful. And even when he realized he wasn't our choice, he was trying to help me out. That day I told him that he is on for the film. He would be Prem.'

Sooraj and Salman were both going through a similar phase in life. The film was a make-or-break for both of them. Salim's career was on the decline in those years, so Salman knew he had to share the responsibility of taking care of the family.

'We could've given our lives to get this film right,' Sooraj tells me.

With Salman on board, the casting for the perfect female lead began. 'My father had gone to Allahabad to look for a heroine because we couldn't find anyone in Mumbai. While travelling he picked up a magazine that had a photograph of Bhagyashree Patwardhan, who was the [TV series] *Kachchi Dhoop* girl. I was supposed to go to Chennai to meet actress Neelam. I was planning to sign her on if she agreed to do the film. But Dad told me to wait, since we knew Bhagyashree's family through one of our aunts. We had a meeting with her and signed her on for the film,' he added.

And now he had found his Suman too.

Once the casting was out of the way, Sooraj heaved a sigh of relief. But the chemistry between Prem and Suman took time to build. The first time they met, they hardly spoke to each other. Bhagyashree was shy and Salman didn't want to overstep.

Bhagyashree warmed up to Salman during a photoshoot that the two were doing for a magazine. She was awkward and rather nervous. The photographer suggested to Salman that he put his arms around her and he refused. He told the photographer, 'Ask the lady if she wants me to put my arms around her. You or I can't decide it.' Bhagyashree was touched.[1]

And that's how the two started becoming friends—through consent and respect. Prem's and Suman's on-screen chemistry was scintillating, and it was the friendship that eased them into performing the toughest scenes.

Salman and Bhagyashree were as different as chalk and cheese in terms of value systems. Salman, by now, was already dating Sangeeta Bijlani and had gone through his share of early romances and heartbreaks. Bhagyashree had led a life protected by her parents.

The film's kissing scene was originally scripted as a traditional kiss, but Bhagyashree, coming from a conservative background, was uncomfortable with the idea. To alleviate her discomfort, Sooraj reimagined the scene—

the kiss was portrayed through a glass door. The film's romantic essence was retained while respecting Bhagyashree's boundaries. Salman was in complete agreement with that. Salman's female co-stars have always maintained that he is a man who cares for their comfort before his own. These were the early beginnings of the man he would become.

The co-stars went on to become close friends through the making of the film. In an interview Bhagyashree said, 'My friendship with Salman got really thick, because of one crazy fact. Salman had a common friend with Himalaya ji [her then boyfriend, now husband], and he came to know about us before the entire world. He was the first person to know. We were shooting for "Dil Deewana Bin Sajna Ke" and we were in Ooty for about a month. Salman comes and starts singing the song in my ear. That particular day, we had press on the set, and Salman had never behaved like this. He would nudge me a little bit, come close and again start singing. And I was like, "Why is he trying to flirt with me? Why is he acting funny?"'[2]

Bhagyashree called him out. 'Behave yourself, what's wrong with you?' she said, to which Salman replied, 'I know where the Dil Deewana is happening.' Salman eventually revealed that he knew about her and Himalaya's relationship. He suggested that she call him to the set so they could spend some time together. 'He can stay with me in my room, and everyone on the set will think he's my friend,' he told her.[3]

The actress tied the knot with Himalaya while she was still shooting for *Maine Pyar Kiya*. When she got married, Salman and Sooraj were the only people from her side because her family didn't attend. 'A month after I got married, I was back on the sets of *Maine Pyar Kiya* to shoot the antakshari sequence. By this time, I was completely at home on the sets. I still felt like a new bride because everyone would keep coming up to congratulate me. Salman came out of the blue and asked me if I was happy and had settled down. He was very concerned and kept on asking me if everything was okay. It was almost like he was my elder brother. Because my parents hadn't come for my wedding, it felt very nice to know that there was someone who cared.'[4]

The two never worked together again but remained in touch even after she quit acting. They took the liberty of being candid with each other—

they could say things as they were. In Rashmi Uchil's book *Raising Stars*, Bhagyashree said, 'When ace photographer Gautam Rajadhyaksha did the photoshoot with Salman and me for the posters of *Maine Pyar Kiya*, I was 5 months pregnant. No one knew. I remember Salman saying, "*Shaadi ke baad moti ho gayi ho* [You've become fat after getting married]."'[5] She remembers laughing about it with him later. During one of the sequences when she fainted on the set, Salman picked her up and took her out of the set. That was their bond!

By virtue of being his first leading co-star, a friend and also someone who saw him through his early relationships and in the process of becoming a star, Bhagyashree was privy to his most intimate thoughts. 'At that period of time as we got to know each other he made one statement which I think rings true. He said, "You know what? I don't want nice girls to fall in love with me." So I said, "Why would you want to say that?" He said, "Because I don't think I am a nice guy. I don't think I can stick with one person for a long time. I get bored very easily and till I get this under control, I would want people to stay away. So I don't allow them to come close to me." I think with him it's more the women who have been really after him than him being after any one of them. And like he has been protective about his family, I think he is also extremely protective about his women, so I guess that sparks off possessiveness to another level, which women today don't like.'[6]

Whatever was happening off-screen in his romantic life didn't matter because, together, Salman and Bhagyashree created one of Hindi cinema's most successful films. In some ways, the film's core idea formed the basis of many of the industry's romantic films over the next decade. Love stems from friendship, an idea alien to the previous generation. The line '*Dosti ki hai, nibhani toh padegi hi* [We are friends now, we have to honour it]' later metamorphosed to '*Pyaar dosti hai* [Love is friendship]' in Karan Johar's *Kuch Kuch Hota Hai* in 1998.

Maine Pyar Kiya set the tone for the shift in movies thereafter. What this film, along with *QSQT*, did was bring in the idea of happily-ever-after after a decade of the Angry Young Man fighting social ills on the silver screen. In the *India Today* cover story dated May 1990, journalist Madhu Jain wrote, 'Puppy love is beginning to straddle the Hindi screen in what is surely one of the biggest cinematic successes in the last decade. The big screen is lovestruck … Salman Khan and Bhagyashree Patwardhan became the country's sweethearts. Everyone is now playing their songs. Even cynics who initially cribbed about this mushy love story are now eating their words. "How can I go against the nation?" asks director [Vidhu] Vinod Chopra. "This film is like candy. Everybody loves it. How can you criticize it?"[7]

The film, made on a budget of Rs 1 crore (about Rs 20 crore today), went on to make Rs 29 crore (about Rs 800 crore) at the box office worldwide.[8] The film's impact extended far beyond Indian audiences, prompting dubbed versions in English (*When Love Calls*) and Spanish (*Te Amo*). It struck a chord in the Caribbean, topping the box office charts in countries such as Guyana and Trinidad and Tobago. In Peru's capital Lima, it enjoyed a successful ten-week theatrical run, underscoring its wide-reaching appeal. Within the first eighteen weeks, the film had positioned itself as a potential competitor to *Sholay*'s numbers, the legendary hit that held audiences for three years in Bombay. It was a big feat, and a full-circle moment, in a way, for the family, as Tarachand Barjatya, Sooraj's grandfather, had been the distributor for *Sholay*.

I was born two weeks after *Maine Pyar Kiya* released. But I like to think my connection with the film began before I even entered the world. My mother, living in a small town in Singrauli, Madhya Pradesh, and barely two weeks from her due date, fell hopelessly in love with the songs. She would hum 'Dil Deewana' and 'Kabootar Ja Ja Ja' all day, catching them on the radio whenever she could. When the film finally released, she decided, without a shred of hesitation, that she would see it in the very first week.

Great pains were taken to drive this heavily pregnant woman from Singrauli to Varanasi, in Uttar Pradesh, which had the best theatre in the area back in the late 1980s. It was a five-hour journey through roads that weren't linear or smooth, but my mother wouldn't budge. My father, unable to talk sense into her, quietly made arrangements for this big movie date. He isn't here to tell me his side of the story today, but knowing him, he must have been silently fuming about the risk. Still, both of us know there's only so much logic that can work with my mother when her mind is made up.

And so, on New Year's Eve, my mother and her mother, my Didu, set off on what would be their last mother–daughter road trip together. They stopped at chaiwallahs, lingered at dhabas serving chole and parathe, and reached the theatre, which was buzzing with excitement. Inside, they found something unexpected—the hall was filled with women. My mother says it was such a refreshing sight.

'In small-town India, cinema halls had long been male-dominated spaces, and women were discouraged from going to the movies without male company. Movies were a family experience. *Maine Pyar Kiya* broke that pattern; it made its way into the very heart of the masses and brought women to the theatres in numbers the industry hadn't planned for,' she says.

Having come from Calcutta, where movie-going was never quite as gendered, my mother could see this was a turning point in north India. Perhaps for the first time in years, film-makers realized women were not just fringe audience. Soon stories and budgets began to shift; romantic comedies, with their equal billing for heroines, became bankable propositions.

Just a year earlier, *QSQT* had brought young love back into fashion, but its tragic ending left audiences with a bittersweet ache. '*Maine Pyar Kiya*, on the other hand, ended in triumph. Love went through a lot of ordeal, but survived and won. That happy ending gave people a reason to leave the theatre smiling, and in the business of cinema, nothing is a surer crowd-pleaser than hope,' she tells me.

The *Maine Pyar Kiya* frenzy was in the air that evening. Even after the film ended, its songs were being sung. She remembers how the theatre had put up makeshift cassette stalls in the lane outside, playing 'Kabootar Ja Ja Ja' on their battered music sets. The alley outside the cinema hall had a swirl of colour. Bright dupattas, bangles clinking. But mostly the crowd couldn't stop talking about Salman Khan and how he had brought the screen alive!

There was a collective sigh from the female audience on his entry sequence, my mother tells me. For many of the women there, this was their first encounter with a hero who was the boy next door. Fresh-faced, with a shy smile, yet radiating charm. Salman didn't carry the swagger of the older generation of leading men—he blushed, stumbled and somehow made vulnerability look heroic. The effect was electric. This was a new kind of male presence in Hindi cinema. *Maine Pyar Kiya* struck a chord with these very small-town women, who were used to being on the fringes. They saw themselves in Bhagyashree and hoped for a Salman who would fight for them!

My mother's childhood friend, Sharmishtha De, tells me that seeing Salman made her go weak in the knees. 'Salman was gorgeous, almost unfairly so. There was a softness to his face that made him instantly approachable. He had an undeniable magnetism. His eyes carried both mischief and sincerity, and the camera seemed to drink him in. This was a whole different standard of beauty. We were all like: Step aside, the brooding masculinity of Vinod Khanna or the towering energy of Amitabh Bachchan. Salman brought with him a boyish radiance and a fresh-faced vulnerability that could disarm you in a heartbeat.'

Word of his looks travelled fast. Suddenly, women across age groups—teenagers, young mothers, even elderly aunts—were making plans to 'see this new boy' at the cinemas. He had a refreshing innocence. My mother tells me, 'Everywhere, from family dinners to college corridors, the question echoed, "Who is this beautiful new man in tinseltown?"'

The love of fans aside, *Maine Pyar Kiya* earned Salman heaps of praise from his own father, something he had always strived for. He saw the rushes of the film late one night. Salman was standing at the door, waiting for his reaction. He called him in and asked, '*Kya lagta hai tujhe, tu star banega* [So you think you are going to be a star]?' Salman looked at him. Salim smiled and patted him on the back, saying, 'You are going to be a cult figure.'[9]

Salim's words were prophetic. Almost overnight, his son became a superstar. It is also serendipitous that Sooraj Barjatya, whose father had launched the career of a young Salim Khan when he had first arrived in Bombay from Indore, was now giving Salman this break into stardom.

Within days of *Maine Pyar Kiya*'s release, Salman became the new sought-after face in Bollywood. The frenzy around him eclipsed even the year-old *QSQT* phenomenon. Aamir Khan had become the poster boy for youthful romance in 1988, but Salman's arrival shifted the audience's focus. Where Aamir's charm was his affability and chocolate-boy looks, Salman brought a rare combination of beauty, vulnerability and mass appeal. His posters adorned both hostel walls and family kitchen cupboards, stitched inside school notebooks and framed in bedrooms across the country.

Renowned British chef Romy Gill, who was a young girl living in West Bengal's Burnpur back then, tells me that she was completely smitten with Salman. 'I remember watching *Maine Pyar Kiya* around a hundred times at the theatre! It was the year I fell in love with Salman, so you can imagine why the film meant so much to me. My friends and I used to skip college to go watch it over and over again. My dad's colleagues saw us once and reported us, and we all got a good telling off from our parents. But for the love of Salman Khan, this was a small price to pay.'

But why *this* film? A 1990 *India Today* piece speaks of a 'generational sweep', noting that, every decade, audiences look for a fresh icon. 'Every ten years, the audience says, "Hey, I've changed,"' the article observed.[10] That's why *QSQT*, and a year later *Maine Pyar Kiya*, struck such a deep chord. Their success was the audience's way of declaring a fresh appetite. The faces were new, the romance felt unjaded and the emotions belonged to the new milieu. In many ways, the same sentiment holds true even in 2025. The big summer release of 2025, *Saiyaara,* has critics scratching their heads, but the truth is simple—films about puppy love, about heroes pining and holding on to impossible hopes, will always find an audience.

I remember asking Mohit Suri before *Saiyaara* released why he thinks this package works. He had an interesting take. He said, 'What I've realized over the years is that while the ways we communicate in love have changed, the emotions themselves haven't. Whether it's a break-up letter in an old film or a one-line DM saying "It's over", it hurts in the exact same place in your body. The butterflies you feel when you get a love letter or a message ... they flutter in the same spot. The medium changes, the language changes, but the feeling is eternal. Relationships were never uncomplicated, not even then. Everyone has a love story, sometimes one they've never told. The joy of telling love stories is not about taking you back in time, but about making you rediscover that longing, to remind you that we all still want to fall in love.'

The emotions a love story rouses in you and the triumph of young love against all odds—that's what made *Maine Pyar Kiya* such a phenomenal success.

Rushika Vora, a homemaker now settled in Doha, Qatar, was nineteen when the film was released. Ratifying this theory, she tells me, 'The innocence of Prem and Suman is something I yearned for in those days and sought in life thereafter. I craved being swept up in love, as shown in that movie. It showed us the tenderness of love—I wanted the silent glances, the stolen letters, a pigeon delivering messages. Even now when I watch the film, I think of the time when love wasn't so rushed as it is these days. The film captures that ache of wanting to be seen, to be chosen, to fight for love when the world said no and winning despite all odds. The first thing we latched on to was the film's music, but then, in Prem, most of us found our first love. I was so smitten with Salman that all the walls of my room were covered with his pictures. People who say Hrithik Roshan is the most beautiful actor have either never seen a young Salman or don't remember what he looked like back then. That iconic black jacket Salman wears (which was inspired by Tom Cruise's in *Top Gun*) pretty much became a symbol of 1990s' romance. After I got married, it was the first gift I gave my husband. And very early on in our relationship, I'd demanded that a pigeon bring me a love note from him. I am still waiting for that to happen.'

Just as Raj became inseparable from Shah Rukh, Prem became inseparable from Salman. Prem became a prototype for women on the marriage market. Funnily enough, many of the film's fans wouldn't even know that Prem wasn't the first choice of name for the character. For months, Sooraj was unsure what to call his hero, and eventually settled on 'Prem' because it was the name of the protagonist in *Dulhan Wahi Jo Piya Man Bhaaye*. An eighty-three-year-old matchmaker from Patna, Sunita Jha, tells me, 'The name became such a rage that men named Prem started getting far more marriage proposals than others. Women sought out Prem. The name stood for decency, stability and a romance untouched by cynicism.' Sunita says that between 1989 and 1991, she got more than twenty-nine women from Bihar married to men named Prem.

The name is in demand even today. Tiasha Karen, a twenty-one-year-old student of political science, says that she understands this character of Prem intimately. Living in the times of dating apps and flaky relationships, she is pretty certain Prem is the ideal type for her. 'Prem isn't a very complex character, but he's a total female fantasy. He's designed to appeal to women, which is pretty rare in Bollywood. Even in romantic films, which women usually enjoy more, the hero is often created to impress male audiences too. Usually, in romcoms, the hero and heroine first spar, and the hero often derides the heroine. But Prem is different. He is never rude or condescending with Suman. He doesn't insult the heroine's intelligence or try to overpower her, which is often done to please male viewers. Even in Sooraj's next film, *Hum Aapke Hain Koun..!* (*HAHK*), you'll see Nisha winning most of their games and pranks, while Prem ends up apologizing to her even when he doesn't need to. This is refreshing even today, because quite often films show harassment as love. Prem is also shown as the ideal son—kind, well behaved, obedient and keeping the family together at all costs. And that is so rare in men these days. Just a simple, kind guy who is also someone your folks approve of. I am not in favour of rebelling for love. My parents aren't stupid that they'll reject a good man for something silly. If they tell me a man is a red flag, I look carefully. But imagine if I took Prem home, life would be so much easier for all of us.'

And just like that, Salman became the nation's heart-throb. 'When love wins in the end, it gives people hope that it can happen for them too,' says Rashika Uppal, a media manager based in Singapore who has watched *Maine Pyar Kiya* at least fifty times.

Six years before Shah Rukh's Raj held out his hand to Simran from a moving train in *Dilwale Dulhania Le Jayenge*, Prem from *Maine Pyar Kiya* asked Suman's permission before applying medicine on her leg and promised to keep his eyes closed as she hitched up her skirt to let him do so. 'There was an unwavering honesty and a willingness to earn love, not just fall in it,' Rashika says. 'In the pantheon of romantic heroes in Indian cinema, Prem stands tall. He was the driving force behind the seismic shift in Bollywood's portrayal of love in the decades to come. He was, in many ways, the prototype of the new-age romantic hero. He was sensitive, family-oriented and rooted in tradition, yet unafraid to step up for love.'

The year 1989 marked a pivotal moment in Indian cinema. *Maine Pyar Kiya* shattered notions. It came as a surprise to everyone because the director, the actor and the actress were all new.

Sincerity was at the core of Prem's mass appeal. When Suman's father challenges Prem to prove his love through physical labour, Prem doesn't flinch. He accepts the challenge, hauling sacks of cement at a construction site to prove he is worthy of his daughter. Aashna Jha, a schoolteacher in Ranchi, believes Sooraj Barjatya redefined masculinity with Prem. 'In contrast to many romances of the 1970s and the 1980s, often steeped in rebellion or force, including *QSQT*, *Maine Pyar Kiya* presented love as a deeply moral, familial pursuit. Prem's story became a template. He was among the first mainstream heroes to place the woman's agency and family approval at the centre of the narrative. He didn't want to elope. He wanted to belong. In doing so, Prem made way for Raj, who would carry forward the same ideals, albeit with a more Western flair and mischievous wit that Shah Rukh infused into the character. Where Prem was raw and grounded, Raj was cosmopolitan and charming. But they were both cut from the same cloth—young men who revered love and were willing to go the distance to honour it within the bounds of tradition.'

It was interesting to hear the myriad versions of their love for Prem from fans of Salman. Usually they love to talk action and punches. It has only been a year since I spoke to Shah Rukh's fans about Raj and Rahul for my last book. Do I agree that Raj and Prem are the same at their very core, as Aashna says? Perhaps. They are both men willing to make the effort and go the extra mile to win over the women they love. But so much of how that plays out depends on the actor. My own memory of watching *Maine Pyar Kiya* is hazy. I never quite warmed up to the movie because I never understood it the way my mother's generation did. But Prem, as played by Salman, has always worked for me. I am not subtle about the fact that I am a big sucker for romances and romcoms. And one of my guilty pleasures is watching *Hum Saath-Saath Hai*. I fast-forward to the parts showing Prem and Preeti, played by Sonali Bendre. Their shy romance is so delightful, and I find Prem's quiet nature charming. There's a gentleness to the way he loves, and a lot of their relationship plays out without dialogues and too many words. And Salman plays up the silence beautifully. He makes Preeti feel like she matters. That, to me, is far more romantic than any grand gesture.

A lot of my love for Prem, be it from *Hum Aapke Hain Koun..!* or *Hum Saath-Saath Hain*, is because of Salman himself. My love for most of the scenes from the former, including the one the title is derived from, comes from my deep love of the slightly awkward smile, the way those eyes soften when he looks at the woman he loves … It's impossible to not get pulled in. Prem doesn't feel like a fantasy prince—he feels like someone you could actually be with if only you were lucky enough. Salman's shy smiles, stolen glances and the expression of a love that builds slowly, almost tenderly, is absolutely my jam. And Salman as Prem is the movie equivalent of comfort food.

Film critic Mayank Shekhar, who is the entertainment editor of the Mumbai tabloid *Mid-day*, is of the belief that Sooraj Barjatya is the real Prem and Salman is merely a vessel conveying his ideas and beliefs to the audience. Sooraj disagrees. 'I am the writer, but it's Salman Bhai and me pitching in 50-50 to make the character. I go to him with a straight scene and he adds the mischief in it. He adds the blushing. The nuances and the spice are all him,' he says.

Well, whatever they did together to construct Prem, they got it right. Almost every time!

The early 1990s was a period of drastic socio-economic change in India. Satellite television was making Western pop culture more accessible. Urban aspirations were growing. Against this backdrop, Hindi cinema was changing fast. Romance was becoming more aspirational, less fatalistic. The idea of romantic love, once considered rebellious, was being repositioned as a legitimate life choice. And the first to catch on was *Maine Pyar Kiya*, because *QSQT* didn't allow its lovers to live happily ever after. Romance had always been central to our cinema, but through the 1970s, the arc of the hero changed to someone seeking revenge for something that might have happened to his family because of the villain. But by the late 1980s and through the 1990s, the films started focusing on romance as the central track instead of relegating it to a side story.

That period witnessed a romantic reawakening of the industry. Hollywood was undergoing its own romcom renaissance. Films such as *When Harry Met Sally* (1989), *Pretty Woman* (1990) and *Sleepless in Seattle* (1993) redefined the genre of romantic comedy for a new generation. These films explored emotional intimacy, flawed characters and the complexities of modern love. Films such as *Ghostbusters* and *Ferris Bueller's Day Off* gave way to movies that struck a fine balance between charm and insight, giving rise to the notion that romance could be both entertaining and emotionally layered.

India, though vastly different in cultural context, mirrored this shift as a whole. *Maine Pyar Kiya* was our *Pretty Woman* moment, minus the urban gloss but steeped in traditional Hindi-film melodrama and spectacular music. It used songs as emotional dialogues with the audience. Every track, from 'Dil Deewana' to 'Kabootar Ja Ja Ja', created the language of desi love, rooted in Indian values but with a modern emotional vocabulary.

Maine Pyar Kiya opened the floodgates for a new kind of storytelling. Romantic films exploded in the early 1990s—*Aashiqui* (1990), *Saajan* (1991), *Dil Hai Ke Manta Nahin* (1991) and Salman's own *Hum Aapke Hain Koun..!* (1994). These were all films that put emotions at the core. Salman was the first in a line of romantic heroes who weren't afraid to cry, apologize or wait for the girl to make her choice.

Samreen Khan, a microbiologist living in Toronto, tells me, 'It's tempting to look back at Prem now through the lens of nostalgia. His simplicity, his gentleness, even his fashion choices—everything about him feels like a relic of a bygone era. Prem was the beginning of a cultural shift, the first hero of modern Bollywood who dared to put kindness at the centre of his romance. Without Prem's success, there might never have been any Raj. Without *Maine Pyar Kiya*, perhaps *Dilwale Dulhania Le Jayenge* wouldn't have been received with such thunderous affection. Raj may have had the train and the Swiss Alps, but Prem paved the way for a strong moral backbone. Both defined love for their generation. Way before I started rooting for Raj, I fantasized about getting my own Prem. *Maine Pyar Kiya* managed to wrap the sincerity, melodrama and youthful optimism into one glittering package with unforgettable music. The reason I moved on to Raj was the relatability (he was a bit more Western), but even today, I watch *Maine Pyar Kiya* and *Hum Aapke Hain Koun..!* very fondly. It sometimes seems unbelievable that this is the same Salman Khan who is the action-hero Bhai we all know today.'

Following *Qayamat Se Qayamat Tak* and *Maine Pyar Kiya*, Aamir and Salman emerged as parallel stars—both Bandra boys, sharing a surname and frequently in contention for the same romantic lead roles. This made them natural rivals in the public eye. Salman himself was keenly aware of the comparison. An ad for *QSQT* read: 'Who is Aamir Khan? Ask the girl next door!'[11]

After *Maine Pyar Kiya*, the female fan following went Salman's way to a large extent. Of the many young girls who were smitten with Salman was a young Shweta Bachchan. In an old interview, she admitted, 'When *Maine Pyar Kiya* released in 1989, I was in boarding school, in the tenth grade at the time. We weren't allowed to watch movies in school, so I actually sat there with a tape recorder and I recorded the whole thing on an audio cassette, and I would listen to it. I loved him and I wanted to wear that little cap that said "Friend",' Shweta revealed. Abhishek Bachchan said that he carried multiple such caps from Mumbai to London for her and their cousins. 'I used to sleep with it under my pillow,' Shweta said.[12]

Salman had women flocking to him everywhere. In a handwritten note published in *Blitz* in 1990, Salman wrote, 'Here is a little something I want you guys to know about me. First of all, I have to thank you for accepting me and for being my fans. I am doing and concentrating on good scripts to the best of my judgement, because I know that whatever I do now will be compared to *Maine Pyar Kiya*. So whenever you hear an announcement, rest assured that it is going to be a good film and I am going to give it my 100%.'[13]

In the later years, Salman would become more candid about the film's success and his surprise at it. Of course, he wasn't very confident of himself, given that everyone around him kept saying he wouldn't make it. But as the universe would have it, he did. 'I was really lucky because *Maine Pyar Kiya* did really well. No Rajshri hero has ever become a star apart from me. I was willing to work with Sooraj as an assistant director on *Maine Pyar Kiya*. He had asked me whether he could watch *Biwi Ho To Aisi*, and I obliged. During the screening he asked me, "Why are your eyes looking so big?" I was shocked. I asked him if that was the only thing he noticed. He said that the film was like a screen test and he was confident of casting me in his film. I had taken my family to see *Biwi Ho To Aisi* and, halfway through, they were all dozing off. Later, I took them to watch the first cut of *Maine Pyar Kiya* and they were sleeping in that film also.'[14]

Prem was the beginning of a cultural shift, the first hero of modern Bollywood who dared to put kindness at the centre of his romance. Without Prem's success, there might never have been any Raj. Without *Maine Pyar Kiya*, perhaps *Dilwale Dulhania Le Jayenge* wouldn't have been received with such thunderous affection. Raj may have had the train and the Swiss Alps, but Prem paved the way for a strong moral backbone.

One would imagine that after a hit of the proportions of *Maine Pyar Kiya*, producers would be lining up at his door. But for many months after, Salman didn't have work. He didn't win many awards either, and his co-star ended up getting more love than him. A teary-eyed Salman recalled in 2022, 'After *Maine Pyar Kiya* released, Bhagyashree decided she didn't want to work any more … *Aur wo pura credit leke chali gayi* (She took all the credit). For six months, I had no movie. And that's when a *"devta saman aadmi"* (God-like man), Ramesh Taurani, entered my life.

My father at that point of time paid 2000 rupees and coaxed producer G.P. Sippy to make a fake announcement in a film-industry magazine that he had signed me for a film. GP did that but there was no picture. But Ramesh Taurani went to Sippy's office and paid Rs 5 lakh for the music of the film. It was because of those 5 lakhs that I finally got a film called *Patthar Ke Phool* (1991).'[15]

He even lost out on awards for the film, even though both Bhagyashree and Sooraj won the Filmfare Awards that year. Perhaps PR was never his thing. Recounting an incident from his first award show at an event in 2023, he said, 'I won't take the name of the editor, but it was just after *Maine Pyar Kiya*, so you can figure out who it was. So I was told I should come for the Filmfare Awards and that the award was going to be given to me. So I went there with my father and the whole family. Then the nominations were announced ... Best Actor goes to ... Salman Khan ... I stood up and another name was taken and then another name was taken. And the award went to Jackie Shroff. My dad said, "*Yeh kya hai* [What is this]?" I was to perform that night for the first time. I went backstage and said, "This is something I cannot do because this is not done. I don't care at all." Then the editor was like, "But you'll have to perform." I said, "No, I cannot." And he then told me, "I'll pay you for this performance." I took a substantial amount at that time, and it was five times more than what they offered to me.'[16]

Salman was heartbroken. It was then that he told himself that awards didn't matter. Rewards did. 'I was never interested in awards. Till today, I'm not. I'm interested in rewards. And the rewards are the love and the respect that I get from my fans, Hindi-film audiences and the people of this country.'[17]

Maine Pyar Kiya ended up being more Bhagyashree's film than Salman's. And that's part of the beauty of Sooraj Barjatya films—the women get greater weightage than the men. This was unheard of in 1990.

But after a lull of eight months, Salman went on a signing spree, where he picked up film after film, starting with *Patthar Ke Phool* and *Baaghi* in

1990, and then on to three more in 1991—*Sanam Bewafa*, *Kurbaan* and *Saajan*—all of which turned out to be major hits.

Salman, in a way, also launched Raveena Tandon in Bollywood with *Patthar Ke Phool*. She admits she did the film only because Salman was her co-star. 'When I said yes, my friends were more excited that I was doing a film with Salman Khan and they said, "*Iske baad tujhe picture nahi karni toh na bol de par yeh toh kar* (If you don't want to do another movie after this it's fine, but at least do this one)."'[18]

The love came late, but when it did, it came as a tidal wave of fandom. By the end of 1991, Salman had become the hottest star in the industry. Some even said that his popularity was second only to Amitabh Bachchan's then. Salman remained aware but unserious about his stardom. Once his goal of earning Rs 10,000 was met, he set new goals for himself. In one of his early interviews, he said, 'Everyone works hard, everyone slogs over every scene and film, but it is the luck factor that is very important. Hard work comes second. But to tell you honestly, this success hasn't changed me drastically. I knew I would make it someday, and I still feel that there's a lot to achieve.' For the first time, Salman was becoming ambitious. And he did enjoy the money it brought in. Like every kid from a film family, Salman was often asked: Does he have it easy because he has something to fall back on? In a 1991 interview, he said, 'Forget a room. I don't even have a pillow to fall back on. It all belongs to Dad. And that's why I want to make it big. I want to make lots of money.'[19]

But along with that came rising animosity from his peers. Once, he was asked if he worried about suffering from the Kumar Gaurav phenomenon (being a one-hit wonder). Salman always knew how to use humour to ease the heat. So he replied, 'Wow! Who wouldn't want to be in Kumar Gaurav's shoes? He's got a beautiful home, is happily married, has a BMW, a Mercedes, he's happily settled and has got work. Besides, he's a nice guy. If I'm compared to him, I take it as a compliment.'[20]

At one point Govinda was quoted as saying, 'Salmans and Shah Rukhs were fleeting occurrences.'[21] Salman agreed that Govinda was more talented. 'He is certainly much more talented than the rest of us. He can sing, dance, do comedy roles and even fight on the screen. It is just that he had signed all the wrong films because he wanted to make money.

I'm sure if he signs up with a good director he can be good. I genuinely believe it,' Salman responded candidly in an interview.[22]

The first thing that makes Salman so likeable for his fans is his lack of envy for those around him. It's the quiet confidence of a man secure in himself, which is the result of being surrounded by a set of people who are sure of him even when box office numbers are not on his side. It was this very security that allowed him to do two-hero films, shift genres and even back unknown directors and producers.

When *Saajan* released in 1991, it got pegged as a Sanjay Dutt film—but Salman was not threatened by it. In an interview with *Stardust*, when he was asked about feeling sidelined, he said, 'Sanjay has been my hero and it's great to see him in his best phase.'[23]

However, early success can often make one fumble and lose sight of the larger goal. The same started to happen with Salman. His golden touch began to lose its charm when he picked up films such as *Suryavanshi* and *Ek Ladka Ek Ladki*, both of which were released in 1992 and turned out to be major flops at the box office. Then came *Dil Tera Aashiq* with Madhuri Dixit and *Chandra Mukhi* with Sridevi in 1993. But unfortunately those flopped too.

Salman's uncle, Naeem Khan, said in Jasim Khan's *Being Salman*, 'Salman was overexcited in the beginning and signed many movies without consulting his father. Once he came home with Rs 2–3 lakh and told his father that he had signed a new movie. Salim was very annoyed at this. He said people are using you, and your unmindful approach will ruin your career. He made Salman return the money and told him to follow his advice. Salman was thinking he had done a big deal by signing a movie for Rs 2–3 lakhs.'

By the end of 1993, people were writing Salman off as a has-been. *Andaz Apna Apna* was on the brink of release then. And though the film was out of theatres in three days, it has, in the past three decades, attained cult-film status. Our generation has been kinder to the film than the theatre-going audience back then. '*Yeh kaisa cult hai* [What sort of cult is this]? Poor Vinay Sinha [producer] wasn't able to make a film after that,' Salman has lamented frequently in interviews. It is ironic that in the week I write this, the film is running to packed theatres in Mumbai, making better numbers than new releases today.

Critics have always been quick to come at Salman, but he has a knack for working his magic, especially when everyone else is busy writing career obituaries for him. In 1994 came one of Hindi cinema's biggest hits of all time—*Hum Aapke Hain Koun..!*

When Keshav Prasad Mishra's novel *Kohbar Ki Shart* went out of print, hardly anyone noticed. It was never a bestseller. First published in 1965, its 2007 reprint had just a little over a thousand copies, and those didn't sell either. But what most people didn't know was that this charming little book inspired *Hum Aapke Hain Koun..! (HAHK)*, the first Bollywood film to cross Rs 100 crore at the box office.[24] It was first made into a Sachin-starrer, *Nadiya Ke Paar*, in 1982, but Sooraj's father wanted the film to have a second lease of life, prompting him to make *HAHK*. In both versions, the tragic tone of the original story was replaced with Rajshri merriment. The film tells the story of Prem and Nisha, and how they go from strangers to lovers.

Sooraj took nearly two years to write the screenplay. From its inception to its release, *HAHK* was a four-year journey. 'The first five months I was trying to write yet another *Maine Pyar Kiya*. And then I realized that there was no point trying to repeat myself all over again,' he said in an interview.[25]

One would assume Salman was a natural casting choice, having debuted with Sooraj only a few years ago. Not many know that it was actually Aamir who was the first choice for Prem in *HAHK*. But the actor neither found the script appealing, nor was he keen on portraying Prem, who was yet to become the phenomenon he is today.[26] Salman's career was in a lull and *HAHK* catapulted him to even greater fame than he had known with *Maine Pyar Kiya*.

The lead role of Nisha was first offered to Sridevi, but she turned it down as she was already shooting for the Malayalam film *Devaraagam* then. Eventually, Madhuri Dixit was approached for the part and she readily agreed, having debuted under the Rajshri banner with *Abodh*.

The film was originally going to be titled 'Dhiktana', after one of the songs in the album. The music was the clinching factor. Raamlaxman composed the music, with lyrics penned by Ravinder Rawal and Dev Kohli. Sooraj had as many as fifty sittings to align the soundtrack with the film's emotional tone. The result was a hugely successful album that topped the charts and became the bestselling Bollywood album of the year.

Lata Mangeshkar lent her voice to eleven songs while S.P. Balasubrahmanyam sang nine. 'Didi Tera Devar Deewana' became a nationwide sensation. It was said to have drawn inspiration from Ustad Nusrat Fateh Ali Khan's 'Saare Nabian'. The song featured Madhuri in the iconic purple sari designed by Anna Singh, reportedly costing $18,000 (Rs 15 lakh) then. She had earlier worked with Sooraj in *Maine Pyar Kiya*. The iconic cap from that song also belonged to her. The film was long: It featured fourteen songs and had a runtime of 3.26 hours. Aditya Chopra, after watching the film in a trial, suggested to Sooraj that he take off one song, which eventually helped trim the film.

The film transformed the way Indian weddings were celebrated, and also redefined wedding fashion. Madhuri became a style icon overnight. Legendary painter M.F. Husain was so mesmerized with her that he is said to have watched the film eighty times, before going on to create several paintings inspired by her and, later, his film *Gaja Gamini*.

When the film opened, its reviews were lukewarm. In her book *The Three Khans and the Emergence of New India*, Kaveree Bamzai wrote, 'Indian rituals, nuptials, and an honouring of the united Hindu joint family, critics rubbished it as an extended wedding video. But viewers loved it so much that it became the highest grosser in recent Bollywood history and got many VCR-addicted audiences back into theatres after a long time.'[27] The credit went largely to the music of the film. As an *India Today* cover story, 'Music Mania', from November 1994 put it, 'The movie, which prompted sniggers in the trade pre-release, is the biggest hit in the eighty-one-year history of Indian cinema.'[28]

So what's the magic, the article asked. Songs, songs and more songs— among them the enormous hit, 'Didi Tera Devar Deewana'.

Everyone in the team put in the work to make it the iconic number it is today. It took sixteen days of rehearsals and nine days of filming to be fine-tuned. Sooraj, in an interview, recounted how Madhuri suggested putting Salman in a nighty. 'We wanted to end it on a high note, with a fun and victorious celebration. I suggested to my father that Salman should wear a nighty for the final scene. While Salman instantly agreed, my father rejected the idea, finding it inappropriate,' he said. It was Madhuri who rallied for it. 'All the dancers, including Madhuri, found the idea hilarious and insisted we go with it. In the end, Madhuri herself did Salman's make-up for the scene.'[29]

The playful finger-snapping 'Joote De Do Paise Le Lo' became another instant hit and turned the fun tradition of stealing the groom's shoes into a must-have ritual at weddings across the country. Madhuri's striking green-and-white outfit became a fashion rage, with every corner garment store across the country displaying versions of it in various colours to attract customers. My own family tailor in Kolkata, Hafiz Azim, tells me that he had, in just one week, got forty-five orders for the same outfit. But that wasn't his favourite song, he tells me. 'It was the bittersweet duet "Mujhse Juda Hokar", sung soulfully by Lata Mangeshkar and S.P. Balasubrahmanyam, as Nisha and Prem come to terms with their feelings. It is something I still hum while working. I love that they stitched in the *Maine Pyar Kiya* music as an interlude,' he says.

HAHK initially released in just one cinema in Mumbai (Liberty) and in a few select theatres across Delhi (Sapna, Satyam), Kolkata (Hind, Menoka), Nagpur (Smriti, Panchsheel) and Bengaluru (Santosh, Galaxy—noon shows only). Despite limited screens, packed theatres showcased the film's success and audience demand.

With nearly 7.5 crore footfalls—equivalent to about Rs 1,000 crore net today—*HAHK* became a historic blockbuster. Interestingly, it hit its highest weekly collections in its twenty-second week, with a slight dip only during Diwali week. From the eighteenth week onwards, it consistently earned over Rs 2 crore net weekly—a phenomenon rarely, if ever, seen. Distributors deliberately kept the release selective to curb piracy.

Made on a budget of Rs 4.25 crore, the film grossed over Rs 250 crore worldwide. It became the first Indian film to cross Rs 100 crore in net collections and emerged as the highest-grossing film of its time.[30]

Yes, Salman was the one who set up the fascinating 100-crore club. Everyone else simply joined it later.

In the domestic market, *HAHK* netted Rs 72.5 crore, which, when adjusted for inflation, equates to approximately Rs 711 crore today, making it the most successful Hindi film since *Sholay* (1975). Incredibly, it earned over Rs 1 crore in every territory it was released in, a feat previously achieved only by *Sholay* and *Coolie* (1983).[31]

As mentioned earlier, *HAHK* opened to a sluggish response and was even considered a flop by many within the industry. Komal Nahta of the trade magazine *Film Information* said that despite a disappointing opening, the film remained in theatres because 'the Rajshris are the distributors themselves; they don't sell their film to anybody, so they had the holding capacity. They were so confident: they couldn't care less what people were saying.'[32]

Turns out they were right.

A large part of why the film worked, according to Nahta, was that audiences were fed up with the standard fare of sex, violence, vendetta and action. '[I]t was just our roots, Indian weddings, and plain emotions that made it a big hit,' she said.[33]

HAHK's cultural impact was far-reaching. In fact, the success of the film is an apt inspiration for theatre owners in 2025. With the OTT boom, it is a common belief today that people are unwilling to invest their energy, time and money on the 70 mm experience. A similar conversation was on in 1994, when this film was released. 'The spectacle that *Hum Aapke Hain Koun..!* offered was a lure, and one that proved the medium still had the potential to attract India's middle class. The initial limited release of the film across "quality theatres" was highly successful. The demand for the film inspired more theatre owners to upgrade their facilities to host the epic film. One could almost say this film was what proved there was still a theatre-goer in this country willing to pay a premium for a better experience, and therefore paved the way for the multiplexes that came later,' journalist Karishma Upadhyay wrote in her Firstpost column in 2019 when the film turned twenty-five.[34]

Sooraj poured everything into the film: a story to root for, a family that loves and laughs together, music, memorable dialogues, bonding over hearty dinner conversations—and a dog. He tells me, 'I love taking lengthy shots of good-looking food. It makes people happy. It's part of the package.' The dog, in fact, was a crucial part of the film. He is the reason the film takes a happy turn at the climax. Sooraj tells me that there were two Tuffys on set—one lazy and one energetic. The running shots and the sitting shots were filmed with two different dogs. The energetic dog's real name was Redo and, contrary to popular belief, he wasn't a Pomeranian but an Indian spitz. Dog breeders have told me that the film was instrumental in making Pomeranians popular in India, the way the old Hutch ads made pugs a desired breed in the country. After the film, Madhuri adopted one of the dogs. He lived till the age of twelve, passing away in 2000.

The only exhausting part of shooting with the large ensemble and a dog were the songs. Sooraj would sometimes spend a week on one song alone.

The film broke the usual film-making norms. Sooraj says, 'During the samdhan song, Madhuri and Salman were in the background. And these actors who were perceived as character actors back then took centre stage. To a director, all his actors are the same. I love them equally, and that showed in the film.'

That was the first time that character actors became so memorable in Hindi cinema. Renuka Shahane, as the universally loved bhabhi (sister-in-law) who dies, believes that till date people don't want to see her in any role that does not uphold her *HAHK* image.

The phenomenal success of the film was a clear indication that even as India was stepping into a new era of globalization and rapid economic change after liberalization, the audience's heart remained rooted in traditional values. There was something so timeless about the film that people want to watch it even today. How else do you explain the packed theatres in the US and Canada when *HAHK* re-released in theatres on Valentine's Day earlier in 2025? Despite the influx of Western influences and modern lifestyles, the film's celebration of close-knit family ties and cultural rituals struck a powerful emotional chord with the audience. No matter how much the world around us Indians evolves, we still seek stories that honour our deep-rooted beliefs about family, duty and tradition.

The film ran for a year in London until its golden jubilee, and in Canada it had a glorious platinum jubilee-run. A theatre company in the UK even made a show based on the movie that the *Times of India* film critic Nikhat Kazmi called 'Fourteen Songs, Two Weddings and a Funeral'.[35]

Its impact extended to the next generation of film-makers too. Aditya Chopra and Karan Johar have both said that *HAHK* was a major influence on their work. For Karan, it was this film that made him want to make movies. He said, 'I find there are little moments in the film that I don't know if people get, but I totally got. It was just the way Salman says, "Shit! I love her!"'[36]

But these still did not explain to me why *HAHK* became a record breaker of that magnitude. The more I dug, the lesser I understood. The film dismantled every textbook rule of a good screenplay. The primary conflict of the film appears in the last thirty minutes. One might even call its climax hurried and its closure rushed. One could argue that the film's runtime is far too long, thus running the risk of making it seem boring to audiences.

So why wasn't anyone bored?

Everyone looked unusually happy in the film. It wasn't realistic either, because in those days very few Indian families had the budget for such elaborate celebrations and never-ending functions.

When I asked my friends abroad why they liked the film, some said it took them back to their roots, that they felt less lonely in an alien land because of it.

But it was only when I read *The Politics of India's Conventional Cinema* by Fareed Kazmi[37] did I understand the social context of the film and the answer I was seeking. Kazmi felt that the reason people were so fond of *HAHK* had been erased from public memory because it followed a deeply scarring time. It was released soon after one of the most violent and divisive periods in post-Independence India. The Mandal Commission had exposed deep divisions within the Hindu society. To cover up these internal conflicts, a common enemy—Muslims—was created, fuelling hate and violence. This led to the demolition of the Babri Masjid in December 1992 and triggered deadly riots across the country, especially in Mumbai in early 1993. There was deep cynicism and growing divisions, and this movie arrived like a breath of fresh air. It offered a world of celebration, love, family life and simple joys. Isn't escapism the whole point of watching movies?

The film also offered an alternate reality. By the late 1980s and the 1990s, heroes in Hindi films had begun to hail from rich, powerful families instead of ordinary backgrounds such as Bachchan's Angry Young Man. In *HAHK*, Prem belongs to a wealthy industrialist family. Yet, he and his family are shown as humble, caring and down-to-earth people, making it easy for regular viewers to connect with them. Scenes such as Prem playing cricket with the family's domestic help and mocking the snobby rich relatives helped blur class lines. Pooja, Renuka Shahane's character, taught the house help Lallu to speak in English. There is even a dialogue where the patriarch introduces Lallu to the new bride, saying, '*Yeh humara beta hai* [He is our son].'

The film also snuck in an anti-dowry statement. When Mamaji says they don't want a rich man's daughter, but a simple, loving daughter-in-law, he spoke to a feeling many Indians shared. It was important to convey the disdain for dowry, and the film subtly criticized it, asking people to value love and care over money and material things. By mocking the 'rich class', even though they were rich themselves, the characters distanced themselves from the negative image of those born into wealth.

In *HAHK*, Sooraj reiterates that Indian society is one big, happy family, without caste, class or conflict. Everyone lives together peacefully: rich and poor, Hindus and Muslims, employers and house helps. Even difficult relationships, such as those between in-laws, are shown to be friendly. The two fathers-in-law reconnect quickly as old friends, the in-laws flirt harmlessly and playful teasing keeps everything light-hearted. The film also shows strong Hindu–Muslim friendships at a time when such a connection would have been fraught with real-world political tensions. You might call this utopian, but I secretly wish we saw more films doing this today. It is the need of the hour. The rabid hate around us is all-consuming, and I can't help but think that if film-makers made movies that brought just a little joy back into our lives instead of money into their bank accounts, we wouldn't be telling each other that cinema is dying.

The world needs a bit of Prem, now more than ever before.

Of the many fans I know of *HAHK*, the one I thought of while writing this was my friend Debanjana Moitra, now a television producer in Mumbai. We have been friends for eighteen years, but I wasn't privy to her undying love for the movie until her wedding. Her craze for the film came to the fore only on the day of her sangeet, when her six-year-old cousin danced to Madhuri Dixit's 'Chocolate, Lime Juice'. When she picked up my call, the first thing she told me was, 'Do you know they knocked off that song because it was making the movie lengthy?' The disappointment she felt at this decision still bothers her.

When I asked her the other day, Debanjana retold her story: 'I first watched the film in 1994 at Kolkata's Priya cinema. I was five years old. I went with my mom, mashi [aunt] and cousins. I remember the theatre was packed with women and children. The film became an instant favourite because I wanted to be like Madhuri. I would enact scenes. I would dress like her. Back then I had short, wavy hair like Madhuri's. So every day after school, I would lock myself in my room and stand in front of the mirror with a towel over my head, letting the wind blow my tresses while playing the opening credit song of the film. And I loved Prem. I always knew that when I grew up, I would find myself a Prem. I had always wanted a house with a red carpet running down the stairs. And it so happened that when I got married, my father-in-law [Lt General Gurpal Sangha, former Chief of Staff for the Indian Army's Western Command] was posted at Fort William in Kolkata. The house had a red carpet going down the stairs. Turns out my Prem had found me! I got to live my *HAHK* dream in real time.'

There is a Raj versus Prem debate among women who have grown up on a staple of romantic films in the 1990s. Between 1994 and 1995, after the success of *HAHK* and *DDLJ*, this dialogue unfolded in the living rooms of Indian families. You either fell for Raj's yuppie charm or Prem's sanskari sweetness. There was no in-between.

Raj belonged to Shah Rukh—suave, messy-haired, with a twinkle in his eye that said he knew exactly what he was doing. Raj was every NRI parent's worst fear and every NRI daughter's daydream. He made rebellion look like a class in good manners. Raj didn't chase girls, but convinced families. His love stories were rooted in risk but always came wrapped in reassurance. He was a contradiction in motion, and that's what made him unforgettable.

Prem, on the other hand, was the man you didn't see coming. Prem didn't have to say he loved you—you just knew. Salman's eyes spoke, like that scene in *HAHK* when Prem says sorry to Nisha after both of them tumble into her bed, breaking it, at the end of the 'Joote De Do' song. He wasn't interested in winning over patriarchs by rebelling. He wanted to feed the dog, crack lame jokes with the family, sing songs at every function and, when the time came, quietly step aside if that was what honour demanded. *HAHK*'s Prem was the peak golden boy of cinema: A charmer without having to try, a man who loved through action and not lofty declarations, willing to sacrifice his own happiness at the altar of the greater good. Raj was aspirational. Prem was familiar. He could quietly slip into becoming a habit, and you wouldn't even notice.

But there was a magic to both characters—they were written as products of a time when love stories were about more than just love. They were about values, community, family. That's why Raj could lean into rebellion, and Prem could stay soft but still hold power. They showed us there was more than one way to be the hero. Nisha and Prem, though modern and intelligent, still obeyed their elders' wishes without question. Even though they loved each other and were heartbroken about parting ways, they accepted their elders' choice because they shared the same traditional values. After fainting from the shock of having to marry her dead sister's husband, Nisha later accepts this as her 'duty', saying she will forget her love for Prem. Prem quietly accepts her decision and that of the elders, even while his eyes betray the pain of loss.

Prem embodied this spirit of sacrifice in the second half of *HAHK*. A new kind of hero had entered Hindi movies, someone who could step aside and let the actress shine. Sooraj tells me that *HAHK* was Nisha's story, but that Salman never had an issue with it. 'For Salman Bhai, the story shining was more important than him being the centre piece. He has a fantastic sense of script, which probably comes from his father,' he says.

The film also brought forth the modern woman of the 1990s. Pooja and Nisha were contemporary, educated, spirited, playful. Nisha skates into our hearts (literally) in a pair of jeans and T-shirt, with a cheeky smile on her face, plays cricket, pulls pranks and lives life with an infectious energy. Prem, in fact, became one of the first men in mainstream Hindi cinema to herald a more equal world for both genders when he sang 'Kudiyon Ka Hai Zamaana'—it's a girls' world!

Nisha and Pooja were lively and independent, but also invested in the home, the family and their relationships. The film didn't erase their careers—it simply chose to celebrate their warmth, their love and their ability to make a house a home.

In a world spinning a little faster each day, *HAHK* and its creator Sooraj Barjatya believed that progress and tradition shouldn't necessarily be at odds. Women led the plot of *HAHK*, and this film was the first of the milieu.

But for many who lived away from India, the film showed them the life they were missing out on. Sheetal Karia, a media professional in Canberra, tells me, 'I was already surrounded by empowered female figures, but I was so alienated from my culture. I grew up in Australia, where India was more an idea than a place. It existed in the smell of my mum's chai, in grainy wedding tapes sent from back home and in the awkward attempts at speaking Hindi during the two-minute family phone calls. But I didn't really know what it felt like to belong to that world. I didn't know what Indian emotions sounded like when they weren't translated or explained. When I watched *Hum Aapke Hain Koun..!*, I didn't know what I was signing up for. VHS tapes with fourteen songs. And a story that seemed to revolve around ceremonies. There is hardly any real conflict until the last forty-five minutes of the film. But what stood out for me was Prem. Salman Khan as Prem wasn't an unattainable hero. He didn't fight or command. He giggled. He blushed. He danced with abandon and cried with softness. He was a favourite with the ladies, especially the aunties and the elder sisters. He adored his family, played with his nephew like a child and looked at the girl he loved with a kind of innocence I'd never seen before. There was something disarmingly gentle about him. His love wasn't about ownership or power. It was in the smallest things. Whether he was feeding Nisha ice cream or silently hurting when she was asked to sacrifice her happiness, Prem made me believe that love could be pure. That a man could be strong without ever raising his voice.'

Sheetal talked about the nostalgia that the film evoked. 'The film itself was like opening a window into the India I had never known. The music, the family rituals, the teasing between siblings, the community of friends and family … I didn't know any of it as a lonely NRI kid. That was a culture I was separated from, but it was suddenly made accessible through a movie. And the way it was made, I almost felt invited into it. Watching *Hum Aapke Hain Koun..!* was the moment I realized that my roots weren't abstract—they were alive in those songs and laughter. Prem became my first love. I had a massive crush on Salman Khan. He gave me a version of love that wasn't cynical or complicated. Even today, when I hear "Pehla Pehla Pyaar Hai", something inside me calms down.'

Over time there have been all kinds of heroes who have captured the imagination of the masses. But Salman has always been thought of as the one who truly knows what the masses want. In 1994, they wanted to be soothed by the films they watched. Life was riling them up and *HAHK*

Sooraj Barjatya tells me that *HAHK* was Nisha's story, but Salman never had an issue with it. 'For Salman Bhai, the story shining was more important than him being the centre piece. He has a fantastic sense of script, which probably comes from his father.'

was the escape they needed. When chaos unfurls, everyone enjoys a comfort watch, and for Sheetal and many like her, this film is that lazy-day watch that they know will heal them. And Prem, like his name, is all about love.

I asked Sheetal if she changed gears and moved to Raj in 1995. She told me something I will never forget. 'I did not. I love both equally, and for me Raj and Prem are different facets of the same man. Bollywood gave us two versions of love, and we were lucky to have grown up with both. I sometimes wonder who robbed us of all the love. How did we end up in a world with bare minimum rom coms and men who never make an effort for us or our families? The men we meet today or the heroes we see in our films just can't be the successors of Prem or Raj!'

Salman had become more than an actor by the end of 1994. He was now part of people's personal love stories. For a boy who had once doubted if he'd even get the part, that was perhaps the sweetest reward. Prem made Salman a star.

In the years that followed, friendships would define his choices, risks would test his mettle and a very different side of Salman Khan, one that went beyond romance, would emerge. The perfect boy next door was about to become Bollywood's most unpredictable hero.

"Ek bar jo maine commitment kar di, uske baad toh main khud ki bhi nahi sunta. "

Wanted, 2009

3

A Heart of Gold

BOLLYWOOD doesn't run on talent. It runs on myth-making. PR representatives build personas, journalists sell them and everyone pretends they are real. Well, they are not. And how do I know it? Because I have interviewed someone as unrehearsed as Salman Khan. We know he is messy, mercurial, unpredictable and inconveniently authentic because he has allowed his life to play out in full public glare.

As someone from the press, I've had a front-row seat to the charade of how stars are created. I know exactly how narratives are spun and just how far from the truth they often are. When I'm at parties and someone gushes 'Oh, he/she's so warm!' about a Bollywood celebrity, more often than not, I can't help but roll my eyes. It is hard to be anything but disdainful towards most of them, because everything they sell you is make-believe. It's performance all the way. I've watched this industry invent warmth. I've seen articles selling charm that no one believed in. There's a well-oiled system behind it—a manager or a publicist reaches out on the pretext of 'work', and before you know it, you are being fed carefully packaged PR lines disguised as insider information. These days, the lines aren't even subtle. They are as crude as, 'Here's the next national crush.' And you are expected to play along. It is all expertly choreographed. Journalists are often systematically brainwashed, flattered with 'exclusives' and, lately, reposts by celebrities. Proximity to fame is a prize. If you are smart, you know it's a clever trap to make you feel special. Most of us are pawns in their PR fantasy.

As a newbie in this world, I didn't understand how and why people liked Salman. It's taken me some time to understand that in all this spin and spectacle, Salman remains one of the few actors who are not PR-manufactured. And I say this with certainty, because the stories of his kindness come from unexpected quarters and have existed since before it became fashionable to use generosity as PR currency. They don't get circulated only when his movies are to be promoted.

There are endless accounts whispered between studio lots and make-up vans—of people crashing at Galaxy Apartments between gigs, of struggling directors and writers being handed their first real break in the industry, of those unable to get a break or to put together a film getting a leg up thanks to a quiet nudge from him. He made the wisdom of Salim Khan accessible to young industry outsiders, inviting them not just into his home, but offering them the kind of perspective that is otherwise gate-kept.

Ego is such a strange thing in show business. It is essential to stardom, but you can't have too much of it. It convinces you that holding your ground is power. But more often than not, ego just gets in the way and blocks growth, disconnects you from people and makes everything personal. The older I get, the more I realize that ego isn't a virtue but a weight.

And that's where Salman surprises you. For someone who has been one of Bollywood's top actors for decades, he really doesn't carry any ego. You might expect him to be guarded or self-important, but he's not. He'll crack a joke at his own expense, quietly help people and never make a fuss about credit.

Take the story of Mohnish Bahl. He wasn't very encouraging of Salman in the early days, but still landed a role in *Maine Pyar Kiya* because Salman put in a word for him. That role changed Bahl's career. He went on to do three more films with Salman and Sooraj, all of them roaring hits. Narrating the incident of how Mohnish got signed on for the film, Salman said in an interview, 'I remember this one time—there used to be this hotel here, Sea Rock, and I was at the gym there. I was doing bench presses when this guy comes up, moves me aside, and says, "Move. Let me sleep." I asked, "That's why you come to the gym?" He replied, "Yeah, I've been working three shifts. I'm tired. I just want God to give me a break." You should never say that. Three days later his film was released and *kuch zyada hi break lag gaya* [the break took a bit too long]! Later, I started going to their home when we became friends and that's where I met Nutanji, Mohnish Bahl's mother. Around that time, *Maine Pyar Kiya* came to me. The role of the antagonist—the bad guy—hadn't been cast yet. So I told Sooraj, "Why don't you try Mohnish Bahl?" I didn't even know how Mohnish would react. Back then, playing a negative role was a big risk. People would say, "You're mad. Why would you take a negative part?" I asked Mohnish, and he was completely open. He said, "It's a damn good role. I'll do it." It was for the character of Jeevan. When I suggested Mohnish, Sooraj said, "No, no … Mohnish Bahl? Nutanji's son? We can't even approach them." So I took matters into my own hands. I went straight to Cuffe Parade, to their home, and spoke to Nutanji. I said, "Please pick up the phone and speak to Raj Babu." She said, "I'm not going to call him—I'll go and meet him in person." So Nutanji and I went together to meet Raj Babu, and he was shocked. He couldn't believe someone from Nutanji's family would take on a negative role. It just wasn't done. Meanwhile, I had this visual stuck in my head of Mohnish—this guy who used to be under cars, fixing up BMWs, Mercedes-Benzes and Mustangs. He used to work out of a mobile garage back then. And now, here he was—about to step into a role that would change his career.'[1]

Interestingly, he narrated this story while promoting the debut film of Pranutan Bahl, Mohnish's daughter, launched by Salman in 2019 in a film named *Notebook*.

You are bound to wonder what kind of debutant—saddled with an underwhelming performance as a second lead in his first screen appearance and staring down the barrel of a do-or-die gun—goes out of their way to uplift someone who once dismissed them. Only someone like Salman.

For all the glitter and grime of this industry, it ultimately runs on relationships and the unshakeable kindness of people. Salman embodies that sentiment like no other. He's the man people turn to when the chips are down.

Need to train and look like a Greek god before your big debut and don't know where to start? Ask Salman. That's Hrithik Roshan's story.

Need a superstar for a cameo in a film that is headlined by his competitor? Well, let's talk to Salman. That's how Karan Johar pulled off a casting coup in *Kuch Kuch Hota Hai*.

Need a star to anchor a sinking project because your producer's neck-deep in debt? That's the origin story of Boney Kapoor's *No Entry*.

The stories are endless, spread by word of mouth like folklore. And not all stories are about him uplifting someone because he believed in them. His kindness is second nature, and sometimes the stories are simply wacky.

Like how a thief ended up befriending Salman. On a chat show with Preity Zinta, Salman recalled, 'One night, after a grand party, Arbaaz and I returned to our bedrooms and went to sleep. Suddenly, I woke up to see a large shadow looming over us, moving around comically. I woke Arbaaz up, and told him to stay silent. Then, a man emerged from the shadow, and he didn't look that big. He seemed to be dancing. I gestured to Arbaaz that at the count of three, we'd jump him. We managed to overpower him, and tied him up. We began to question the thief, who confessed that it was his first time trying a robbery. He was dancing because he was wearing a Walkman that he'd stolen from the house. When I asked what all he'd taken, the thief presented Rs 5, which is all they had as kids. I asked the thief if he'd eaten, and when the thief said he hadn't, I gave him some food. By then, my mother had come, and she was like, "Who is this man?" I told her that he's a thief, and she was like, "Why are you feeding him?"'[2]

That's Salman for you. And what happened to the thief? Oh well, he escaped after eating well. We can only hope he didn't go back to petty thefts and made something better of his life.

Show business may be built on illusion, but Salman remains one of the few who operate on instinct. He is impulsive. He is hopelessly loyal. There's no knowing what makes him do a film. More often than not, it depends on how much he likes the people who are making it.

Usually after a humongous success such as *Hum Aapke Hain Koun..!*, any star would want to scale up. Capitalize on the market, so to say. But not Salman. Interestingly around the same time as this monstrous hit, he starred in two films—one with Shah Rukh, another with Aamir, instead of choosing only single-hero movies that would build him up further.

The year 1994 was a turning point for Salman, not just because he had delivered a blockbuster such as *HAHK* but because of how the industry began to perceive his star power. With the right director and the right story, he became a darling of the masses. Smart directors noticed that. Everyone from David Dhawan to Sanjay Leela Bhansali queued up to offer him work.

Salman wasn't known for his comedy until *Andaz Apna Apna*, released later that year. And it became a genre that Salman aced once he started pairing up with directors who knew how to use him well.

We might love the movie now, but *Andaz Apna Apna* was made under duress and led to a host of misunderstandings off-screen. Though the camaraderie between Amar (Aamir) and Prem (Salman) lit up the screen, behind the scenes, the two actors barely spoke to each other. The same was true of Karisma Kapoor and Raveena Tandon, the two female leads, whose cold war gave ample fodder to Bollywood gossip columns. Karisma, then in a relationship with Ajay Devgn, reportedly didn't want him around Raveena, an old friend of his.

Salman, on his part, remained unbothered. But Aamir found Salman 'moody' and 'mercurial', which was just Salman's unpredictable nature. In one of the *Koffee with Karan* episodes, Aamir admitted, 'In *Andaz Apna Apna* I had a very bad experience working with Salman Khan. I didn't like him then. I found him rude and inconsiderate. After tasting the experience of working with him I just wanted to stay away from Salman.'[3]

Originally planned as a quick shoot, the film ended up taking nearly two years to complete, derailed by the egos of the men on set. Salman and

Aamir, two starkly different personalities, often clashed. What really got to Salman was Aamir's closeness with director Rajkumar Santoshi. Aamir would sit in on script discussions and offer inputs on edits. Santoshi said in an old interview from that year, 'Very often he would come up with very good lines of dialogue. Most of the time I would give the lines he suggested to Aamir, because they were more suitable to Aamir's character. Salman did not mind that.'[4] However, Salman, known to usually go with the flow, did feel sidelined. He later admitted that he felt short-changed. And yet, here's the thing that makes him so incredible—none of that ever showed on-screen.

In the final cut, Salman didn't just hold his own against Aamir, Bollywood's Mr Perfectionist, but sparkled and made sure he got an entry into the much-loved comedy genre. Even when Salman wasn't given the upper hand, he left a mark. His comic timing has since been recognized as pure gold.

And thankfully, film-makers such as David Dhawan saw the full extent of that potential. Five years later, in *Biwi No. 1*, Salman's comic energy would explode on-screen. The film, a massive hit, cemented what his fans always knew: that Salman didn't need perfect scripts or tailored scenes—he just needed the camera to roll. The rest—the charm, the laughs, the magic—he brought on his own.

But Aamir and Salman did find their way back to each other after *Andaz Apna Apna*. When Aamir and his wife Reena got divorced, it was Salman's company that brought Aamir solace. He admitted, 'Salman walked back into my life when I was at my lowest. I had gone through a divorce with my wife. But later we bumped into each other and he expressed his wish to meet me. We met again and drank together and we connected. And it began as a genuine friendship and it has only grown.'[5]

The ill feelings from the past, the competition, none of it mattered then. Aamir believes Salman is a bigger star than him. At the launch of *Dhoom 3*, Aamir said, 'Salman is my friend. He is a bigger star than me. When I see him in *Dabangg*, I feel very happy. Salman doesn't need to do anything. He is a powerhouse of star power. *Woh sirf belt hilaata hai, chashme theek karta hai* [He only moves his belt and fixes his sunglasses], and see his magic.'[6]

Their friendship has seen quite an arc. On Aamir's grand sixtieth, Salman, along with Shah Rukh, paid him a visit at home before the bash. And that was enough to get everyone talking of a movie starring the three. A swan song before they retired? And Aamir did talk to the press about it that day. He said, 'About six months back, Shah Rukh, Salman and I were together and we did speak about this. I was the person who brought this up and told Shah Rukh and Salman that it would be really sad if the three of us didn't do a film together. I think Salman and Shah Rukh were equally in agreement and said, "Yes, we must do a film together. The three of us." Hopefully, it will happen soon. It will need the right kind of story. So, we'll have to wait for the right script. We are all looking forward to it.'[7]

Now that is a film we all want to see! But by the looks of it, the Khans are still going strong. The swan song will probably have to wait.

But not just Aamir and Salman, the friendship of Shah Rukh and Salman, too, has had its own trajectory—falling out and then reforging that bond. We will get to their infamous fight later in the book, but the seeds of friendship were there all along and started in 1992, when Shah Rukh first moved to Mumbai from Delhi.

On a 2018 episode of *10 Ka Dum*, Shah Rukh talked about how Salman's family welcomed him when he first came to Mumbai. 'Salman is younger than me by one-and-a-half months. *Lekin (Salman ne) bade bhai se bhi zyada kiya hai. Aur inki family ne mera bahot dhyan rakha. Aur sirf dhakke hi nahin khaaye, maine inke ghar ka khaana bhi khaaya hai* (Salman took care of me more like an elder brother, along with his family. And I didn't just struggle, I have also eaten home-cooked food at his house).'[8]

The first time the two actors got together on-screen was for Rakesh Roshan's *Karan Arjun* (1995), and the crowds went crazy. Just last year, the film was re-released to packed theatres again. Salman and Shah Rukh fans joined forces to throng the halls and keep the business of films running.

In Bhopal, graphic designer Liso Perry requested both stars' fan clubs to host a joint screening of the film on 24 November 2024. And it was a smash hit with the members! 'The moment the "*Bhaag, Arjun, Bhaag* [Run, Arjun, Run]" dialogue came on-screen, you couldn't hear the rest of the dialogue—the cheer was so loud! And this is always the case with

Salman's films, but this time even Shah Rukh's fans, usually civil in their cheering, went ballistic. That film really cuts through the rivalries of the two fandoms. Salman and Shah Rukh have this easy chemistry. They look effortless on-screen, especially in this film. Even in that scene in *Tiger 3*, where Pathaan comes to rescue Tiger, they look like two old friends. The same energy lights up the screen in *Pathaan* when Shah Rukh tells Salman, "Can't leave the big work to kids!" It was a smart meta reference and makes their on-screen camaraderie shine brighter. And when you watch *Karan Arjun* on the big screen so many years later, you can see where that all started.'

It was on the set of *HAHK* at Filmistan Studio that Rakesh Roshan met Salman to pitch this film. Ajay Devgn had just walked out of the film, and Rakesh offered the role to Salman. He said yes on the spot. And that's one thing that all his friends say about him: He is game for anything, and loyal to his film-makers. There is no ego to get a bigger part or a bigger share of the pie.

A co-star from *Karan Arjun* who doesn't wish to be named tells me, 'Shah Rukh doesn't wish to compete with you, but he is inherently competitive. That's the essence of his journey. And he wouldn't have reached where he is now if it weren't for this competitive spirit. He is a sportsman who wins fair and square. But Salman simply doesn't care to compete. He cares for the movie. He cares to work. He loves the film set, the people. But he is like a tiger. He knows he will rule and doesn't see any reason to feel threatened. If Shah Rukh does better than him, he'll say: Good for the film! If he doesn't get as praised as Shah Rukh, he will say: He is better than me. He isn't competing at all. That's not his goal.'

And it is on this attitude that the aura of Salman Khan is built.

Govinda has a famous line about Salman: *Salman Khan ek hi jagah time pe pahuchta hai, jab kisi ko takleef hoti hai* [Salman Khan only reaches on time when he knows someone is in pain].[9] Obviously when one is successful, it is a lot easier to hold your hand out to others. If youth affords one greater bandwidth, success gives them the power to help others. The latter is easier. But when you are on shaky ground yourself, or emotionally distraught, how do you do that?

In 1994, right before the success of *HAHK*, Salman was on the brink of getting married. The wedding cards had gone out. Though Salman had been dating girls since he was thirteen, he came close to marriage only once. He was going steady with Sangeeta Bijlani since 1986. It was assumed that the two would tie the knot sooner or later. *Stardust* had reported that Salman and Sangeeta were to wed on 27 May 1994. But the split wasn't a snap decision for either of them. Sangeeta was really close to the Khan family and in interviews later, she admitted that it took them nearly four months to call it quits.

In an interview she said, 'I got the feeling that all was not well before our marriage. I started following him and soon found out that he does not deserve it. Far from that. He is not even worth having as a boyfriend. It was emotionally traumatic and a terrible experience.'[10] It was speculated that Salman had been involved with British actress Somy Ali while he was seeing Sangeeta. Somy had debuted in Bollywood in 1992 and made it to Salman's friends' circle. 'I was so ambitious that I forgot Salman was with somebody else. This was morally wrong,' Somy admitted in an interview to *The New York Times* in 2012.

Why is this story relevant when discussing Salman's kindness? Much of the discourse around Salman has suffered from broad-stroking. And it is assumed that his kindness is a PR gimmick to camouflage his mistakes. The fallout from Salman's highly publicized break-up didn't just fracture a relationship, it also fractured his image. For years Salman had been the face of selfless love, thanks to his portrayal of Prem, a character etched in public imagination as kind, pure-hearted and gentle. But when the off-screen narrative clashed with that ideal, public opinion shifted.

Salman's aversion to the press only solidified things. The media, already shaping first impressions, found in Salman a figure who refused to play along. At a time when Aamir was charming journalists with literary references, Salman remained aloof. A 1995 piece by Khalid Mohammed[11] tried to strike a balance, praising Salman's charisma while lamenting his lack of introspection as an artiste. But the deeper story—of someone retreating from public discourse even as his image came under siege—was largely missed.

This is where the question of kindness gets muddled. When you're not seen explaining yourself, every gesture of kindness, however small, can look like strategy.

His public break-up created a certain opinion about him. He was stubborn, impulsive and often his worst enemy. But to reduce him to just those traits is to miss the complicated, contradictory and often generous man behind the headlines.

There's something to be said about people who are broken but still manage to give. Salman's compassion doesn't come from a place of perfection—it comes from knowing the ways in which life can bring someone to their knees. For someone who is branded difficult and volatile, he has consistently been the person who shows up for those who need help. In a 'no one needs to know' kind of way. In 2013, Salman sent 2,500 water tankers to drought-hit villages in Marathwada (rural Maharashtra). In 2015, while shooting for *Bajrangi Bhaijaan* in Pahalgam, he hired an elderly woman's grandson as part of his film crew so the family wouldn't starve.[12] According to a report in *The Times of India* Kanpur, Salman paid the fines for nearly 400 inmates stuck in jail despite completing their sentences, simply because they were too poor to pay. It was close to Rs 40 lakh, and it all came from his own pocket.[13]

So when we talk about kindness, we have to ask: Does kindness count only if you are squeaky clean? Or does it, perhaps, mean more if you are deeply flawed? Someone who has known rejection, ridicule and heartbreak, and still chooses to extend a helping hand to others?

There are innumerable stories of how Salman has paid for medical bills of junior artistes, supported families of late technicians, launched the careers of people who had no backing and stood by friends when their own families didn't. He doesn't always like to talk about them. He's famously awkward when asked about his philanthropy. Almost dismissive. Because maybe, for him, it is some form of duty.

And perhaps that's why his goodness is often met with suspicion. Because it's inconsistent with his public image.

But maybe that's the point. Human beings are rarely ever just one thing or the other. Especially those who have lived under the weight of fame since their youth. With Salman, the truth has always existed in the shadow area—the flawed man who's capable of immense affection; the superstar who draws media ire by giving the most politically incorrect answers; the friend who stands by you like a rock, come what may.

He doesn't give himself enough credit, but around the same time that he was going through the personal turmoil of his split with Sangeeta, he was also helping launch the careers of two of the most well-known filmmakers today, Karan Johar and Sanjay Leela Bhansali.

Before *Kuch Kuch Hota Hai* (1998), Karan Johar's father had had five flops in a row. 'What I inherited from my father was goodwill, not money,' Karan said in an interview recently.[14]

At that time, the two actors who agreed to his film were Shah Rukh Khan and Kajol. He was relaunching Rani Mukerji after *Raja Ki Aayegi Baraat* didn't fare well at the box office. But who'd play Aman? Everyone from Saif Ali Khan to Chandrachur Singh had passed. Karan spoke about it during an episode of the reality show *Yaaron Ki Baraat*. 'With Shah Rukh Khan and Kajol as the lead actors, no one said yes to the role of the second lead. I was very disappointed and, with my sad face, I went to attend a party at Chunky Panday's house, where I met Salman,' he said.[15]

In his book *An Unsuitable Boy*, Karan writes, 'Salman Khan was there at that party. His sister, Alvira, had told him that Karan was in search of an actor to play this other guy's role—a twelve- to fifteen-day part. Salman said, "What role is it?" I began telling him. He said, "Nobody's going to do this role. No hero will want to do this role. There's only one idiot in the industry who'll do it, and that's me. My sister says you're a nice guy. Come and narrate it to me tomorrow." I thought, Salman Khan? Now who would have thought of it? My father said, "*Paagal hai? Woh kabhi nahi karne wala* [Are you mad? He'll never do it].'"[16]

Salman at that time was shooting for *Jab Pyaar Kisise Hota Hai* with Twinkle Khanna. She, too, had passed on this film, despite being Karan's childhood friend. In fact, the film had been passed on by Karisma Kapoor, Raveena Tandon, Tabu, Urmila Matondkar, Shilpa Shetty and even Aishwarya Rai.

Salman heard the first half and said, 'I will do the film.' Karan writes, 'I got worried as I wondered if he thought I was offering him Shah Rukh's role. I told him, "*Sir aapka role aaya nahi abhi tak* [I haven't narrated your role yet]. Salman said the role is immaterial as he knows my father and is doing the film for him.'

Before the usual cries of nepotism start, about how Bollywood is just famous people backing other famous people and their children, let's talk about the part of the story that rarely gets told. When film-maker Nikkhil Advani and his mentor Karan Johar went through a split, Salman decided to champion Nikkhil despite his love for Karan. Nikkhil said, 'Salman Khan prides himself on being the messiah of the industry, so the minute I walked out of the doors of Dharma Productions, I got a call from Salman saying, "Come and meet me." (He then said) *[sic]* "Now you will work for me, you will make a film for me." And I appreciate that.' Salman headlined the ambitious ensemble film *Salaam-e-Ishq* for Nikkhil, which also starred Anil Kapoor, Govinda, John Abraham, Vidya Balan, Priyanka Chopra, Juhi Chawla, Akshaye Khanna and Ayesha Takia. Screentime is never an important feature in Salman's scheme of things.[17]

Nikkhil rightly calls him a messiah. 'In case of emergency, call Salman. He could be in the middle of his biggest action sequence and he'd still show up to help you out,' Nikkhil added.[18]

The same happened for Sanjay Leela Bhansali, who was assisting Vidhu Vinod Chopra when he met Salman for his first film, *Khamoshi*. Sanjay was born into a household struggling to make ends meet. His father, Navin Bhansali, had been a film producer in the 1950s, known for films such as *Jahazi Lutera* and *Pak Daman*, but none had found success. Disillusioned, Navin had turned to alcoholism, leaving the family in financial distress. His mother, Leela, became the backbone of the family, sewing and selling saris door to door to make ends meet. Father and son had a deeply troubled relationship, but in some ways, Navin influenced Sanjay's cinema, urging him to watch *Mughal-e-Azam* repeatedly and introducing him to the music of Bade Ghulam Ali Khan and Naushad.[19]

Around 1995, Sanjay reached out to his sister Bela with his first script—the emotionally charged story of *Khamoshi: The Musical*. While Sanjay had been honing his skills in direction, Bela had trained in editing under the legendary Renu Saluja, working on films such as *Pestonjee* (1987) and *Parinda* (1989). As Sanjay narrated the story of Annie

Braganza and her deaf–mute parents, Bela was moved to tears. Though fictional, *Khamoshi* was deeply personal, echoing their own childhood. Like Annie's mother Flavy, played by Seema Biswas in the film, Sanjay's mother Leela had once stitched clothes to sustain the family. And Joseph's (Nana Patekar's) rage against Annie's passion mirrored moments from Sanjay's own fraught relationship with his father.

Salman, in his free time on set, still reads scripts of assistant directors. And that's how he first met Sanjay. 'He has always believed in giving newcomers a chance, because he remembers what it means to be a newcomer. When Sanjay Leela Bhansali was struggling to make *Khamoshi*, Salman supported him. There are hundreds of assistants who keep on coming up to him and telling [him] that they want to make a movie. Salman sits and listens to all their scripts in the middle of shots,' Salim said in an interview to *Stardust*.[20]

Any film with a debutant director needs a superstar's backing. Salman requested Helen to do a special appearance in the film, which she agreed to only for him. Manisha Koirala's character was originally written for Madhuri, but due to logistical reasons she couldn't do the film. Manisha said, 'I was not his first choice for the role. I remember, we had become friends and Sanjay just said, "Manisha, I have written this script, just go through it. You are not acting in it, Kajol and Madhuri are my choices."'[21]

Salman loved the story. And more than that, he found a friend in Sanjay. The two forged a bond. In 2022, in an interview, Sanjay said, '*Khamoshi* couldn't have been made without Salman's support.'[22]

Editor Jabeen Merchant, who worked with Bela on the film, said in an interview, 'For all of us it was special because we didn't know what would happen to the film eventually, whether it would be a success … This was the beginning of something. We were on something that meant a lot.'[23]

Despite the excitement on set, resources were limited. Sanjay was determined to incorporate everything he envisioned. For instance, for a sequence he needed twenty metres of red satin cloth to achieve the perfect effect, and the production could only provide him ten. But none of this budgetary strain shows in the film.

Anil Mehta, an FTII graduate and assistant cinematographer, met Sanjay through a friend. Despite initial financial concerns, he agreed to work on the film after reading the script overnight, captivated by the passion of its maker. *Khamoshi* was his first feature film as a cinematographer, and he later went on to become the director of photography for movies such as *Lagaan, Veer-Zaara* and Sanjay's later superhit film *Hum Dil De Chuke Sanam*.

Khamoshi was shot entirely in Goa. The production designer, Nitin Desai, searched extensively along the Goan coast to find the perfect spot for the Braganza home, eventually settling on Morjim beach. Because most scenes were set indoors, they decided to build a house at the location. That gave the film a richer sense of place, enhancing the film's realism.

Music was a big highlight of the film, right from its inception. Sanjay knew Babloo Chakravarty, an arranger who worked with the music director duo Jatin–Lalit, and it was through this connection that he approached them. Jatin later said in an interview, 'When Sanjay came we knew in an instant that we liked him. He was very non-filmy and had a great script and song situations, everything he narrated to us, and we were very comfortable with him. He knew exactly what he wanted for the music, and that included the lyrics. He roped in the veteran Majrooh Sultanpuri and as usual, the 77-year-old tapped into the teenager in him with tracks such as *"Aaj main ooparlAasman neeche"*, *"Jaana suno/Hum tumpe marte hain"* and the eternal favourite of cover singers, *"Baahon ke darmiyan/Do pyaar mil rahe hain"* … Sanjay had specific briefs for his composers … I had never done anything like that before and I've never done anything like that since.'[24]

Jatin–Lalit joined *Khamoshi* after the success of *Dilwale Dulhania Le Jayenge* (1995), drawn by lyricist Majrooh Sultanpuri's thoughtful and character-driven writing. Sanjay pushed them creatively, even allowing them to experiment with long, unique song structures.

But sometimes one can put everything into a film and it can still not work. Today it is a cult movie, but back then it was a washout, despite love from the critics. When he gained some perspective after a few years, he realized why this gem of a film did not strike gold at the box office.

'*Khamoshi* … had emotions but lacked colour and glamour,' Sanjay said in a 1999 interview.[25]

When *Khamoshi* flopped, Sanjay lost faith in himself. 'I was shattered. I thought my journey as a film-maker had ended even before it began. I've to thank two people: Majrooh Sultanpuri and Salman Khan. They kept reminding me what a wonderful film I had made. But I kept thinking if *Khamoshi* was so wonderful, why did the audience reject it? Was it because it was a dark film? No wonder, I gravitated to something far more celebratory and happy in my next film *Hum Dil De Chuke Sanam*.'[26] And, of course, he had Salman's backing even then.

A good movie can sometimes go unappreciated at first, but it is bound to find its audience. Salman's and Sanjay's passion project, too, found the love it was destined for. In 2022, after *CODA* won the Oscar for Best Picture, someone on Twitter (now X) pointed out that the film, directed by Sian Heder and starring Emilia Jones, Troy Kotsur, Daniel Durant and Marlee Matlin, had an uncanny similarity to *Khamoshi*.

CODA made history as the first film from Apple TV—any OTT platform, for that matter—to win the Academy Award for Best Picture. An acronym for 'Child of Deaf Adults', the film tells the story of Ruby, the only hearing member in her family, as she struggles to balance her responsibilities at home with her dream of becoming a singer.

It turned out that the film was a remake of the 2014 French movie *La Famille Bélier*, which, interestingly, draws clear inspiration from *Khamoshi: The Musical*. When asked about it, Sanjay said, 'I wouldn't like to see it like that. A good story can be interpreted in many ways. *CODA* is a different film from mine.'[27]

Regardless, a unique film-maker was born because of Salman's backing. Today, Sanjay is one of Indian cinema's most revered film-makers. The industry believes his name is enough to sell a movie. Even at a time when theatres had been shut for a year during the Covid-19 lockdown, his female-led film, *Gangubai Kathiawadi*, headlined by Alia Bhatt and released a month after the Omicron outbreak, raked in over Rs 120 crore for its domestic box office run.

Sanjay believes he owes his career to Salman. He reiterated this to me during a conversation in his Juhu office after the release of *Padmaavat*.

'I have [the] utmost regard and respect for the person who did *Khamoshi* for me, who did *Hum Dil De Chuke Sanam* for me, and who stood by in *Saawariya*. So he has been a very important part of who I am today and I will always respect him for it,' he said.[28]

The duo went on to deliver the memorable *Hum Dil De Chuke Sanam*, but, unfortunately, had quite a few public clashes. Both temperamental men, Sanjay and Salman have had their share of love and war. The latest split came when Salman walked out of Sanjay's now-shelved film, *Inshallah*, co-starring Alia Bhatt and slated for a 2022 release, following creative differences. But in an industry where rivalries persist for decades and often turn ugly in public, Salman and Sanjay have not let their fights overshadow the love they have for each other.

Sanjay had even discussed this in an interview. 'The only person that I'm still friendly with is Salman Khan. Even if *Inshallah* didn't happen, he stands by me. He'll call me; he'll care for me. "Are you okay? Is there anything (you need)? You've goofed up, you messed up." I enjoy his humour so much. It (a phone call) comes once in three months, once in five months, but it comes because he doesn't care about my film. He cares about me. "You, bro, you've done so many films with me, it doesn't matter. Are you okay?" And that is what it is all about. On work, we may have sparred, we may have not had our moment correct, and it didn't fall into place. But after one month, he called me, and I called him, and we talked. So that is a friend. In that sense, I'm fortunate enough to have that friend who once in six months will speak and will exactly start from where we left off.'[29]

Bollywood is often branded as a dog-eat-dog world. Time and again that impression gets played up, because nothing feeds voyeurism and garners TRPs like it. Stories of people helping each other often get lost in this sea of negativity. Initially, all you know about this man is what the press reports tell you, and then slowly your circle widens and you get to meet people across departments and social classes who tell you stories of his kindness.

Over the course of my research for this book, I have been warned over and over by senior journalists not to gloss over Salman's missteps. 'That'd be a gross misrepresentation of this man-child, who lives in his father's house till date and refuses to grow up. It's not endearing—it's a cautionary tale of what happens to a man who doesn't grow up,' a furious senior editor told me over the phone when I called them about a piece he'd written on Salman in the early 1990s.

The same day I was interviewing a textile seller, Sushil Nihar, from Ujjain, Madhya Pradesh. He laughed out loud when I told him about the editor's tirade. 'The truth is we are all just busy boxing everyone into good and bad, instead of letting people be. He is a good man ... he is a bad man ... but people are just people. They have good deeds and bad deeds. Eventually every man is a sum total of all of this,' he said.

Sushil then poignantly asked me, 'Has this editor ever saved someone's life? This good-man-versus-bad-man conversation could go on. But I feel not enough gets said about a public figure who has made a tangible difference to cancer treatment across the country. Do you know Salman Khan was the first bone marrow donor of the country? And ever since, people have registered to donate their marrow simply because Bhai has asked them to. Celebrities have so much power but how many use it to make others' lives better? He does. And if he could get so much hate for the wrong things he does, let's take a moment to praise him for the good he does as well.'

He told me about Pooja, the four-year-old who was saved by the bone marrow Salman donated in 2010.

Later that night, I read up about Salman's contribution to bone marrow donation. Dr Sunil Parekh, former board member of Marrow Donor Registry India (MDRI), said in an interview, 'Salman had read about Pooja, a little girl who was in need of a bone marrow transplant. He got his entire football team to come and donate marrow. Unfortunately, they all backed out at the last minute, and only Salman and Arbaaz (Salman's brother actor Arbaaz Khan) landed up donating and became the first donors.'[30]

Suniel Shetty once called Salman God's favourite child because of the good he does,[31] and Sushil agrees. He tells me, 'The good you spread comes back to you. I know it sounds idealistic and simple, but it is actually that simple. Be a good human being and do good deeds.'

Because of Sushil, the conversation in my head about Salman shifted. I routinely get lambasted by self-righteous people for writing about a man they believe is a monster seeking forgiveness through stray good deeds. To that Sushil says, 'No good deed is stray. It benefits someone. Yes, the man may never fully grow up, as his critics say, but perhaps that's the point. Maybe it takes a man-child to believe he can still change the world. And sometimes he does.'

I don't want to reduce Salman's philanthropy to a footnote. His fans wouldn't let me, and this is a book told from their perspective. The good Salman does deserves its own chapter. And we'll get to that soon.

For now let's go back to his movies.

"Muscle dekha hai, muscle? Masal ke rakh doonga!"

Andaz Apna Apna, 1994

4

Muscle Man

I T was the late 1990s. Aamir was playing the cute boy in *Raja Hindustani*, Shah Rukh was the quintessential chocolate boy in *Kuch Kuch Hota Hai* … and what was Salman doing? Well, he was dropping shirts!

There's an idea bandied about in Bollywood that clings to our hero like a shadow: *Jiss film mein Bhai ka shirt nahi utarta, woh picture pitt jati hai.* The film that does not see Bhai take off his shirt, gets slammed at the box office. This is an old saying, and perhaps for good reason. Like they say, never question the juju. Trade gurus have time and again told me that when Bhai bares his chest, the box office surrenders.

The mania might have started when the movie *Pyaar Kiya To Darna Kya* (1998) hit the screens, but Bhai had gone shirtless in many memorable films before that, including for the poster of *Veergati* (1995), in which he stands facing the camera with a bloodied, bare torso, fists clenched and muscles rippling. Ever since his first film, shirtless Salman was a recurrent feature directors were happy to incorporate. But with that iconic entry scene in *Pyaar Kiya To Darna Kya*, where he strums a guitar, flashes a

89

charming grin and says, 'I love you all', and bursts into 'O O Jaane Jaana', he changed the game and elevated shirtless Salman to another level. The audience swooned, girls screamed, boys hit the gym and directors knew one thing for sure—Salman taking off his shirt was a *moment*. From that point on, baring his torso became part of his signature—equal parts fan service, fantasy and flex.

A trendsetter ahead of his time, Salman showed men the importance of incorporating fitness regimes into their lives when taking care of their bodies and looks had still not become fashionable. 'Salman Khan bared his chest at a time when Bollywood heroes bared their hearts,' Junaid Afzal, a Bhai fan from Darbhanga, Bihar, told me over a late-evening phone call. He runs a local Bhai fan club called 'Superman, Salman Ka Fan', after a song from the 2014 film *Tevar*. Junaid and a bunch of twenty boys put in their hard-earned money to buy a shack that doubles as their makeshift gym and entertainment centre.

Junaid believes that Salman dropping his shirt on-screen gave birth to a new mould of Bollywood hero. The brooding poets and velvet-voiced charmers now had to coexist with the hero who was dripping with attitude, and muscle, like Bhai.

Junaid tells me, 'I was probably four when I saw Bhai in *Pyaar Kiya To Darna Kya*. My house didn't have a TV set then, so I would go to a friend's house. Both of us would take our shirts off and dance to "O O Jaane Jaana". To this day, every time Bhai goes shirtless, theatres erupt and fans hoot and whistle. Men copy him in front of mirrors and flex their biceps. Before Bhai, the gym was a place for bodybuilders, a few actors such as Sanjay Dutt who had an enviable physique, and wealthy boys with money to spend. After Salman, it almost became a rite of passage for boys as they stepped into manhood. In the 1970s and the 1980s, India's leading men had different signature appeals—Rajesh Khanna's melancholic smile made him a favourite with the ladies, Amitabh Bachchan's towering presence and baritone made him the dashing Angry Young Man, Mithun Chakraborty's smooth dance moves established him as the Disco Dancer. The men largely embodied a relatable masculinity. They were men you could imagine at your cousin's wedding or at the corner chai shop. Their bodies were secondary. But Bhai made us believe that the dream body was achievable. For as far back as I can remember, I have been working out. I work out every day. I saved up pocket money to buy dumb-bells. We at the gym watch training videos on YouTube because we can't afford trainers. Before YouTube was a thing, we would bribe the PT [physical training] teacher at our school to help us. He would even let us use the school premises after hours to exercise. The confidence I have now, even to talk to you, is because of Bhai. Someone with more education, more money doesn't intimidate me because I feel good in my skin!'

Junaid believes Salman was the reason behind the fitness revolution of the mid-1990s. Even Salman's brother Arbaaz thinks so. At the launch of a gym, he told the press, 'Salman is the one who actually started the gym culture in this country. If you see earlier, people did exercise, there were "akhadas" and other gyms, but nothing that was state-of-the-art. Salman is the one who revolutionized everything. Almost in every suburb or every lane, there is a gym. One fine day people are going to realize that the contribution has come from him. If youth have got inspired to start working out, it's purely because of him. Salman has been the pioneer in this, and he continues to do that,' he said.[1]

It wouldn't be erroneous to say that Salman transformed the very idea of male fitness in India. Long before Instagram reels and protein shakes became an obsession, Salman would bribe the staff at his gym with a hundred bucks just to sneak in a few extra reps when no one was looking. His family thought he was wasting time chasing the impossible dream of becoming an actor. They also discouraged him from gymming. 'What does acting have to do with bodybuilding anyway?' was a common retort in his household.

But Salman was too busy creating a new mould for Bollywood heroes. His fans tell me that even when he was briefly in jail, the man didn't quit. With no fancy equipment or air-conditioned space, he requested the guards for two buckets of water, which were his makeshift weights, so he wouldn't lose a single inch of that hard-earned muscle. That shirtless Salman you see on-screen, abs glistening under studio lights, is a result of sweat, dedication and a refusal to bow down to any obstacle.

Salman's fitness is an integral part of his identity. It's the myth that built the superstar. When that viral photo of him with a belly bulge hit the internet in May this year, fans panicked. 'My first thought was: Is he depressed? Why doesn't he care about himself any more?' his fan Sharib Khaimar told me. Sharib is a twenty-three-year-old fitness trainer in a small village off Versova in Mumbai. He's been running a modest gym since he turned twenty, teaching local kids the basics of bodybuilding. Every morning they run on the Versova beach and, if you are lucky, you might see them play the most nail-biting game of football.

His fanboying started when he watched *Dabangg* in 2010. For Sharib, Salman is a symbol of raw masculinity, a man who could single-handedly take care of his family. 'I've always admired his fitness, the way he's always looked so strong, no matter what. And he had once said this: "*Agar dikhana hai, beat karna hai, maarna hai, toh mehnat karke apna level badha ke kaam se maaro* [If you want to show the world, to beat, to defeat, then work hard, raise your level and defeat through your work]. Nothing better than working hard." Whatever I have in life is because I have followed Bhai and worked hard. Now I help others work hard and be the best version of themselves. If you look good and feel good, you'll fare well,' Sharib said matter-of-factly.

For him, Salman's chiselled body became the gold standard of manhood. That's why the viral photo hit him hard. 'Salman is the reason I started working out in the first place. When I saw that photo, it felt like my hero had stopped caring,' he said, adjusting the weights on a battered barbell. 'It felt like he'd given up. But I know everyone has tough times. I hope he bounces back. It might sound strange but Salman's body is not just his—it's part of us too. We own that myth of Salman Khan. Of course, he's allowed to age, become fat, catch his breath and lie low. But this is a man who built his stardom on sweat and pushed all of us to take care of ourselves. This is the man who knew the effect his bare-chested walk would have on both men and women. To see him let go is … catastrophic.'

Isn't he being dramatic, I casually queried. 'Dramatic?' he fired back, his voice rising. 'Salman's body is a national treasure! When he rips off his shirt, the entire country holds its breath. You think we're overreacting? We're talking about the man who taught India how to dream of having a body like that. He's the original fitness god. If he gives up, it's like the temple's falling apart.'

We were sitting in a dusty local gym in Versova gaon, and there was a life-size poster of Salman, all veins and intensity, staring down at us from a wall. Next to the poster, Salman's quote stands in bold, his words thundering, 'The older you get, the better you have to look, the higher you have to kick, the harder you have to work.'

Sharib tells me that his gym is a Salman centre. He and his bantais (blokes) watch a Bhai film every day. The evening we met, they were to screen *Wanted*. 'This gym is my little shrine to Salman. We are complete Salmaniacs. Even when we work out, we play his songs. A lot of Salman's mania comes from his fitness. There is an entire generation of men who grew up wanting to be him. And he inspires us every day, even when he isn't in his best shape. He has this burning drive in him. It's Bhai, *woh sabko masal denge* [he will squash everyone]!'

'It might sound strange but Salman's body is not just his—it's part of us too. We own that myth of Salman Khan. Of course, he's allowed to age, become fat, catch his breath and lie low. But this is a man who built his stardom on sweat and pushed all of us to take care of ourselves.'

Most actors are celebrated for their acting chops, the weight of their filmography or the charm they wield on-screen. When Shah Rukh was serenading women with roses and romantic declarations, Salman was inspiring young men by redefining what it meant to be a man. Before Salman, 'well turned out' meant a sharp shirt, a combed quiff and a polite smile. Then came Bhai, shirtless and ripped, and turned the idea of masculinity on its head.

Through the early 1990s, he gave fitness a whole new meaning. He showed Indian men that building a body equals confidence. He showed everyone that a man can be both rugged and romantic, vulnerable and invincible. That's the blueprint that transformed not just how heroes looked but how millions of men saw themselves.

Saikat Kundu, a software engineer from Burdwan, West Bengal, tells me, 'I was an obnoxiously obese child. In Bengali households, physical fitness is somehow never prioritized. And food is a little too important. Through my younger years, I was a glutton. I wasn't fit at all. I did great in class, but wasn't part of any sports team. I believed I wasn't cut out for it. My parents never encouraged me to give sports a shot, not even football, which Bengalis usually love. It was always about more and more studying, and getting higher marks. I would go from one tuition to the next and just chase grades. It was when I turned thirteen that something shifted in me. I remember sitting with a girl, my friend whom I had a bit of a crush on, and she told me how she loved Salman's body. I still remember her words: That's how men should look. I was so unnaturally jealous. He looked perfect, and I looked at myself and realized that I could never have his good looks! Worse, I wasn't even trying. That week was the first time I woke up at 5 a.m. to walk instead of to study. I have stuck to my fitness journey ever since, and this year I will be trekking to Dayara Bugyal for a week. I wouldn't have become this version of myself if it weren't for Salman. It started with hate and then turned to awe. I will never forget to thank him for who I have become now. Over time, I became a huge fan of Salman. When I started dating my wife, she was a bit stumped to see how much I adored Salman. Shah Rukh fans, especially women, don't like Salman fanboys. We are a little too excited and understandably intimidating, because we celebrate traditional masculinity. But every Salman fan only has a rough exterior—they are softies inside. We grow on people over time. Even my wife took some time to get that about me. Initially, I was taking her for films such as *Dabangg,* and she wasn't very enthusiastic. The first time I realized she loved me was when she surprised me with tickets for a 7 a.m. show of a Bhai film. It was the best date we have ever had. This is a man who has changed my life. I could have been a fat geek rotting away in a library, but he showed me that I could have a shot at a grander and a more wholesome life if only I invested in myself.'

Saikat also introduced us to Oindrilla Biswas (name changed), now based in Paris, the crush who had led him to Salman. She continues to be a massive fan of the superstar. But as a teenager, her love for Salman was just about his looks! She admits to me, 'Men are never shy to admit how they love someone just for their looks. But young girls back in the 1990s could not do so openly. At least I couldn't. Everyone around me loved Shah Rukh because of how he made them feel. I liked him too, yes, but he was never the kind of looker who would blow my mind. Salman was that guy! His face, his smile and his body had a major role to play in drawing me in. I love him in *Karan Arjun*. He is brooding and sexy. There is this obscure film with Neelam called *Ek Ladka Ek Ladki*, which not many love, but I loved Salman in it. There is a throwaway scene in *Kuch Kuch Hota Hai*, where he is doing push-ups, in which he seems so physically appealing. Think of the 1990s and small-town India. As a teenager, understanding sexuality was complex. There was so much shame attached to dating. We weren't encouraged to speak to boys. If we liked someone, we would be grounded. Salman was the first man I ever saw topless, because no one else would show us what their bodies looked like. Right after his smile got us giddy, it was his bare chest and big biceps that made you crush on him. He has a major role to play in my sexual awakening. This might sound lusty, but I mean it in the most matter-of-fact way. I liked his body so much that it became an ideal for me. Waxed chest, toned muscles and a man who knows the effect he has on women.'

'Shah Rukh fans, especially women, don't like Salman fanboys. We are a little too excited and understandably intimidating, because we celebrate traditional masculinity. But every Salman fan only has a rough exterior—they are softies inside. We grow on people over time.'

I tell her that Salman doesn't wax. Madhuri Dixit reportedly asked him during the shooting of *Hum Aapke Hain Koun..!* if he did, and he replied, unfazed, 'I am a man, I shave it.'

In case men are taking notes, that's what Bhai does!

The 1990s were seeing a cultural pivot. India, newly liberalized, found itself seduced by the trappings of a globalized world. With liberalization in 1991, India's economic doors swung open to the West. There was a shift happening alongside a deeper societal churn. Satellite television brought Hollywood blockbusters and music videos into middle-class living rooms. International magazines featuring fitness icons such as Arnold Schwarzenegger and Sylvester Stallone were making the aesthetic of the ripped hero a household aspiration. The ripple effect in Bollywood was seismic. Salman was among the first Indian heroes to capitalize on this visual grammar, making muscles a mainstream, even essential, part of stardom.

The first time Salman went shirtless was in a scene in *Maine Pyar Kiya*. It didn't register as prominently as the puppy-romance plot did, but by the time *Pyaar Kiya To Darna Kya* was released in 1998, it became his signature. He had the six-pack abs, the bulging biceps and the confidence of a man who looked like he could wrestle a bear and charm a princess both at once. Cinema, which until then had been content with a more laid-back masculinity, suddenly realized that to be a hero, you had to look the part.

Salman's most iconic shirtless avatar was born of an accident when the team was shooting 'O O Jaane Jaana' in Madh Island. Salman narrated the story on a chat show: 'I had built muscles at that time. Vikram Phadnis was the designer for the film. When he brought my shirts on set, they all fitted like a blouse on my body. New costumes would have taken time. So I decided to shoot it without a shirt and the director, Sohail Khan, agreed. When we saw the shots, all of us liked it and we decided to keep it as it is.'[2]

It later became a trend, as film-makers started using the shirtless scene as a gift to his fans. And it goes with Salman's vibe. That's who he is, how he is—if you've got it, flaunt it! In an old interview, he said, 'I realized that a good body was an asset and hence I cast my shirt off for the film. When you have a good body, why shouldn't you show it off, man? Walking around bare-chested is not new for me. Even in my house, I never wear a shirt. You will always find me in just shorts. If I am driving or walking down the road, and if I feel hot, I just take off my shirt and carry on. I do not care what people say. If you have a problem, get lost.'[3]

However, it might not be wholly accurate to credit this trend of going shirtless entirely to Salman. Indeed, Sanjay Dutt has a strong claim to being the first major Hindi film star to bring bodybuilding into the Bollywood fold, thanks to his buffed-up look in films such as *Rocky* (1981) and *Naam* (1986). He is Bollywood's first 'bodybuilder hero'. But where for Sanjay the chiselled male body was only a side character, Salman made sure the glistening six-pack abs were front and centre.

Zayed K., who trains at Sharib's gym, tells me that right after he watched Salman's films from the 1990s, he wanted to be like him. 'I didn't resonate with Sanjay Dutt. He was so tall and looked like a gentle giant. But Bhai looked like one of us. I wanted Bhai's arms, his chest, his attitude,' he says, eyes lighting up as he gestures to the collage of Salman posters on a wall behind him. 'I wanted his biceps, his six-pack, his entire look. Before Salman, only big-time bodybuilders cared about gyms. After him, every guy with even a scrap of confidence wanted to be like him. We'd go to the gym with Bhai's posters rolled up and then pin them on the wall beside the mirror. We'd stand there, flexing, trying to match his abs. Every cut, every vein, every muscle was examined. If it didn't look like Bhai's, we'd push harder, do more reps. We'd check the mirror every single day, like maniacs, measuring our biceps with a tape and comparing them to the photos. The day someone's arms looked even a little like Bhai's, we'd buy biryani and run to Galaxy Apartments to celebrate under his balcony, screaming "Bhai!" at the top of our lungs. That's how deep it ran. That's how much he changed us.'

'When you have a good body, why shouldn't you show it off, man? Walking around bare-chested is not new for me. Even in my house, I never wear a shirt. You will always find me in just shorts. If I am driving or walking down the road, and if I feel hot, I just take off my shirt and carry on. I do not care what people say. If you have a problem, get lost.'

Zayed says gyms that once looked like dingy basements with rusty weights transformed into glass-fronted spaces, filled with international workout gear, and a clientele chasing the dream of a Salman-like body. The notion of masculinity had a new dimension. Along with being a provider and a protector, being sculpted was necessary. After all, everyone must look the part they play! Zayed says, 'Suddenly, every hero, starting with Hrithik Roshan in 2001 to Ranveer Singh and Varun Dhawan in

2011–12, was flexing their muscles. A hero's body became important. Salman Khan didn't just change how men looked, but also how they felt about themselves. He gave them permission to embrace a Westernized look of masculinity without feeling less Indian. Think of someone like me—I don't come from a high social class, but what's common between me and Rakesh Roshan's son? We have both achieved that level of fitness and physique. Bhai was the one who made me believe it was possible. For me, fitness is an equalizer.'

That evening, I understood what he meant. Zayed also runs a famous kebab joint in Versova gaon, near the jetty area. 'People ask me how I manage to look like this when I have greasy kebabs at my disposal all day long. But Bhai eats everything and still looks like he can bulldoze ten men single-handedly. It's such a terrible idea that you can't eat what you like, which people have lately started promoting. Nutrition is a big part of fitness. Happiness is a big part of fitness. If you toil at the gym for four hours and don't eat, you'll look scrawny. *Jam ke khao, aur bharpur workout karo* [Eat as much as you like but also work out equally hard],' he says. Between serving me kebabs and eating some of them, he pulled up his shirt to show me and my friend his abs.

Zayed also enthusiastically introduced us to Milind Sawant, his workout buddy. He bowed out of the greasy kebabs we were gorging on, because it was his Mangalvar ka vrat (Tuesday fast), but he had a lot to say about Salman. He started with quoting Siddhant Chaturvedi's line from an interview to us, '*Shah Rukh saab ka pyaar jawani mein samajh aata hai. Bhaijaan toh humare bachpan ka pyaar hai* [You understand Shah Rukh sir's version of love when you grow older. But Bhaijaan's love goes back to our childhood].'

Zayed and Milind laugh as they explain to me how love for Salman has often been the foundation of deep male friendships, like theirs. Milind tells me, 'Zayed and I have nothing in common. I am an introvert. He is a chatterbox. I am Hindu, he is Muslim. We do have similar economic backgrounds, but we are two people who otherwise would have never been friends. We met while watching a Salman film and it's been fifteen years now that we are friends. Men aren't great at friendships the way social media promotes it. We are emotionally closed. We struggle to have deep conversations. We don't know how to be vulnerable. So our way of friendship is founded on drinking and cigarettes, both of which Zayed and I haven't taken to. So love for Bhai became that binding factor between us. We started working out together because we both wanted to be like Bhai. And then we became friends and each other's confidantes. Over the years, my family has come to think of him as their son and vice versa. We celebrate each other's festivals, dance during Ganpati visarjan and go to Mohammad Ali Road during Ramzan. And mostly never miss the first day first show of Bhai's movies. I am very grateful to Salman because he gave me a brother I would have never known otherwise.'

Milind admires the fact that Salman promoted the idea of bodybuilding that was desi and yet had a global appeal. He never rejected his roots to bring in a new idea. 'Salman's looks, and by extension his entire persona, has never been about rejecting India's roots but about blending them with a new world order. The dhoti-clad hero with a dholak was giving way to the gym-honed superstar in ripped jeans. Before him was Sanjay Dutt. Not sure how many people know this, but Gavin Packard, the Irish actor often seen in Hindi films, used to train him. Gavin used to work in south Indian and Hindi films. Before them was Dharmendraji and Dara Singhji, who brought in that rugged masculinity but kept it desi. But Bhai took that raw masculinity and fused it with Western gym culture. He was forging a new kind of hero—one who could charm the girls and still punch through walls. He made fitness all about swagger. It's this swagger that sells his films.'

It's possible Salman's love for fitness comes from his role model Dharmendra. The two of them share a special bond. The thespian met Salman while working with Salim on films such as *Sholay*, and today thinks of him as his own son. In many interviews, Dharmendra has been quoted as saying, 'Salman is like my third son!'[4] In a 2021 interview, Salman admitted that he aspired to be fit like Dharmendra. 'I have always followed Dharamji. He has this innocence on his face. He is a good-looking man with vulnerabilities and a good physique.'[5]

This transformation was not without its critics, though. Some argued that the rise of the body-obsessed hero marked a move away from substance. It's a criticism against Salman that has persisted. Could a six-pack overshadow a script? Could a hero's abs be a substitute for acting chops? These questions were valid then and still are. But Milind and Zayed say that a film is made primarily for entertainment. Zayed says, 'Look at my life. I am happy and content, but this isn't a life of privilege. When I go to the movies, I want to have three hours of good time. Don't preach to me, because I have zero energy for that. Every time I see a preachy film, I think to myself that these actors and directors have the privilege to preach while my entire day goes in just trying to make ends meet. If I am spending my hard-earned money on you, just give me what I want—a break from my mundane existence. Show me three hours of Bhai beating up goons and showing his abs. It really gives me the drive to exist.'

'Salman's looks, and by extension his entire persona, has never been about rejecting India's roots but about blending them with a new world order. The dhoti-clad hero with a dholak was giving way to the gym-honed superstar in ripped jeans ... Bhai took that raw masculinity and fused it with Western gym culture. He was forging a new kind of hero — one who could charm the girls and still punch through walls.'

Zayed and Milind break into a loud laugh and go back to discussing details of their gully cricket match the next day. We have often asked what the audience wants from their favourite stars, especially in 2025, when films are barely working their magic at the ticket counters. Turns out it's that basic, even escapist: Just show the audience a good time.

Salman's fitness reshaped the expectations of both audiences and film-makers and what goes into making a successful Hindi film hero! It's thus no surprise that Salman was instrumental in launching one of Bollywood's biggest stars—Hrithik Roshan. No one in tinseltown has ever had a bigger success with their debut film than Hrithik Roshan. It was a dream launch, and Hrithik became an overnight star. The one person who made sure

Hrithik looked like a Greek god and came across as a well-rounded hero was Salman.

In an old episode of *Rendezvous with Simi Garewal*, Hrithik admitted, 'Things got decided that I was going to be in Dad's next film. There was no time, and I was skinny as hell. I was half of this, so you can imagine [pointing to his body]. I asked myself who was the best in the business and the name popped up—Salman Khan! I got his number and called him up just out of the blue. I had to remind him who I was ... Rakesh Roshan's son Duggu, do you remember? He's such a nice guy. He just took me in.'[6]

Salman, true to his role as an elder brother in Hrithik's life, would sometimes call him at 2 a.m. to work out. When Hrithik found it hard to be enthusiastic about it, Salman joined Hrithik for the workout session. 'The characters had to look different. I knew the physicality was very important, especially for this film where I was doing a double role—Rohit in the first part and Raj in the second half. I thought it would be nice if I could, even physically, show the difference between the two characters. So, I was training myself for a year, but I was not seeing the kind of results I wanted to see,'[7] Hrithik added.

Hrithik feels indebted to Salman even today for the emotional support he received. 'Along with training me, the moral support that he gave me was incredible. He was one of the few people who really believed that I would be a phenomenon. I had read that Salman is insecure but (you should see) when he's around me, you know, he's always pushing me. He's like a brother.'[8]

It's important to note that while Salman may have pioneered fitness, the entire machinery of Bollywood—from costume designers and choreographers to directors—aligned itself with this new aesthetic he brought on. Stunt masters created more stylized action sequences to cater to his fan base. Songs were shot in a way that highlighted the hero's physique. Even love stories now featured at least one scene of the hero flexing his muscles.

Kolkata-based sociologist Susmita Bandhopadhyay tells me that she believes Salman's body has been objectified in a way only women's bodies have been. 'The female body is to be lusted after; the male body by design is not considered alluring. The way Salman Khan's body began to be portrayed marked a pivotal shift in the gendered aesthetics of Bollywood. For a very long time, the male star was the subject of action, power and moral authority, but rarely the object of erotic desire. The female body, by contrast, was repeatedly framed through the lens of male fantasy—lingering camera shots, song sequences designed to titillate, the choreography of seduction. What happened with Salman, especially *Pyaar Kiya To Darna Kya* onwards, is that the male body itself became stylized, aestheticized and deliberately placed under an erotic gaze. In many ways, Salman's stardom challenged the traditional binaries of gaze and gender. His body was strong, yet sensual. It invited desire. And this was unprecedented. Male stars before him had certainly been attractive, but rarely had their bodies been so consistently, and consciously, displayed for visual pleasure. This repeated exposure, the ritual of the shirtless scene, made his body a spectacle. In this sense, he was both reinforcing and disrupting normative ideas of gender on-screen.'

But like in the case of women, the pitfall of this is that the body is not allowed to age. And it is subjected to disproportionate criticism when there is even the tiniest slip. Susmita explains, 'The body becomes a prison of its own making. It is not allowed to age or falter. When the body is central to a star's value, it is also subject to intense scrutiny and criticism at the slightest sign of change. While female stars have long faced harsh judgement over ageing or physical transformation, male stars, once relatively shielded, are now entering a similar cycle of aesthetic anxiety. Both the audience and the system demand youthful virility. Endorsement deals, action-heavy scripts, hero-centric narratives all demand the perpetuation of that sculpted, ageless ideal. Salman has the pressure of upholding an entire fantasy of masculinity that the industry has come to bank on. And in 2025, with the trolling he faced for putting on some weight, we have come to realize how punishing such ideals can be.'

Salman's career has often had to negotiate this tension between the man who cries and the man who fights. In doing so, his stardom inadvertently holds up a mirror to the changing, and often conflicted, expectations we place on male celebrities today.

The ideal set by Salman also feeds an entire industry. His rise gave birth to a whole new vocation in the industry, what eventually came to be known as fitness coaches. The term itself has diversified as specializations grew, but a large part of the credit for Salman's fitness must go to the celebrity trainers who helped him achieve this body and maintain it over the years.

So what is this regimen, really? There's no method to his madness, said Salman's trainer from 2001, Manish Advilkar, in a 2008 interview. Just consistency, perhaps. 'No matter how punishing his shooting schedule, Salman will find the time to exercise. He even calls me up at 3–4 a.m. for a training session. Salman goes cycling for three hours to Panvel. He does unbelievable stuff like 1,000 push-ups a day or 2,000 sit-ups a day,' he said.[9]

Another of his early trainers, known in industry circles as just 'D'Souza', said that Salman works out for at least two hours continuously. 'His workout includes one hour of cardio, concentrating on any two body parts each time—triceps, legs, back and biceps. He is very particular and serious about his workout and once in the gym, nothing affects his concentration. While in the gym, if someone approaches him for an autograph or a photograph, he asks them to wait until he is finished with his training. He has got perfect abs and works a lot to keep them in shape. He can do five hundred crunches, pull-ups and chin-ups.'[10]

There is no secret formula, no shortcuts, just a brutal grind fuelled by sheer willpower, says every trainer who has worked with Salman. But I wanted to hear it all from the man who lives Salman's fitness with him, Rakkesh R. Uddiyar. The celebrity trainer was at a shoot in Hyderabad when he sat down to give me an interview for this book after weeks of chasing. 'I can never stop speaking about how wonderful Bhai is,' he tells me right at the start of our conversation.

It's been more than a decade of association now. Rakkesh tells me what he admires the most about the actor is that he doesn't try to follow fads. 'He is not in for short gains. He is in it for the long haul. No one trains like him. Just bring in any newcomer and ask them to keep pace with him at the gym for half an hour—they won't last. As a trainer, I've seen first-hand how relentless he is. Actors come to train with Salman and can't even make it through one session. Some give up and leave, and I've even seen people throw up trying to keep up with his pace,' he tells me.

He reaffirmed what Zayed told me about Salman. 'A big part of fitness is to have a good relationship with food. Salman's a huge fan of eating, but even on his cheat days, he doesn't let things get out of control. Salman allows himself one cheat meal a week, but he never crosses 2,000 calories. And he eats biryani quite frequently. I see celebrities these days go on gluten-free, vegan or sugar-free diets. Bhai eats what he wants. He loves eating home food cooked by his mother. No matter what fancy food you bring him, he will say, "*Ghar ka khana do. Mummy ne jo banaya wahi khana lagao. Wahi khaunga* [Give me home-cooked food. Give me what Mom has made. I will have only that]." He loves eating vegetables. His salads are a must for him. It's a lifestyle for him. His fitness is not based on his movies or shoots. This is who he is.'

Another habit that Salman has is keeping his workout attuned with nature. Rakkesh says, 'People say *kya farak padhta hai*, but *farak padhta hai* [People say it doesn't matter, but it does]. He doesn't like using a fan or an AC while training. Even during cardio, he prefers walking under the sun. *Shiddat ki baat hoti hai* [It's really a matter of passion]. He loves cycling. So many times we've cycled from Bandra to Panvel and worked out in the open at his farmhouse.'

Rakkesh laughs when I tell him stories of fans and their frenzy around Salman's body. 'People are mad about his body. I understand when young boys say, "*Bhai jaisi body chahiye* [I want a body like Bhai's]." And I always tell everyone that this is a man who has never gone to sleep without cardio and weights for over forty years now! *Logo ke bas ki nahi hai Bhai ke takkar tak aane ki* [Matching up to Bhai is not everyone's cup of tea]!' he tells me.

In 2018, Salman put four decades of learning into launching his own chain of gymnasiums—the SK-27 Gym—and joined hands with the Fit India Movement, which is a nationwide initiative in India that promotes a healthy lifestyle by encouraging people to incorporate physical activities and sports into daily life. The pre-Covid plan was to instal 300 gyms across India by 2020. In a statement, Salman said he was on a mission to create a healthier, stronger India, one gym at a time. The idea was to make fitness affordable and accessible to everyone. 'He would like fitness to reach every village, town and city in India, which can also create job opportunities for entrepreneurs and sportspersons of the country,' the press release announcing the venture said.[11]

But often, celebrities are unable to walk the talk. Kartik Sharma, who goes to the gym's branch in Gurgaon, says, 'I work at a call centre. I have been able to enrol at this gym for as low as Rs 750 a month, when most other places were charging as much as Rs 5,000 a month or Rs 8,000 a quarter. The only reason I am fit is because this gym makes room for people from lower-income groups too. Not everyone can afford high-end gyms. I certainly can't. I make about Rs 25,000 a month. Coupled with rent, commute and conveniences, I can't shell out any more than a grand a month. People ask me why I even need a gym—I could go for a run—but where is the space in India to run? There are no fitness parks or tracks for runners, or space for cyclists. Gyms give you a sense of discipline and routine. I wish more people would sign up for this gym, but the rich people of Gurgaon feel it's beneath them to work out with people like us! This has affected the gym's business, but they have still stuck to this model. I have friends who work in high-end companies such as Apple, who want to go only to luxury gyms, but I prefer it here. They have a value system they stand by. And that is so rare these days. That comes from Salman Bhai. He genuinely believes fitness is for everyone!'

In March this year, Union Minister of Parliamentary Affairs Kiren Rijiju also spoke about Salman's role as a fitness inspiration and how he has gone above and beyond to promote a lifestyle that focuses on fitness. Speaking at the India Today Conclave, Rijiju said, 'I am thankful to Salman for promoting the Fit India Movement. He also joined me in promoting adventure sports and cycling in Arunachal Pradesh, leaving his shooting commitments just to be with me. His kindness knows no bounds.'[12]

The casual words of wisdom Salman throws his fans' way hold a deeper meaning for him. He really believes in the words, and unlike most of us, walks the talk.

His fans also respect his resilience in the face of the painful disease he has been battling for nearly two decades now. The actor's battle with trigeminal neuralgia, often called the suicide disease, began around 2007, when he first experienced a searing, electric-shock-like pain in his forehead while filming *Partner* (2007). The diagnosis itself took close to six years. The pain gradually spread to his cheeks and jaws during the shooting of *Veer* (2010), growing so severe by 2011 that during the action-heavy sequences of *Bodyguard*, it became unbearable. Seeking medical help in the US, Salman underwent surgery for it that very year. What was meant to be a brief thirty-minute procedure stretched to eight hours, during which doctors performed a Gamma Knife treatment, an invasive surgery designed to target and calm the overactive nerve responsible for the pain.

After the surgery, doctors told Salman to take it easy. They said relief from trigeminal neuralgia could either last a short while or, if he was fortunate, several years. In spite of that uncertainty, Salman went straight back to work and continued delivering some of the biggest hits of his career. It was only in 2025 that he openly talked about it on *The Great Indian Kapil Show*, saying that trigeminal neuralgia wasn't his only battle and that he had also been diagnosed with a brain aneurysm, which could burst any moment and lead to a brain haemorrhage, and an arteriovenous malformation (AVM), known to trigger seizures. Both conditions are serious, and yet he carries on at the same relentless pace, refusing to let illness dictate his life.

Even at sixty, within three weeks of being trolled by netizens for an accidental show of his belly at a dance performance in the Middle East, he showed up for a shoot at Film City, having shed all of that extra weight.

I asked Rakkesh how Salman manages to bounce back so quickly. He just repeated to me, 'Told you *Bhai ke takkar ka koi hai hi nahi!*' And he quotes a line Salman often uses, '*Upar wala izzat de aur sehat de, shohrat kama lenge uske baad* [May God give us respect and health, we will earn fame after that].' And for that sehat (health) he does everything it takes.

Funnily enough, while writing this chapter, I had the chance to interview Salman. We barely had a few minutes between preps for his new film and other topics. I asked how he managed to pick himself up and work on his physical health while battling the painful trigeminal neuralgia and AVM.

He smiled, and with his trademark honesty, replied, 'With each passing year, month and day, fitness becomes more challenging. I have to invest a lot more time now. Earlier, I could get into shape in just a week or two. Someone cannot be ripped all the time. But every day you have to eat right. And you have to work out. You have to sleep. Repeat this every single day. Don't take a break. And the older you grow, the harder you need to work because it's not as easy any more. There are no short cuts.'

And with that commitment, four months before his sixtieth birthday, Salman is off to shoot a war film with high-end action and underwater stunts! Every few weeks he posts a picture of himself at the gym. But like a fan commented on his post, 'Bhaijaan will rise like never before—prepare YOURSELF.'

" Aap Devil ke peeche, Devil aapke peeche ... Too much fun. "

Kick, 2014

5

Unbeatable and Untamed

YOU can tell a lot about a man by the home he builds. In the case of Shah Rukh, Mannat is a metaphor. An outsider—or anyone who has ever dared to dream big in a city that can eat people alive— looks at this house and remembers that inside lives a man who built his kingdom brick by brick, starting out with nothing but a suitcase. This year, when he temporarily left Mannat as it underwent renovation and moved into an apartment, fans continued to drop by as if Mannat were their shrine.

Salman has never bothered with that kind of symbolism. His home in Galaxy Apartments has remained the same through the decades. No high walls. No flash. No big, heavy gates that keep the world at bay—the crowds outside are the only sign that this is where one of the biggest superstars of Bollywood lives. It tells you he doesn't need his success to reflect in marble floors or manicured balconies. It's about comfort, routine and maybe even a refusal to give in to the industry's obsession with the trappings of stardom.

But it's the farmhouse in Panvel, Arpita Farms, that gives you a window into the man behind the myth. In Mumbai, he lives in the home his father built. But the farm in Panvel has been constructed by him brick by brick. He got it in the first decade of his career, as early as 1996. When the land was initially acquired, it had only two or three small structures. Over time, the family developed the property into a rustic, yet luxurious estate with multiple cottages, a swimming pool, a full gym, stables for horses, open fields and a riding area. By 2018, the farm had grown to at least eleven separate buildings. The farmhouse is a deeply personal refuge for Salman. This is where he goes to escape the chaos of Mumbai, where he farms his own rice, drives tractors, rides horses and hosts his closest friends.

Salman loves to farm. Talking about it on *The Kapil Sharma Show*, Salman said, '*Uske andar pura din bhi chala jata hai, aur aisa lagta hai ki kuchh kiya hai din mein. Aap fasal bhi uga rahe ho* [You spend an entire day there, and you feel like you've done something. You're also growing crops there].'[1]

It is where he celebrates birthdays, New Year's Eve and private gatherings. It's sprawling, quiet and, on most days, it's just him and his animals. Especially his horses. He's said on numerous occasions that the place calms him down. But it runs deeper than that. For instance, his attachment to horses shows a lot about how he functions. Horses don't respond to power, they respond to energy. That's exactly who Salman is too, in his most honest state.

The man who lives in that farmhouse in Panvel is probably the real Salman Khan. It's him minus the cameras, the crowds. It's the one place where Salman Khan doesn't have to be Salman Khan.

There's a reason people compare him to a stallion. He's unpredictable. You can't domesticate him. You can't contain him. He moves on instinct, never on instruction. Always a little wild and a little dangerous.

But if you look closer, a stallion is also one of the most loyal in the animal kingdom. Much like Salman. It doesn't seek glory, but when it runs, you can't look away. You may try to understand Salman through films, headlines and gossip, but it's in Panvel that the metaphor comes alive.

By the mid-1990s, Salman was unstoppable when it came to his star power, box office numbers and aura in industry circles. His stature as a star in the 1990s becomes evident when one glances through trade figures.

If one were to pull up the lifetime collections of the top Hindi films of the decade, one would see Salman dominate that list. He gave huge blockbusters such as *Hum Aapke Hain Koun..!* (1994), *Karan Arjun* (1995) with Shah Rukh, *Jeet* (1996), *Judwaa* (1997), *Pyaar Kiya To Darna Kya* (1998), *Hum Saath-Saath Hain* (1999), *Biwi No. 1* (1999) and *Hum Dil De Chuke Sanam* (1999). The cumulative domestic box office business of these films stands at Rs 224.90 crore, which if adjusted for inflation roughly stands at Rs 1,500 crore today.

He played the lead in *Hum Aapke Hain Koun..!* and *Biwi No. 1*, and made a strong impact despite shared screen space in *Karan Arjun*, *Jeet* and *Hum Dil De Chuke Sanam*. Even his extended cameo in *Kuch Kuch Hota Hai* (1998), which was a Shah Rukh movie, was memorable and talked about. In a decade where he was up against formidable contemporaries such as Shah Rukh, Aamir, Govinda, Sunny Deol and Anil Kapoor, Salman's dominance on box office charts showed his power with the people.

Throughout his career, Salman has never made claims about the superiority of his craft or immersed himself into a character or transformed entirely for a role. He knows where his strengths lie and embraces them. The audience doesn't expect him to disappear into a character like a trained method actor might; instead, they come to watch Salman Khan— him playing a character, or sometimes even himself in roles. That's what fans celebrate. And yet, Salman has had a surprising range of genres—from romance to action to comedy—and has been successful in each one of them. This is a feat uncommon in Bollywood.

Still, in February 1997, when *Filmfare* did a cover story on the reigning Khans of Bollywood, Salman was conspicuously absent from the conversation.[2] The magazine focused almost entirely on Aamir and Shah Rukh—both were fresh and had apparently freed Bollywood from the looming legacy of Amitabh Bachchan, their creative choices instrumental in shaking Indian cinema out of its slump of the late 1980s. They were on the cusp of redefining the industry on their own terms.

The article noted that at thirty-one, both Aamir and Shah Rukh stood on the brink of greatness. The question before them was how far they were willing to push the envelope. How adventurous could they afford to be, now that the industry had recognized their power?

The story offered a solid SWOT analysis of the two, breaking down their strengths, weaknesses, opportunities and threats. And yet, amid all this introspection on the future of the Khans, Salman remained absent.

Let's rewind to understand why. By 1994, Salman's relationship with the press had begun to fray. While his stardom was undeniable, the headlines around him increasingly centred on his personal life—volatile relationships, temperamental behaviour and brushes with controversy. The media, in turn, found its own rhythm in portraying him as a troubled star, someone unpredictable and difficult to access.

In contrast, both Shah Rukh and Aamir had cultivated a far smoother rapport with the press. Shah Rukh, though branded arrogant initially, found a way in with his natural charm, wit and readiness to engage with journalists. He quickly became a media darling. He knew how to give a great quote, how to be candid without being reckless and, most importantly, how to remain in control of his own narrative. Aamir commanded respect for the intelligence and integrity that marked his demeanour. Even in his silence, he projected thoughtfulness, and the media played along.

Salman, however, was cut from a different cloth. His aversion to the media often played out publicly. He called out reporters, walked out of interviews and severed relationships with several top magazines, including *Cine Blitz*. In an interview author-journalist Bhawana Somaaya did with Salman, he said, 'It's so long ago, that it's almost impossible to go back in a chronological order, but let me try. It was immediately after the release of *Patthar Ke Phool*. It was the mahurat of my new film, *Sangdil Sanam*, and there was this usual rush for pictures. Suddenly, while we were all posing for the stills, one of the senior photographers said, "*Yeh apne aap ko Amitabh Bachchan samajhta hai, isko nikalo* [He thinks he's Amitabh Bachchan. Get him out]." Everyone was stunned. I moved away. The photographer's wrath was directed at me, because earlier I'd refused to pose with Rekha for him, when he had visited the filming of *Biwi Ho To Aisi*. He felt that as a newcomer I had no right to a mind of my own. I would have let go of the incident, but a few days later, as I was driving home, I spotted Ketan Desai shooting an advertisement film (Four Square) with

Jackie Shroff on the street outside my building. Naturally, I stopped to say hello. A bunch of photographers were hanging around. That particular cameraman was there too. No sooner had he seen me than he put on a condescending expression. Something just snapped within me. I grabbed his collar and would have hammered him had my father not intervened.'[3]

When Somaaya asked what had made him so angry, he said, 'People's attitudes. I hadn't gone there with war in mind. Just because somebody is refused an interview or a photo session, must he turn so vicious? Do they have a right to be so patronizing? On another occasion, a weekly tabloid sent their photographer to my sets. I was splashed with mud and was doing a difficult shot. When the photographer clicked, I looked at him and said, "Don't. Not now." But he did it again. This time the director noticed it too and pulled him up. The whole thing was blown out of proportion and became a major issue. The editor of the paper preferred to believe the photographer's word to mine, and so the war continued. I've met only a couple of them and most of the time the experience has been weird *(smiles)*. It's not as if I don't give interviews at all. I've talked a couple of times to a couple of magazines, but I can't go on and on about myself every two months. What's there to say? Besides, I've exhausted all the topics. I've talked about my career, my family. I've even talked about Helen aunty. They've written about my failures, my friends, even my girlfriends. I have nothing more to say, so I pleaded for silence. They took affront and began attacking me in print. That really put me off.'[4]

This marked the beginning of a long and bitter estrangement between Salman and the mainstream film media, which only deepened as personal slights, editorial bias and sensational headlines eroded whatever trust there was left between them.

In an old interview, Salman says, 'If I want to meet you and you don't want to meet me, and I keep trying again and again, then I must be a pathetic man. If you don't want to meet me, I shouldn't want to meet you either. End of story. If [I say] terrible things about you, would you still entertain them? If someone abuses your father, your mother, your girlfriend—or insults you—would you maintain a relationship with them?

Of course not. That's it. Neither do I. If someone pushes me into the water, I won't start screaming, "Help! Save me!" I'll swim. I know how. I know my job.'

He added, 'Maybe I'm not the best, but I can do comedy reasonably well. I look decent, I can pull off romantic scenes okay. I can handle action too. I do my bit. That's it. And most importantly, my audience and fans—they are die-hard. Even during my bad phases, they've loved me. That's the only reason I'm still here. Now if I ask you, "Who's your girlfriend? What's your relationship with her?" You'd say, "Why are you asking me that? That's my private life."

'So why is it okay to ask me that all the time? Who I sleep with, who I fight with, it's my personal matter. Not yours. Why don't you write about my performance instead? Say I was bad, say the film was terrible—fair enough. But why comment on my personal life?'[5]

Salman was obviously referring to his rather public break-up with longtime partner former Miss India and actor Sangeeta Bijlani. The press had a field day writing about how she caught him with someone else. What was reported wasn't off the mark, because soon after that split began his romance with model and actor Somy Ali.

In a 2024 interview, Somy confirmed some of the rumours and said they used to meet each other behind Sangeeta's back and that the latter had caught them red-handed.

Somy said, 'Yes, that's absolutely true … Salman used to climb the pipes and come to my room through my window. I found this act of Salman utterly romantic. It was a two-bedroom apartment. However, I remember one day he came over at around 10.30 a.m. Salman and I were sitting and talking in my room and Sangeeta walked in suddenly. She looked at Salman and said, "This is it. You have to make a choice." Salman told me, "Somy, I'll be back in 10 minutes." I assumed that he would go ahead and marry Sangeeta, since the wedding cards had already been printed. But he came back to the room and told me that he had broken up with Sangeeta.'[6]

Soon after, their love affair began. Disturbing rumours started doing the rounds, including stories of Salman allegedly dragging Somy by the hair, humiliating her in public and, in one incident, reportedly pouring a drink on her head because, despite his own indulgence in alcohol, he disapproved of his partner drinking.

After their relationship ended, Somy relocated to the US and eventually started No More Tears, a non-profit dedicated to supporting survivors of domestic violence, to which Salman Khan made a generous contribution. 'Salman's friends donated $150,000 last year. He and I are friends now, we've moved past what happened, and he's very supportive of No More Tears,' she said.[7]

When prodded about whether their history of domestic violence had prompted her to start the support group, Somy set the record straight by saying, 'I was out with some friends and had a rum and Coke; he felt I was in the wrong company and didn't want me drinking, so he poured it on the table. Now I think he did the right thing. But a media guy blew it out of proportion. It went from one thing to another, that he broke the bottle on my head, that he dumped it on my head, but he just poured it on the table and said, "You shouldn't be drinking." He's just overprotective, that's how Salman is in relationships. He has the most generous heart I've ever seen. He will give the shirt off his back to someone.'[8]

In 2024, when Sangeeta was seen celebrating Eid with Salman's family, the internet talked about how their sour relationship had given way to a solid friendship. Over the years, Sangeeta has established that there is no bad blood between them. In an old interview, she even said, 'Connections don't break. Connections never go away. The love between your partners, school friends never goes away. People will come and go. Nobody will be permanent in life. That does not mean you will feel bitter or angry. At one point you evolve. There was a point in time of my life [sic] where I was childish and stupid, but I am a grown-up now. Life is full of experiences.'[9]

To feed people's love for voyeurism, Salman's actions were widely reported. Another infamous story from those years is how Salman slapped film-maker Subhash Ghai at a party. In late November 1998, Salman allegedly hit Ghai at a party hosted by Kailash and Aarti Surendranath to celebrate their wedding anniversary. The tension between Salman and Ghai had been simmering for years after the latter had passed over Salman for *Saudagar*, casting Vivek Mushran instead. So when Ghai later approached Salman for a film, the actor, reportedly drunk that evening, didn't take it kindly. Salman confessed to slapping Ghai in an interview and revealed that he apologized to the film-maker the next day. Salman said, 'I have hurt myself all over. I cannot hurt anyone else. I have only hit Subhash Ghai. Yet, I apologized to him the next day. That person hit me with a spoon, almost broke a plate on my face, urinated on my shoes and grabbed me by the neck. I couldn't control myself. And look what happened. The next day, I had to go and apologize.'[10] The altercation made headlines, but the following day, Salman's father, Salim, stepped in and ensured his son apologized to Ghai, putting an end to the episode. Ghai spoke about how that incident turned them into friends. 'Salman came and stood in front of me like a guilty child. I smiled and asked him, "What happened to you last night?" and he said, "I have come here because my father told me to do so." I said, "So you are not sorry?" and he replied, "Of course I am." That's how we broke the ice,' said the film-maker.[11]

The incident was tabloid gold. A reigning superstar, a bruised veteran director and a high-profile party had every element of a juicy scandal. The press gleefully dissected Salman's temper. For days, the headlines screamed about the actor's volatile streak, with gossip columns savouring and recounting every detail of the showdown.

But Salman, being Salman, gave it right back! He spoke candidly about his messy equation with the press. In a 1998 interview, he said, 'Call me arrogant or whatever you like. I am like this. I try to put forward myself very clearly. I am not scared of speaking the truth. I have been labelled arrogant by a section of the film press, especially those magazines which want me to run around them and accept whatever they write about me. If I call you names, if I write rubbish about your family, will you like it? It can spoil your relationships with your colleagues and family and also land you in a soup. Just because somebody wants to sell his magazine, does it mean I should allow them to make use of me? If I am so bad then why aren't people scared of me? Why do children run and come to me for autographs? Why don't parents hesitate to introduce me to their children? Do I behave like a real-life villain? The truth is that only those people are scared of me, who, when I was going through a low phase, wrote a lot of rubbish about me. I was rude to people because of their own mistakes. Most of them were journalists who indulged in yellow journalism, and I refused to give them interviews. Since I stopped entertaining them, they wrote a load of bullshit about me. Why should I take all that shit? I am a man who has his principles and will adhere to it.'[12]

Another facet of his bitter equation with the press was that he was faulted for not trying to do better. A March 1995 interview even said that he wasn't trying to display more intelligence than he possessed—which is a strange mix of a compliment and a snarky remark. In that same piece, when the interviewer asked him if he aspired to do a *Devdas* like Dilip Kumar or a *Deewaar* like Amitabh Bachchan, Salman honestly revealed that he didn't think he could ever do those.[13] This kind of honesty, while refreshing, fed the narrative that he was content being a safe entertainer rather than an actor who aimed for greatness. Critics felt he wasn't striving to evolve, but only resting on his stardom, showing little ambition to build beyond his established persona. Over time the media began to wonder if it was really only his fans who were putting Salman on a pedestal rather than any real acting prowess.

Rauf Ahmed, who was the *Filmfare* magazine's editor in 1989, admitted that he and the team didn't think much of Salman's performance in *Maine Pyar Kiya*. While in 1989, the Filmfare Most Sensational Debut Award had gone to Aamir Khan for *Qayamat Se Qayamat Tak*, in 1990 the same award went not to Salman, but to Sooraj Barjatya for *Maine Pyar Kiya*. On the other hand, Bhagyashree was awarded the Most Outstanding New Face in 1990. The snub couldn't have been clearer. When asked, Ahmed said the award was never intended for acting alone. He said the editors believed the director's work was more deserving than Salman's acting. 'We didn't think Salman's was a great performance, but they had all assumed it would go to Salman because I had earlier given it to Aamir,' Ahmed said. According to him, it was only from the following year that awards were given specifically for debutant male and female actors. Shah Rukh bagged the award in 1992 for *Deewana*. Ahmed added, 'He [Salman] stopped talking to me, there was a cooling off with his family and he did not turn up for the awards the next year. They were upset because they felt I had deliberately avoided giving the award to Salman.

So I said, it is not charity that I would give it to him. The performance did not merit the award.'[14]

The sentiment among many in the press was clear, and it's an impression that has persisted. They knew Salman commanded massive star power and loyalty, but exhibited minimal curiosity or hunger to transcend that fame. He appeared content being a superstar and didn't seem interested in pushing himself towards the kind of legacy-making pursued by his peers.

Another veteran critic, Subhash K. Jha, once described a conversation where Salman started out by taunting him over a personal matter, then insulted an actor he had had a dispute with and abruptly hung up on him, later calling back only to check whether Jha intended to write it down. 'It is between you and your conscience,' he warned. In his column, Jha said, 'Here is what the unspoken deal between a superstar, specially a superstar called Salman Khan, and the media is: he can say and do what he likes. But the media persons must say and do what Salman likes.'[15]

Despite a slew of big gainers at the box office, he was snubbed repeatedly when it came to the awards. While there is merit to Rauf's stand, part of the reason lay in how the award circuit functioned. Beyond talent, it often required careful behind-the-scenes effort—building the right relationships, attending the right events, staying on good terms with organizers, sponsors and jury members. It wasn't just about the work on-screen—it was also about playing the game off it.

And that is how it works the world over. The road to an Academy Award, too, isn't as straightforward as just being part of a great film. It's often about how well a film is campaigned for. Studios spend months planning how to get the attention of Academy Award voters. That might mean hosting private screenings in Los Angeles or New York, sending voters carefully packaged screeners or placing subtle ads in trade magazines such as *Variety* and *The Hollywood Reporter*. It's also common to see actors and directors making the rounds of film festivals, doing Q&A sessions or turning up at brunches and events, just to stay visible. More often than not, the film that wins isn't the best of the year—it's the one that stays on top of people's minds. Now adapt the same model to Bollywood.

Salman was never particularly good at any of this. He didn't see the point of networking for applause or charming people just to stay in their good books. There was a bluntness to him that didn't always sit well with an ecosystem built on social niceties and quid pro quo. Not one to master strategic warmth, Salman remained distant and often uninterested in seeking validation from a room he didn't feel the need to impress. On bad days, he was quite vocal about this. 'I think only people who lack confidence in themselves chase awards. I will not go up and pick up a Filmfare Award. I won't go just because someone from a magazine calls and says, "We've got to give you an award to come perform." Then they sell sponsorship to a pan masala brand or something. And we sit there in tuxedos like idiots, accepting those trophies. It's like tomorrow, my driver, my servant, my spot boy says, "Baba, we're giving you an award." Ridiculous!'[16]

But despite this, he showed up at award shows for his friends. Everyone remembers his easy camaraderie with Shah Rukh at the Filmfare Awards the year *Dil To Pagal Hai* swept the stage. Shah Rukh called Salman up to share the moment, joking that Salman should take it since he 'never wins anything'. Playing along, Salman stepped up, pretended to tear up in mock gratitude and walked off with the trophy, much to the audience's amusement.

I tracked down an old magazine editor to get his views on why magazines never gave the most popular star awards to Salman. He told me, 'Bollywood award shows are a glossy farce—part PR circus, part dance concert—and barely about merit. Once aired live with the suspense intact, they are now chopped into carefully edited telecasts teased for weeks to maximize ad revenue. Awards come in too many flavours—Popular, Critics' Choice, Jury—so everyone leaves with something. Winners are often tipped off in advance, turning the night into a transaction: Reduce your performance fee, and we'll hand you a trophy. There's zero clarity on who's voting, how selections are made or why genuinely deserving performances are overlooked.

'But Salman had a different problem altogether. He was a crowd favourite, but which movie of Salman's can be called good or award-worthy? For some reason, he never featured as a possible winner!

With Salman, the love was always from the audience, not the intelligentsia. He was the guy people whistled for in single-screens, not someone critics wrote odes about. Award juries didn't know what to do with him. His performances were magnetic, sure, but not nuanced in a way that fit their idea of "good acting". So even if he pulled in crowds larger than any contemporary, he remained the superstar no one thought to vote for. He didn't campaign, didn't play nice—and frankly didn't care to. And that indifference? It cost him trophies, but perhaps earned him something rarer—longevity.'

By 1997, Salman had just about begun to recalibrate his relationship with the press. He went all out to promote *Auzaar*, a film directed by his youngest brother, Sohail Khan. He held a press conference with Sanjay Kapoor, where he specifically spoke about the film. He refused to get riled up at questions that didn't fit the rulebook. He walked everyone through the plot of *Auzaar*. 'So our film is about one boy in love with another boy's girl, and his best friend doesn't even know who he's in love with. Shilpa, Sanjay and I are friends. But because our lives take very different paths, I have to move away. When I return, I'm happy that they got married and all that. I've got a very cool role. I don't have any girl opposite me. I just do my thing. The film is fun. The music is exceptionally good. It's a very simple story. In this movie, there's no typical triangle drama. There's no "boyfriend suspects the friend of having an affair with the girlfriend" kind of situation. It's a straight-up, simple, commercial kind of film, with all the usual ingredients. Sohail is a good director. He tells me what to do, and I do it. He knows my strengths and weaknesses. So he cuts the weak stuff out. I'm very comfortable. I can even tell Sohail if I don't like something.'[17] When he was brazenly asked if Sohail was partial to him, Salman retorted, 'We didn't want that someone says later on that Sanjay *ka role nahi tha* [Sanjay didn't have any role]! We have given him a great role. I hope this film does well for him!' When asked who the weapon, auzaar, was in the film, Salman beamed and said, 'He is the weapon!', referring to Sanjay.

Salman went all out to put Sanjay front and centre, because casting for this film had been difficult. Many actors, including Aamir Khan, Sanjay Dutt and Sunny Deol, had turned down the negative role of Yash, which Sanjay played. In an interview in 2024, Sanjay recounted, 'I was a hot newcomer and despite it being a negative role, I agreed to do it at once when Sohail called me. Salman was a superstar by this time and I don't know if Salman would remember this, but over a drink, he said to me, "When you become a producer, I will do your film."'[18]

By the time *Auzaar* released, Salman was soaring at the box office and the producers decided to give Salman better billing than Sanjay on promotional material. Salman fought back, according to Sanjay. He said, 'When the hoardings of *Auzaar* came up, it had a big Salman picture and a small picture of mine, even though I had a better role. He called up our producer and said, "If you want to have this kind of publicity, then don't put my name also. Sanjay stood by us." Salman made sure that my picture was more than his only and not less. That is how Salman is.'[19]

The film did well, but more than anything else, the music clicked with the audience. The soundtrack, composed by Anu Malik, became one of the film's biggest draws, with foot-tapping numbers such as 'I Love You' becoming instant crowd favourites. It was an album that was the first of its kind and featured an unprecedented ensemble of fifteen to sixteen playback singers.

But where there is Anu Malik, there's also controversy. Pakistani qawwali maestro the late Nusrat Fateh Ali Khan publicly hauled up the makers for distorting his spiritual number, 'Allahu'. He accused Malik of transforming a devotional piece into a romantic pop song, saying, 'He has taken my devotional song "Allahu" and converted it into "I Love You". He should at least respect my religious songs.'[20]

Another number, 'Dil Le Le Lena', came under fire for being an unofficial reworking of the global hit 'Macarena' by Los Del Río. Malik acknowledged the source, candidly stating, 'That's not my music at all and everyone knows that. The group called D-Funk, we worked upon this song to suit the Indian people. People have been dancing to this song. I wrote the lyrics for the song, [but] I won't take credit for the song as I did not compose it.'[21] Producer Ramesh Taurani even defended him, saying, 'So what if it's been lifted? We've presented it well.'[22]

Unfazed, they put all their might into a high-visibility promotion strategy. They launched an on-ground campaign involving a fleet of bikers in uniform riding across the city to announce the film's arrival. The event was flagged off by Salman himself. Additionally, a massive contest was launched, offering prizes to lucky viewers, which was, again, among the first and most ambitious fan-engagement tactics used to promote a film.

Rohit Malhotra, a techie based in Gurgaon, remembers the *Auzaar* songs from his graduation party at Delhi's iconic Ghungroo. '"Dil Le Le Lena" was our very own "Macarena", and no '90s music CD was complete without it. I still remember our college farewell. We were all in shimmery shirts, trying to copy Salman's steps, completely offbeat but full of josh. My best friend twisted his ankle midstep, another guy tore his trousers doing that weird pelvic move and I was so into it that I didn't realize that one of our teachers was watching us! I remember how that song made us feel like we were in a Bollywood music video. Total madness, total nostalgia. No one does cool better than Salman Bhai.'

The following year, Sohail Khan stepped into the role of producer with *Pyaar Kiya To Darna Kya*. This time Salman and Arbaaz both starred in the film, along with Kajol and Dharmendra. Kajol plays a free-spirited girl who falls in love with a mischievous boy, who then must convince her overprotective brother to accept their relationship. The film was a classic Salman crowd-pleaser, and it worked with the audiences.

While *Auzaar* had fared well, doubling its investment upon release, the press had expected far more from it. But it was an action film, and the 1990s were all about romance—unlike our post-pandemic world, where action movies are ruling the roost! *Pyaar Kiya To Darna Kya* was more aligned with audience expectations, as it was a sweet, funny romance with generous doses of emotion thrown in. With Sohail producing the film, it was in some ways a home production, and Salman, with his experience, stepped in to shoulder more responsibilities. During one of the press interactions, Salman made it clear that his movies would be clean entertainers. 'You haven't seen me in a film that has exposure or cruelty. I do very clean films,' he said during an interview for the film's promotions.[23]

Pyaar Kiya To Darna Kya wasn't expected to be a blockbuster, but it turned into one of the biggest hits of 1998. It had all the right ingredients—Salman at his charming best, Kajol bringing heart to the film and a soundtrack that got everyone crooning. 'O O Jaane Jaana' became the feather in its cap. It was this song that gave Salman's abs a fan following of their own.

'O O Jaane Jaana' was a song Salman had liked for years. Talking about it, Salman said, 'I had this song on a CD for almost 6 years and was rejected by many big music companies at that point in time. I loved the song so much that I decided to use it for my upcoming film of that time *Pyaar Kiya To Darna Kya* and told Sohail that we should use this song for our movie.'[24] It was initially to be part of the film *Jab Pyaar Kisise Hota Hai*, but got rejected by the makers. Salman recounted in an interview, 'I heard this song and it was like the most fabulous song that I had heard. So I tried to put it in that movie, then I tried to put it in some other movie and some other movie. Nobody took that song from me. Then we started *Pyaar Kiya To Darna Kya*, so I said, "If I like the song so much, I'm going to put it in my movie."'[25]

The film threw everything into the mix—romance, family drama, comedy, action—the full 1990s Bollywood thali. Salman was the cheeky lover boy pulling every trick in the book to impress Kajol, all while dodging the glares of her overprotective brother, played by Arbaaz Khan. At a time when most young boys were sneaking notes into their crush's notebooks or blushing their way through stolen glances, this film made them feel bold, like their love was worth fighting for. Many men who were teenagers in the 1990s will vouch for how this film encouraged them to ready their abs, guitar and wit to win over their lady love!

The film didn't bother much with logic, but it wasn't trying to. It leaned into emotion, fun and big gestures—stuff that worked for the audiences of the time. Critics were lukewarm, but the public had a blast. And for Salman, it was just more proof that he could carry a naughty romance and a family drama at the same time.

This was also the period when Salman's on-screen image was shifting. He was itching to break out of the mould he had created for himself. No matter what had gone wrong in his life, work was always a good distraction for him. While recovering from his broken engagement, he was delivering back-to-back hits. Even when the court cases against him were in their final stages, he was shooting for *Bajrangi Bhaijaan*. Because of his good looks and the fact that romance as a genre was booming at that time, he was being offered rom com leads. After all, he had given two of Bollywood's most iconic romantic hits as Prem! With *Judwaa* (1997), he moved away from the morally upright, clean-cut Barjatya hero that audiences had come to associate him with, and embraced a more boisterous, masala-driven double role. He knew that as a man of the masses, with little support from the press, his longevity would come from his fans—and that the loyalty of fans was won by surprising them every time. In David Dhawan's zany universe of *Judwaa*, Salman played both Prem, a well-mannered, naive gentleman, and Raja, the wisecracking, reckless tapori, with equal ease and charm. The film's story circles around twin brothers separated at birth—one raised as an NRI in the US (Prem) and the other on the streets of Mumbai (Raja)—who cross paths years later and swap lives, leading to a plot full of chaos and comedy. Their identical appearance gives rise to utter confusion among the characters, and the two eventually team up to defeat the main villain of the film. The film is a remake of the Telugu film *Hello Brother* (1994), which, in turn, was based on the Jackie Chan film *Twin Dragons* (1992). Mamta Kulkarni was approached for the second female lead in *Judwaa*, but was later replaced by Rambha, whose voice was lent by Tabu.

Double roles have always worked in Bollywood. From Dilip Kumar's *Ram Aur Shyam* (1967) and Hema Malini's *Seeta Aur Geeta* (1972), to Sridevi's *Chaalbaaz* (1989) and Anil Kapoor's *Kishen Kanhaiya* (1990), the trope of twins or lookalikes separated by circumstances has been used to explore themes such as nature versus nurture, class divides and order versus chaos. Usually these stories place one character in a controlled, often urban, setting and the other in a rougher environment, letting actors flex their skill range while doubling the drama and comedy. *Judwaa* was both a continuation of a beloved formula and a redesigning of it.

Judwaa was Salman's first major foray into broad, physical comedy, because it allowed him to embody two sharply contrasting personas in the same film. In Raja, the street-smart, smart-alecky, slightly raunchy tapori, Salman discovered the beginnings of a new screen identity that was far less polished, far more unpredictable and infinitely more mass-friendly.

If Prem was the last gasp of the Barjatya-era hero, Raja was the prototype of the 'Bhai' avatar that Salman perfected in the years to come. There was an easy swagger and a comic sharpness that made Salman instantly relatable to the front-bencher crowd. His slang, his body language, even his dance moves, were drawn from the streets, and the audiences lapped it up.

But how did he land the film? There are many stories to it. 'I have known Salim saab since long before I knew Salman,' David Dhawan warmly recalled on the phone call with me one evening. Their association goes back to the mid-1980s, when Dhawan was editing *Naam* (1986), a hard-hitting Mahesh Bhatt film that Salim had scripted after his split with Javed Akhtar. 'That was the first time I met Salim saab. He had such a sharp mind and such clarity in his writing. It left an impression,' Dhawan said.

Years later, when he was looking to become a director, fate brought Salman into the picture. *Judwaa* was originally written with Govinda in mind. But then I met Salman. I saw in him something I hadn't seen before. He had that raw star power, the ability to effortlessly switch between charm and mischief.'

But if Govinda is to be believed, Salman called and requested him to drop out of the film. 'I was at the top of my game at the time when a film called *Banarasi Babu* was being filmed. I was also working on *Judwaa* at that time. While the shooting for *Judwaa* was on, Salman Khan called me one night at around 2–3 a.m. and asked me, "Chichi Bhaiyya, how many hits will you give?" I asked him, "Why, what happened?" He said, "The film which you are shooting right now—*Judwaa*—please withdraw yourself from the project and please give the movie to me. You also have to give me the director of the film."'[26]

Whatever the case may be, the film changed Salman's fate and gave the industry an actor–director pairing for keeps. *Judwaa* allowed Salman to be goofy, cocky, flirtatious and aggressive, often all in the same scene. And as Salman juggled Prem and Raja with infectious energy, he proved that he could not only carry a comedy but also create space for a new kind of hero, who didn't need critical validation as long as the crowds were cheering.

Backed by Sajid Nadiawala, who ensured the film was mounted on a grand scale, and steered by David Dhawan, with his instinctive knack for comedy, *Judwaa* turned out to be a huge commercial success. Released across 220 screens, the film opened to one of the strongest box office responses of the time. It raked in Rs 76 lakh on the first day and collected Rs 2.19 crore over its opening weekend. To reiterate, this was 1997—the same year the Filmfare article on the Khans was published. The film went on to earn a total net of Rs 13.14 crore in India, which was a significant figure in the pre-multiplex era. Overseas, it added another $250,000 to its tally. With a worldwide gross of Rs 24.28 crore, *Judwaa* cemented itself as a commercial success and reaffirmed Salman's stardom. The amount is today equivalent to Rs 233.42 crore when adjusted for inflation.[27]

A superstar's stardom can play out in many ways. Some get comfortable and serve more of the same. Some get experimental and try to push forward with bolder ideas. Salman is an interesting case study in diversifying. Early on he realized that he worked well in romance leads. But by the mid-1990s he was considering what else he could do, and his association with David Dhawan showed that he could also make people laugh!

Judwaa can be seen as a big shift—the first of many he would take in his career—in terms of switching up things and taking risks. *Judwaa* showed Salman's hunger to constantly reinvent himself, be it through genre shifts, character quirks or even dance styles.

Dhawan believed that the dichotomy of the characters was what had attracted the audience. 'Prem had masoomiyat (innocence), while Raja had badmashi (mischief), and Salman got both spot-on. For the cast and crew, the shoot was more picnic than project. The film embraced my formula: *Zyaada hasao, thoda rulaao* [Make them laugh a lot, and cry a little],' he told me.

'Salman is a seasoned actor. When he gives a shot, you might feel that he is not interested, but in reality he is the most interested actor on the set. He does a good job. He works from the heart, there is "thehrav" (stillness) in his performance. It was my first film with Salman, and it was superb working with him.'[28]

The David–Salman duo went on to make many more movies together—including *Biwi No. 1* (1999), *Dulhan Hum Le Jayenge* (2000), *Chal Mere Bhai* (2000), *Mujhse Shaadi Karogi* (2004) and *Partner* (2007).

Judwaa brought in another friend in Salman's life, producer Sajid Nadiadwala. In *Hall of Fame*, recounting the exact moment during the film's shoot when Sajid knew Salman was a friend he'd always want in his life, he said, 'We were returning one night after shooting for *Judwaa* at Mukesh Mills in Mumbai. At Worli I spotted an accident through my rear-view mirror and mentioned it to Salman. He insisted that I reverse, so we could help the people in the car. There were a couple of teenage boys stuck in the car and they couldn't come out as the doors were jammed. Salman broke the glass and hurt himself but didn't give up. He was bleeding and crying because he felt he couldn't help the boys. We tried to stop a bunch of extras who were travelling in another car, but no one stopped because they didn't want to get involved. When we finally reached the hospital, the doctors refused to treat the victims until a police case was filed. This is where Salman totally lost it and started screaming at the doctor. He couldn't understand how the doctor could stand around and talk about procedures while there were lives in danger. Salman was behaving as if those boys were his family members, even though he had no clue about who they were.'[29]

Audiences know Sajid and Salman as a hit jodi today, but their friendship was founded on that incident. 'He is a kind man, and that's what matters more than the star he is!' Sajid said.

Judwaa also laid down two unwritten rules for a typical Salman Khan entertainer: an Eid release and catchy music with hook steps. There is a DNA to this genre of Salman films—slapstick humour, foot-tapping music and a carefree disregard for logic. And the success of this genre proved that audiences didn't come for the plot of the film—they came for the vibe: the larger-than-life persona, the punchlines, the dancing and, above all, the attitude.

Judwaa's now-iconic tracks 'Oonchi Hai Building' and 'Tan Tana Tan' didn't merely play in clubs or weddings—the songs introduced a new grammar to dance that was equal parts silly and cool. Young fans began imitating his exaggerated moves.

'I was in college when *Judwaa* released, and I remember people going "Tan Tana Tan Tan Tan Tara" like it was a greeting,' recalls Vishal K., a bank official and a long-time Salman fan from Kanpur. 'Every time the song played at a party, someone would *have* to do the Salman step. It wasn't even about being a good dancer—it was just about being fearless, like him. He made it cool to look ridiculous. For the first time, dancing like a bit of a cartoon became aspirational.'

There is a DNA to this genre of Salman film—slapstick humour, foot-tapping music and a carefree disregard for logic. And the success of this genre proved that audiences didn't come for the plot of the film, they came for the vibe: the larger-than-life persona, the punchlines, the dancing and, above all, the attitude.

It's not very different even today. A regular Sunday night at Radio Bar in Khar, Mumbai, lights up every time there's a Salman song. DJ Bobby tells me, 'We have a schedule for this. After every ten minutes, we play a Salman banger and the crowds come alive. Most of his films from the 1990s had impeccable music.' So what are the crowd favourites? 'Usually *Judwaa* and *Jab Pyaar Kisise Hota Hai* songs. "O Janaa" is a hit. And, of course, "Janam Samjha Karo"!'

The year 1998 turned out to be a stellar one for Salman at the box office. *Pyaar Kiya To Darna Kya* struck gold, followed by *Jab Pyaar Kisise Hota Hai* with Twinkle Khanna. Even *Bandhan*, which trade analysts prematurely dismissed, surprised everyone by performing well. In some ways, he bounced back from the shaky ground his personal life was on. In an interview during the *Bandhan* promotions, he said, 'I was always considered the black sheep of the family. But then, the situation is not the same any more. I have done a lot of good work. I have given so many hits, and the number of flops that I have given is much less than anyone else in the industry today. I am not here today to prove a point. I have already proved my worth by giving hits like *Hum Aapke Hain Koun..!* and *Karan Arjun,* apart from *Judwaa* and other films. I was neither disillusioned nor disheartened when my career took a turn for the worse. In fact, I accepted my fate as part of the job. Highs and lows are part of the profession ... I just indulged myself and had a good time. Sitting and regretting things is silly and idiotic. The past is gone. We have to concentrate on the present and get a better future. But that does not mean that you slog your ass out. You have to work hard, but then you have to enjoy what you are doing, so that you do not ruminate and cry over it if it does not work.'[30]

Salman was having fun working and finding himself. Even cameos such as in *Kuch Kuch Hota Hai* made a lasting impression. Farida Jalal, who played Shah Rukh's mother in the film, remembers how the crowd erupted into shrieks when Salman made an entry to the tune of 'Saajanji Ghar Aaye'. Ranveer Singh even called it Bhai's best entry on *Koffee with Karan*. '*Aaya bhi toh chappar phaad ke* [He entered the scene in his full glory]!; that back shot is iconic,' he said during the rapid fire round.[31]

In fact, Salman's Aman has seen a surge of love in the past few years. Younger filmgoers have been raging about Aman getting a raw deal. I spoke to Lisa Mendes, a baker who lives in Panjim. She said, 'When I rewatched *Kuch Kuch Hota Hai* after binge-watching *The Summer I Turned Pretty*, it hit me that Aman was the ultimate green flag. He's kind, secure, respectful and, most importantly, never made Anjali feel anything but precious. Think about it—Rahul took her for granted in college, laughed at her feelings and only realized he "loved" her when Tina was gone. Meanwhile, Aman saw Anjali exactly as she was and loved her for it. He didn't want to change her, didn't mock her, didn't gaslight her. He was steady, patient and so emotionally mature. He never once made her feel trapped. He was ready to marry her, but the second he realized where her heart really was, he stepped aside with so much grace. Honestly, I don't get why we as an audience still root for Rahul. Anjali should've chosen Aman. Because in real life, Rahul is the red flag—you don't want a man who only sees your worth after you glow up. You want an Aman, who sees your worth from day one.

We're always told to chase the complicated bad boy, when the good guy has been the prize all along. Watching Aman now, as a Gen-Z kid, I just kept thinking that the world needs more of him. We don't need another Rahul—we need men who make us feel safe, seen and celebrated. Anjali deserved that. We all do.'

But little did audiences know that that beautifully suited-up man on-screen actually came to the set wearing distressed jeans and would have been happy to keep them on for the scene. Karan Johar narrated the story on a chat show. 'We were filming the song "Saajan Ji Ghar Aaye" and Salman came in wearing torn jeans and a black T-shirt. We had a suit made for him. I was very scared of Salman, and I am still. At that moment, he said, "You know what, no dulha has ever worn torn jeans and made it a trend." I reluctantly said no and then burst out crying in front of him.' Karan started pleading with him to wear the suit, saying that it was his first film. 'He quickly agreed to wear the suit and asked me to stop crying,' the film-maker recalled during a conversation with Prabal Gurung.[32]

The idiosyncrasies notwithstanding, Salman was having a ball.

Jab Pyaar Kisise Hota Hai was another film of the time that worked wonders with the audience and has aged into a crowd favourite over the years. Salman plays Sooraj, a charming spoilt brat who's used to getting what he wants, thanks to his good looks and smooth talk, until he meets Komal (Twinkle Khanna), a woman who doesn't fall for the act. For the first time, he wants to change, to be better, to deserve someone. But just as he begins to shed his old ways, life throws him a curveball: A young boy shows up claiming to be his son. Played by Aditya Narayan, the child, Kabir, becomes a mirror to Sooraj's past mistakes. Suddenly, love is about earning Komal's respect while owning up to his past and learning what it truly means to take accountability. *Jab Pyaar Kisise Hota Hai* is as much about romance as it is about redemption, told through the story of a man who stumbles his way around fatherhood and emotional maturity. Written by Honey Irani and directed by Deepak Sareen, the film helped Salman tap into a demographic he hadn't focused on until then—kids.

In the film Salman was adorable with Aditya, a motif that stuck. During an appearance on *SaReGaMaPa*, which Aditya hosted, Salman said, 'I had worked with Aditya when he was young. We shot for *Jab Pyaar Kisise Hota Hai*. I used to wipe his nose when he was a kid.' Aditya added, 'I always had a runny nose, and he was there for my rescue. But look how I've grown up, but Salman Bhai is still the same young, dashing man.'[33]

Children responded to that softness. In a decade filled with towering male heroes or overly stylized romantic leads, Salman in *Jab Pyaar Kisise Hota Hai* played a man trying to do right by a child he didn't know he had. Around 1997, Aamir was dazzling audiences in *Ishq* with his prankster energy, Shah Rukh was redefining the template of romance in *Dil To Pagal Hai* and Sunny Deol was roaring his way through *Ziddi* with fists of fury. Against that backdrop, Salman was on-screen fumbling with Kabir's shoelaces. He didn't start off as a father figure, but watching him grow into one in the film, trying to cook for Kabir and playing games with him made him an endearing figure with viewers.

Many teenagers who watched the film in the late 1990s wanted a dad like him. 'That mix of childlike mischief and adult care he showed towards Aditya Narayan's character set him apart,' says my friend Namit Kapoor, who remembers he told his father to watch the film and be a bit more like Salman Khan. Did it work? 'Papa did try, but we obviously can't expect regular dads to miraculously become emotionally involved, because they didn't see it in their fathers. This film showed us how a dad could really be a son's best friend. Most films even now show difficult father–son equations. Salman's character in the film was a cricket coach, a confidant and a goofy but loving dad. Some of this was also seen in Aamir Khan's *Akele Hum Akele Tum*, but in that the father–son relationship came second to the husband–wife romance.'

There are many opinions on the film's complex gender politics, especially the ending, where Twinkle's character forgives him when it is revealed that Kabir is his son. Mehseen Sadiq, a Salman fan who is now a teacher in Dubai, tells me, '*Jab Pyaar Kisise Hota Hai* is peak pre-millennium Bollywood morality, the kind where a hero can have a past and an illegitimate child, and still walk away with the heroine on his arm and the audience's applause. The film never bothers to ask important questions, because it's too busy rewarding the hero's charm. The script plays into a well-worn trope: Men get to mess up, 'grow' and still end up with the girl, and women have to be the ones to absorb the emotional debt. Twinkle Khanna's character might have set conditions for love, but once the man was excused, the heavy lifting, forgiving, accommodating and adapting all fell squarely on her. It's the kind of narrative 1990s' Bollywood excelled at espousing. It was dressing up male redemption as romantic destiny. The child's innocence is used as a shortcut to absolution, and Salman's charisma does the rest. The politics is highly questionable, but the packaging is irresistible. And maybe that's the most telling part— the film doesn't just rehabilitate its hero, it makes you root for him while he's being let off the hook.'

Mehseen's sister, Khadija, contradicts this critique of the film by pointing out that it mirrors the classic Salman trope the audiences fall for. 'In *Jab Pyaar Kisise Hota Hai*, he plays a man who messes up but tries to fix things, and that's why you root for him. He makes being flawed feel real. It could be any of us. But can we undo our past? That sudden shift from charm to guilt feels like the guy next door trying to figure things out. That's what makes the character irresistible. He can be a skirt-chaser one moment and a doting father the next. Both are equally him. So is he good or bad? It's Salman. Someone who always messes up, but has a good heart and never stops trying!'

Like always, Salman ditched the discourse about the politics of his films and dove into his next. In 1999, David Dhawan reunited with him for *Biwi No. 1*, casting him as a two-timing husband whose charm lay in his role as a loving father and a dutiful son. When I asked Dhawan what the secret behind these relentless successes was, he said, 'Cinema is the cheapest and the only entertainment for middle-class India. It's escapism. That is what most of the films are about.'

It was this idea of escapism that stitched together the Salman–David collaborations. If *Judwaa* opened the gate for a more mischievous, masala-driven Salman, *Biwi No. 1* took it forward. The morality was messy, but the entertainment was intact.

Salman fan Mahesh N., an engineer from Vizag, says, 'By the late 1990s, Bollywood had room for everything. The era of soft romances and shy heroes existed parallelly with masala flicks, full of swagger, slapstick and sex appeal. *Judwaa* arrived right at that pivot, and Salman Khan, with David Dhawan, caught the pulse before most. *Biwi No. 1* took that prototype and ran with it. The cheating husband, instead of being condemned, was rewarded with laughs, sympathy, even redemption. It was the kind of film where moral ambiguity didn't matter as long as the punchlines landed and the music worked. David Dhawan understood better than anyone that the audience wasn't looking for lessons—they were looking for an escape. And Salman, with his shirt unbuttoned and smirk in place, gave them exactly that. He was chasing fun. And in doing so, he became endlessly watchable.'

The film starred Karisma Kapoor and Sushmita Sen, along with Anil Kapoor and Tabu. In fact, for a young Sushmita, this was a dream come true. She was so smitten with Salman that she had his posters all over her room! But she wasn't the first co-star to have had a crush on him. During a chat show, Kareena Kapoor admitted that Salman was Karisma's first crush too!

When I asked David Dhawan what the secret behind these relentless successes was, he said, 'Cinema is the cheapest and the only entertainment for middle-class India. It's escapism. That is what most of the films are about.'

Sushmita, however, was very open about her love for Salman. She admitted in an interview that she used to spend all her pocket money on Salman's posters back in the day. She even had a picture of the famous kabootar (pigeon) from *Maine Pyar Kiya*. 'Whatever pocket money I got, I would buy Salman Khan posters with … My parents always said that if the homework is not done on time, we will remove those posters so I would always finish my homework on time because those posters were sacrosanct. I was in love with this man,' she recalled.[34]

Salman didn't believe Sushmita until he saw it with his own eyes. 'We became friends and I told him this story. Then one day, he told me that he saw a picture of me as a 15-year-old and there's a poster of his film behind me so I said I told you that I had a poster in my room. So he asked, "Which was your favourite film?" I said, *"Maine Pyar Kiya"*. He went to Dhawan and he said, "We have to make *Maine Pyaar Kyun Kiya* with Sushmita Sen."'[35]

Salman is one of Sushmita's favourite co-stars. She said that during the shoot of 'Chunnari Chunnari', David Dhawan told her not to wear heels because of Salman's height. Sushmita went on the set wearing flats. She recalls Salman saying, 'Nice outfit but why are you wearing those chappals?' So she said, 'You're short, na.' He burst out laughing and said, '*Ja na, heel pehen ke aa* [Go, wear your heels]. I'll manage my height; you manage yours.'[36]

The actress, who attended Salman's fifty-third birthday party, posted a video of her dancing with the man of the hour on 'Chunnari Chunnari' and sent the internet into a tizzy. 'Whenever life gives us a chance to sit it out or dance… we dance,' she wrote.[37] *Biwi No. 1* was a powerhouse at the box office. Made on a Rs 12 crore budget, it netted Rs 25.58 crore in India (around Rs 35.5 crore gross) and added roughly Rs 6 crore from overseas, bringing its total to approximately Rs 49.8 crore worldwide, which placed it among the top four Hindi film grossers of the year. Even more remarkable: When adjusted for inflation, *Biwi No. 1*'s Indian net collection is about Rs 189.9 crore, placing it in the top seventy all-time Bollywood grossers. The enduring strength of the Salman–David formula continued to resonate decades later. Their legacy is proof that this brand of escapist comedy still holds commercial power.[38]

But beneath the slapstick lay a curious case study in shifting gender politics. Harshali Mehta, who is a film student in Paris, tells me, 'At a time when Bollywood's moral compass was swinging, the film walked the thin line between humour and subversion. The plot, which was centred on a philandering husband juggling a wife and a mistress, could have easily turned into a morality tale. Instead, it became something else entirely. Salman Khan's character was indulged. A flawed male lead could still be desirable, forgivable and loveable … But *Biwi No. 1* didn't just focus on its leading man. Karisma Kapoor and Sushmita Sen were more than romantic foils—they became the emotional spine of the film. Karisma wasn't just the "wronged wife" but her journey involved heartbreak, defiance and transformation. She leaves her husband, rebuilds her self-worth and then decides whether or not to return—not out of compulsion, but from a place of choice. That arc gave her a level of agency rarely afforded to women in such plots. Meanwhile, Sushmita's modern "other woman" role wasn't villainous but vulnerable, complicating the viewer's allegiance. Together, the film played out like a comedy, but the emotional stakes and the subtext offered a surprisingly progressive lens for its time.'

With this film, David Dhawan turned his 'No. 1' films into a genre of their own—films that somehow always landed. And in the middle of that madness, Salman was always there to put a smile on your face.

That same year, in 1999, *Hum Dil De Chuke Sanam* was released. In Sanjay Leela Bhansali's sweeping, larger-than-life romance, Salman starred opposite Aishwarya Rai, kick-starting one of Bollywood's most-talked-about real-life love stories. It was also the year when *Hum Saath-Saath Hain* became a big success as Salman went back to playing the much-loved Barjatya 'Prem'. And while it could be called a banner year for the star, it was also one that was marred by too many controversies, more than Salman could count.

While filming in Jodhpur in 1997, Salman was accused of hunting the endangered blackbuck, an act that led to a years-long legal battle. He was booked under multiple charges, including under the Arms Act, 1959 and the Wildlife Protection Act, 1972. He was arrested briefly in 1998 but was granted bail shortly after. What began as a wildlife law violation spiralled into one of the most high-profile celebrity court cases in India. In 2018, he was convicted and sentenced to five years in prison, only to be granted bail again. The incident would cast a long shadow over his career, becoming inseparable from his public image, even today.

In the biography *Being Salman*, Jasim Khan wrote, 'His first tryst with infamy came in 1998. In the months of September–October, Salman was shooting for the movie *Hum Saath-Saath Hain* ... in Jodhpur. He was accused of poaching the endangered chinkara (blackbuck) in the vicinity of Jodhpur, and also of possessing illegal weapons. Saif Ali Khan, Sonali Bendre, Tabu and Neelam are the others accused in the case. However, Salman is alleged to have indulged in poaching on other occasions as well: once in Jodhpur at Ghoda Farm near Mathani, and in two other cases in Bhawad, all three instances involving deer. Controversies have thus been his constant companion.'[39]

As per a 1998 news report, H.L. Meena, conservator of forests, Jodhpur, told Rediff on the NeT in an interview that Harish, driver of the white Gypsy in which Salman and his friends travelled, and five people who had accompanied them, had turned approvers. According to their testimony, Salman was the prime accused, since he was the one to kill all five animals with a .22 rifle and a revolver. The other accused, actors Saif Ali Khan, Tabu, Sonali Bendre and Neelam, were onlookers, out to have some fun and adventure. Some villagers who were woken up in the night by the sound of gunfire also testified in the case. Meena said that they chased the culprits, but the Gypsy was too fast for them. But the villagers were still confident that the actors were the culprits because they had been spotted earlier in the day surveying the place.[40]

There are many conflicting stories about what happened that night. In a 2008 interview, Salman denied shooting the blackbuck. 'It's a long story there and I wasn't the one who shot the blackbuck. There's no point. This hunting case, that case, he is ill-mannered, he has hit this person ... you don't even know what 1% of the truth is. Just because I would not say things. ... Because I don't need to speak about anything or anybody and I will not. You have your own dignity, you have your own loyalty and priorities in life. And I chose not to speak about it ... If it involves somebody else then you don't have the right to speak about them. I believe in Karma and whatever wrong happens, I have to pay for it the next day.'[41]

Salman said he only fed the blackbuck. But whatever the truth may be, the incident also cast a shadow over Salman's and Sooraj's long friendship, said the press reports of the time. A family friend of the Barjatyas was quoted as saying, 'Salman and Sooraj were very close. When on the sets, Salman instinctively knew what Sooraj wanted him to do. But Barjatya could never come to terms with Salman's bratty personality. He's a very composed person and couldn't cope with Salman's rebellious streak. Soorajji didn't say a word to Salman but [has] maintained his distance from him ever since.'[42]

Despite the storm brewing behind the scenes, the film was met with thunderous applause. *Hum Saath-Saath Hain* eventually became the biggest Bollywood film of 1999, grossing approximately Rs 39.18 crore net domestically (Rs 54.42 crore gross) and Rs 15.16 crore overseas, with a worldwide total of around Rs 69.58 crore. Produced on a budget of roughly Rs 17 crore, the film was labelled a 'blockbuster' by Box Office India. When adjusted for inflation, its net Indian collection equals about Rs 274.26 crore, placing it among the top thirty highest-grossing Hindi films of all time. The film sold nearly 28.5 million tickets, an extraordinary figure that showed its mass appeal.[43]

But for many Salman fans, the film is a bittersweet indulgence. Jigar Jain, a businessman from Jaisalmer, says, 'Hum Saath-Saath Hain is nostalgia. I grew up watching it with my family every Diwali. But whenever I watch it, I think of the blackbuck case. There's this weird guilt that creeps in. Salman as Prem was all about values and being the perfect son. But off-screen, it felt like he was living a totally different life. That gap between Prem and Salman is too wide to ignore. It's a guilty pleasure, no doubt, but it always makes me realize that actors are not what they say they are.'

But there are those who can separate the art from the artist. As Ruchi Nair, a painter based in Mumbai, puts it, 'Whatever was happening off-screen, on-screen he was Prem. If we start holding grudges against our favourite celebrities, we would have to stop watching everything. Starting with Woody Allen to Justin Baldoni to Hugh Jackman, and even Tom Cruise and Brad Pitt. Maybe there is some truth to the fact that women like bad boys—we think we can change them. Most women have a saviour complex and that's why we go for Salman. He is a man I want to save and protect. Because beneath all the macho is a "pookie". Salman is actually Prem pretending to be dabangg. That's the core feeling from which his female fans operate.'

Why do women wish to save this man who keeps landing himself in trouble? Ruchi tells me that most women in the 1990s were happy to be rehab centres for 'badly behaved', 'commitment-phobic' men. 'How is Salman any different from Sex and the City's Mr Big? He is the Mr Big of India, and because life cannot be like our TV shows, or Barjatya movies, there hasn't been a single woman yet who can tame this man. Or as Carrie Bradshaw would say, he is probably yet to find someone just as wild as him to run with.'

But not all women endorse the film or Salman. Anika Verma, a sociology student from Delhi, lashes out during our chat. 'Watching *Hum Saath-Saath Hain* as a child, I was enchanted by the songs, the wedding shenanigans, the spectacle of togetherness. But growing up, it hit me how suffocatingly idealized these women were—always graceful, never angry and constantly virtuous through silence and service. They were ornaments to the men's emotional arcs, not people with inner lives. It's frustrating because the film equates feminine goodness with self-erasure. That glossy family portrait suddenly feels like a gilded cage. And as for Salman, he is not Prem—he *plays* Prem. We should have that neatly distinguished in our heads.'

Well, love him or hate him, this character—and the man who plays him—has clearly been seared into everyone's minds for the past three decades.

Every once in a while, an actor feels the need to scale up to reach for something more than box office numbers. Salman was already being celebrated by trade but was probably hoping to be seen as more than just a bankable star. He wanted to add some mettle to his résumé and prove that he had the emotional chops to carry a film. Or perhaps he simply wanted to back Sanjay Leela Bhansali, who was truly a film-maker with grand ambitions that demanded more from his actors. Salman knew he had to rise to Sanjay's vision. And he did so in what is among the most memorable and heartbreaking performances of his career. The film's story starts with Sameer (Salman), a carefree NRI, who arrives in India to learn classical music from a respected guru. There, he falls in love with the guru's daughter, Nandini (Aishwarya Rai). Their romance blossoms in secret, but when they are discovered, Sameer is asked to leave. Nandini is married off to Vanraj (Ajay Devgn), a kind-hearted man who senses her unhappiness. When he learns of her past love, he decides to reunite the lovers. Bhansali was over the moon when the film clicked with audiences and critics alike. After the failure of *Khamoshi* he didn't know how to bounce back, but with Salman's encouragement yet again, Sanjay made a film that struck a chord with audiences and hit the jackpot at the box office.

In an interview, Salman was asked why he decided to take a punt on Bhansali despite the dismal box office performance of *Khamoshi*. Salman explained, 'When Sanjay came to me with *Khamoshi*, I really liked the script. I did the film when no one was doing it at that time. He is the same Bhansali for me even today. He has passion for cinema and will always do his best to give a good film. No wonder he goes over budget at times *(laughs)*. I have always taken risks in my life. The trend in our film industry is that no one wants to work with a new guy. If you are a newcomer, you will remain a newcomer. I think it is the ability in me to understand good script. I am a writer's son. I have it in my genes. Though I don't write films, I understand the film at the script level—whether it will work or not.'[44]

And the film worked wonders, kick-starting Bhansali's golden run, which continues till date. In one of the first interviews after its release, Bhansali said, 'One can put emotions, craft and hard work into films but without the audience's approval, the art of film-making is incomplete … After *Khamoshi*, I decided I had to bring the audiences to the theatres, but without compromising. After the failure of *Khamoshi*, for two months, I was sleepless and angry … I channelized my anger positively. I worked 24 hours a day …'[45]

Sanjay's films have a distinct quality, primarily that they serve as the perfect escape for audiences through their elaborate sets, over-the-top drama, and heroes and heroines who look ethereal. He said, '*Sachhai bahut dekh li* (I've seen enough of reality). I want to meet nice people and see nice people. The characters of Salman and Ajay are nice people. I show what should happen and not what happens in life. You know, I don't read newspapers because I don't want to start a day with anguish. Bad news disturbs me.'[46]

The film also remains etched in the memory of fans as the starting point of the iconic but troubled relationship between Salman and Aishwarya. News reports[47] say that it was Salman who suggested Aishwarya be cast in this film, who until that point, hadn't delivered a single hit. People on set knew Salman was obsessed with her, but Ash didn't give in initially. When she came on board, they weren't seeing each other. But for Salman it was more than just a passing infatuation. When he was initially offered the role of Aishwarya's on-screen brother in Mansoor Khan's *Josh*, he turned it down. The part eventually went to Shah Rukh.[48]

As Bhansali said in an interview recently, love was in the air.[49] Ash wanted to make a career and was dreaming big, but Salman eventually managed to woo her with his persistence!

On set, the two were completely immersed in Sanjay's world—living and breathing his opulent vision. They fell in love under grand chandeliers, among the golden dunes of Rajasthan, draped in breathtaking costumes. What stood out was the unmistakable tenderness in their eyes for each other. The heady, all-consuming kind that marks the early flush of love, beautifully framed and captured by Bhansali. Despite pressure, he refused to alter the ending of the film, in which Ash's character Nandini returns to her husband Vanraj. 'I was forced to shoot an alternate, happy ending for *Khamoshi* due to pressure from distributors, who didn't want a tragic conclusion. But with *Hum Dil De Chuke Sanam*, I stood firm on the ending I had envisioned from the beginning,' he said.[50]

Clearly Salman wasn't on board with Bhansali's climax for the film. He even said in an interview, 'I did not agree with the ending in *Hum Dil De Chuke Sanam*. Sanjay Bhansali told me that he wanted a depressive high. ... But if you are making a traditional film, then *(cuss word)* love. Nandini (Aishwarya) should have left her husband and gone with the guy she loved (Salman). Her husband (Ajay Devgan) was like a god to her for what he did. If I had made *Hum Dil De Chuke Sanam*, I would have let her go with the guy she loved.'[51]

Visually, the film was stunning and was deemed a must-watch for that reason alone. It brought poetry to life on-screen without tipping into pretension. *Hum Dil De Chuke Sanam* felt personal and larger-than-life at once. At the centre was the crackling chemistry between Salman and Aishwarya, which was made all the more intense by whispers of their off-screen romance. It gave the love story an ache, a thrill, a sense of reality under all the fantasy.

Salman gave his all to the film. He allowed his spontaneity to show, and he stripped his emotions bare on-screen, something he usually didn't allow himself to do. Recounting the experience of shooting the song

'Tadap Tadap Ke' in a hot desert, cinematographer Anil Mehta said, 'I remember, in the desert, Salman just went with the scene. Otherwise, which hero is going to lie down in the hot sand and ask people to put that sand on him. He was doing it himself and that's infectious. You are drawing from that energy and then he started doing some random stuff. I took the camera off the tripod and then I was with Salman in that moment. I soaked in what he was doing and later the camera also pointed at the sun which was a "no, no" at the time. Today, it is the norm. But, it was the energy of the piece and the performance and then, of course, there was the master of drama at work—Sanjay.'[52]

Ismail Darbar's music lent the film an enchanting aura, as it beautifully blended traditional Indian music with the allure of exotic foreign landscapes. The film felt like a dream. Songs like 'Tadap Tadap Ke' and 'Aankhon Ki Gustakhiyan' became a rage with people. The film's success brought with it it's fair share of controversy, one of them being Darbar's proud declaration that he was better than his rival, A.R. Rahman. He said in an interview, 'My work has always been better than his. *Hum Dil De Chuke Sanam* was better than *Taal*. Even *Devdas* was better than *Saathiya*. But it is destiny that he got international fame … Whenever my work is good and he takes the awards, I feel bad. I wonder why people run after name and fame, and not good work. *Kyunki humare yahan bahut kum akal ke log hai* (Because we have very few intelligent people here). We see some foreigners holding someone's hand, and he becomes a big man. But the foreigners have also praised my work in *Hum Dil De Chuke Sanam*.'[53]

The film premiered at the Berlin Film Festival on the recommendation of the taxi driver who was ferrying the official festival representative around in India when she had come to take her pick of films for the movie gala. 'The Berlin Film Festival's representative for South Asia, Dorothy Wenner, was in Mumbai. One evening she asked her taxi driver if he had seen any good films lately. The driver—God bless him— immediately recommended *Hum Dil De Chuke Sanam*. That's how she ended up seeing the film, loving it and inviting it to Berlin. I owe that taxi driver a big thank you,' Bhansali said at an interview during the premier of his 2022 movie, *Gangubai Kathiawadi*, at the same festival.[54]

Salman, who until then was a hero who had always won, knew that this time he had shown how to lose with grace. Usually it's the women who gush about the film, but Arjun Rao, an ad film-maker, tells me that Bhansali showed to the world an untapped and softer side of Salman, which fans had not seen till then. 'I was thirteen when I watched *Hum Dil De Chuke Sanam* in a packed theatre in Bandra, and I remember my father tearing up in the last scene, something I'd never seen him do before. Salman had always been the cool guy to me, the one who danced, fought, made you laugh. But in this film, he wasn't trying to win, but learning to let go. I didn't even know he was capable of that! That moment, when he silently watches her leave, was devastating, and stayed with me. Who were these men Sanjay wrote? How were they so devoid of the male ego that saw women as possessions? It taught me something about love I didn't understand till then. Sometimes, the truest love is the one that doesn't ask for anything in return. Years later, when I went through my first heartbreak, I found solace in this film. That boyish stubbornness, the hope that love alone is enough—it all felt too close. Salman made it real. That's why this film will always be more than a love story to me. It's a mirror. It's a reminder to do better!'

Women echo the same sentiment. Mehak Singh, a twenty-nine-year-old lawyer from Delhi, tells me that she is an Aishwarya fan who grew to appreciate Salman because of the film. 'I went to watch *Hum Dil De Chuke Sanam* for Aishwarya, because I was obsessed with her beauty. But halfway through the film, it was Salman's Sameer who completely disarmed me. He wasn't the perfect man. He was childlike, innocent and silly. He had a lot of growing up to do! But there was something heartbreakingly earnest about the way he loved. You could see every emotion play out on his face. It's Salman's purest performance, perhaps. The visuals, the framing—it's how the camera romances Salman in this film that is so perfect. You see the jealousy, joy, hurt, hope on his face. And when he stepped back in the end, it broke me. This was a man coming to terms with his limits. I didn't expect Salman to make me feel that much, but he did. That performance stayed with me, because it wasn't about getting the girl, but about learning to let her go. And I don't think we talk enough about how quietly powerful that is. Women notice that. We're so used to

Only Salman can turn a random step into a nationwide trend.

Back when Salman and Revathy made 'first love' feel real.

The abandon with which Salman dances hasn't changed since the 1990s.

Someone call the stylist, because Salman has misplaced his shirt again!

The chaos behind Salman's most brooding love story, *Tere Naam*.

Decades later, still towel-twirling like it's his first time.

BTS from Bollywood's original *Baaghi*.

Salman, mid-move, grooving to the anthem 'Suno Gaur Se Duniyawalo' that defined an era.

Khandaan—the original blockbuster ensemble.

Brothers in arms—the Khan trio
with producer Bunty Walia (right) from
the making of *Pyaar Kiya To Darna Kya*.

With several hits to their name, Salman and David Dhawan are partners in punchlines and still in on the same joke.

Action doesn't start with the clapboard.
It starts when Salman enters the frame.

India's favourite spies Pathaan and Tiger, friends and co-stars since the 1990s.

With Salman, Priyanka and Akshay, comedy already had its dream team in *Mujhse Shaadi Karogi*.

Prabhu Deva: 'Follow the step!'; Salman: 'Step will follow me!'

Salman and Chandni
from the shoot of
Sanam Bewafa, the
kind of old-school
romance Bollywood
rarely makes now.

Aamir and Salman, still in perfect sync
even decades later.

Sweat, grass, sunset—somehow,
Salman makes it all look good.

Peak 1990s flashback—Amar, Prem and the queen of all their troubles, Karisma.

When Bhai meets Chi Chi on the dance floor—or in comedy gold such as *Partner*—it's always a hit.

A young Salman with Ayesha Jhulka, all smiles in a softer, sweeter time.

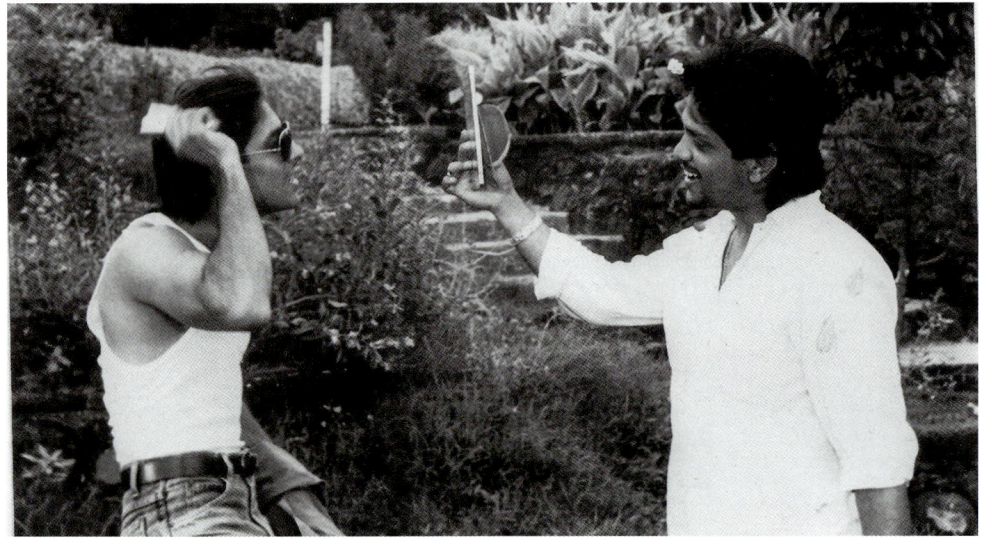

When the BTS looks better than the actual film—Salman at the shoot of a Punjabi music video in the 1990s.

Bhai and Baba, the OG bad boys
of Bollywood.

Steps change, but the swagger stays the same.

Bollywood's iconic spy couple. It's candids such as this that make you root for their chemistry.

All eyes on Salman as the man gears up to strike.

From *Patthar Ke Phool* to *Andaz Apna Apna*, from drama to comedy, Raveena and Salman have always been a hit pair.

Koffee is best served with a side of Bhai humour.

O teri! When Salman shows up, the ladies line up ...

Bhaijaan is the happiest with his Bajrangi; Salman with director Kabir Khan at the trailer launch of *Bajrangi Bhaijaan* in 2015.

In Hindi movies, when the hero picks up a dafli, you know the song's about to be iconic.

Salman in *Bigg Boss* has a cult following, with the whole country tuning in every Saturday and Sunday for 'Weekend ka Vaar'.

male characters trying to possess women in love stories that Sameer was so different—he was one of the few who let her choose. That kind of dignity, even in heartbreak, is rare and deeply attractive.'

Interestingly, another fan, Shamsher Singh, a scientist in Cape Town, South Africa, tells me that he believes there are some obvious parallels between this film and *The Bengali Night* starring Hugh Grant and Supriya Pathak. The film is based on a 1933 Romanian novel, *Bengali Nights*, written by Mircea Eliade. It retells his real-life affair with Maitreyi Devi, who later wrote a rebuttal (*It Does Not Die*) to reclaim her voice and counter Eliade's portrayal. Shamsher tells me, 'In both films, the central love is never fulfilled. Maitreyi is forcibly separated from the narrator due to societal and familial pressure. In *Hum Dil De Chuke Sanam*, Nandini is separated from Sameer by her family and is married off to Vanraj instead. Even when she travels across continents to reunite with Sameer, she ultimately chooses to stay in her marriage, again leading to a love that remains unconsummated. What I love is that both films reflect the idea that love is not always possession—it's often about letting go, learning and evolving.'

'It was Salman's Sameer who completely disarmed me. He wasn't the perfect man. He was childlike, innocent and silly. He had a lot of growing up to do! But there was something heartbreakingly earnest about the way he loved. You could see every emotion play out on his face. It's Salman's purest performance, perhaps. The visuals, the framing—it's how the camera romances Salman in this film that is so perfect.'

Hum Dil De Chuke Sanam was a major commercial success. Domestically, it amassed Rs 24.76 crore in net earnings (Rs 34.39 crore gross) and nearly Rs 9.47 crore overseas ($2.20 million), pushing its global gross to about Rs 43.86 crore. Adjusted for inflation, it ranks impressively among Bollywood's top performers: It earned a net of Rs 24.76 crore in 1999, which equates to approximately Rs 171.7 crore today. Notably, it was the second-highest-grossing Hindi film of 1999 (after *Hum Saath-Saath Hain*), with worldwide revenues around Rs 51.38 crore. Adjusted for inflation, the film made a little over Rs 200 crore worldwide.[55]

The film was a critical and commercial triumph, and Salman had quietly delivered one of the most emotionally resonant performances of his career. He welcomed the new millennium on a high, with his artistic credibility finally aligning with his box office clout. But even as he basked in the glow of both audience love and a sweeping on- and off-screen romance, he couldn't have foreseen how dark the path ahead would be. The year had been tainted by some controversy, but everyone had hoped it would pass. But the storm clouds were only beginning to gather. The next decade would test his stardom and his very sense of self. He had no idea that his off-screen life was about to steal the spotlight.

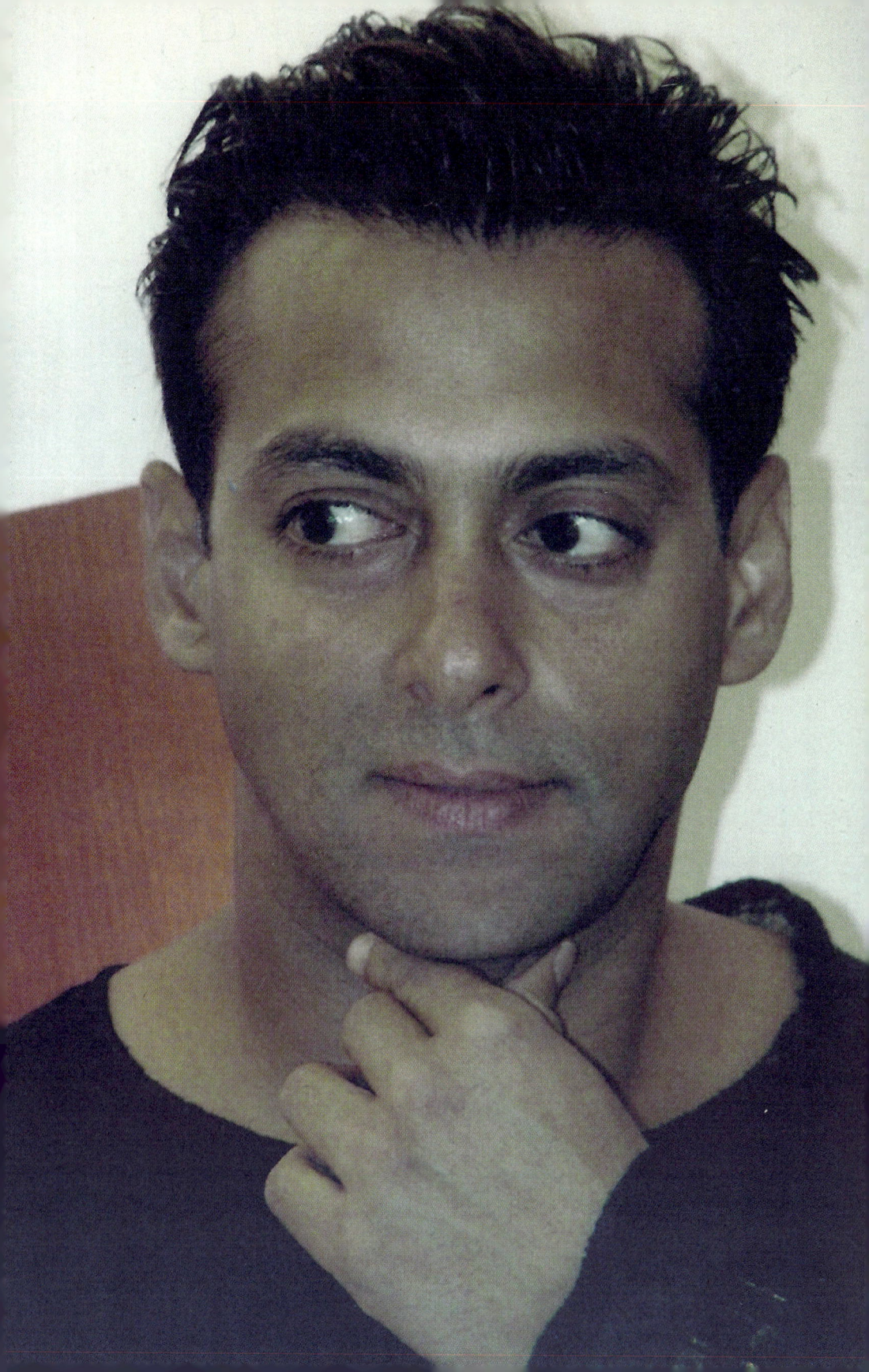

" " I am a bad boy. Thoda sa ziddi, thoda sa awara, thoda sa pagal, thoda sa nakara. " "

Yuvvraaj, 2008

6

The Irresistible Bad Boy

ET'S address the core question at the heart of every discourse on Salman: Our obsession with the flawed hero.

We routinely have a discussion on this topic with friends, and it sparks endless debates around dinner tables. The reason this familiar trope—of a rebel without a cause but with a heart of gold—just does not seem to get old is because Bollywood itself has long romanticized it, and few stars embody this archetype more fully than Salman Khan.

Stardom is a loop that thrives on extremes, feeds contradictions and survives on our collective willingness to blur morality in the face of charisma. In India, we worship our stars, project on to them and defend them. The more problematic they are, the more conversations they generate, the more they register in our collective consciousness and the deeper our fascination grows. In that sense, one could argue that the veneer of a 'bad boy' itself has a role to play in mass appeal.

The audience may know better, but they often don't want better. The fantasy of reforming the bad boy, or simply living vicariously through his defiance, seems far more thrilling than the predictability of a nice guy.

A 2016 dissertation by C.J. DeBuse broke down male archetypes neatly into four categories: the nice guy, the bad boy, the hero and the loser.[1] Bad boys and heroes were seen as the most dominant, assertive and confident. They were the ones who took charge. The research went deeper to understand what made some women lean towards the bad boy. DeBuse's study, mostly centred on women, found that those who were made to feel avoidant (emotionally distant or closed off) by their families, especially parents while growing up, became less interested in supportive men. In contrast, when they were made to feel anxious, they gravitated towards dominant men. Emotional insecurity, in other words, fuelled attraction to unpredictable man.

The same could be used to explain the Salman frenzy.

Introducing Salman in an early 2000 interview, the host said, 'He is number 1 for real but equally controversial. Lately, there have been rumours that he's drinking heavily, skipping shoots and leaving producers worried. That he's fallen in love and is on a path to self-destruction.'[2]

This introduction might just be an apt one, as, by the year 2000, drama and danger were happening *to* Salman incessantly. And he was flowing with it, swept up in the storm. Rumours swirled, and when such things happen, most people pause, take stock and course-correct. But Salman was in the thick of a heady mix of success, power and the madness of new love. It was chaos. He was living the full-blown messy arc of a hero. The standout from that interview is when the host asks Salman about how he contradicts himself, a recurring thought most of us echo about him to date. 'How can I define myself when I have a hundred different shades—most of them contradicting each other? With every new situation, your personality evolves. And if it doesn't, that's sad, because that means you're not growing. People say I contradict myself—but that's a good thing. It means I'm evolving, I've changed my mind about something. It means I've grown.'[3]

And grow up he did. Between 2000 and 2008, Salman was in a churn. He was stumbling, learning, shedding layers and making a lot of mistakes. He was changing form. The contradictions began to settle. It was a rite of passage and somewhere along the way, he had to figure out why stardom was such a huge responsibility. Many years later, Salim Khan was quoted as saying, 'You know, a person has to discover himself every time. This is a continuous process of evolution. Salman has also discovered himself so many times. He has started taking his career very seriously for the last few years. He did not know how to handle the media during the initial years. He is a normal boy, who was not aware of his responsibilities as a superstar. He did not realize that he can't lead a normal life. Everything he does would be looked at through a magnifying glass and become news.'[4]

But before that realization dawned on him, his torrid love affair nearly destroyed him. Salman was still dating Somy Ali when he and Aishwarya met. The relationship with Somy had run its course and by the time *Hum Dil De Chuke Sanam* wrapped up, Salman and Ash had decided to give their feelings for each other a serious shot.

It is said that the volatile nature of the relationship and the anxiety associated with it was keeping him distracted. It started reflecting in Salman's work. The year 2000 was tepid for him. He stopped bothering to experiment. He was collaborating with only those he trusted and showed no inclination to up his game after *Hum Dil De Chuke Sanam*, choosing to do a series of monotonous romances, ironically fuelled by his real-life romance. *Dulhan Hum Le Jayenge*, a reunion with hitmakers David Dhawan and Karisma Kapoor, didn't fare well at the box office. *Chal Mere Bhai*, another Dhawan–Karisma combo, with Sanjay Dutt starring alongside, also landed on its face, though his easy on-screen chemistry with off-screen friend Sanjay Dutt was appreciated. *Har Dil Jo Pyar Karega...*, backed by his long-time friend Sajid Nadiadwala and featuring a starry cameo by Shah Rukh, performed averagely. The year closed with *Kahin Pyaar Na Ho Jaaye*, which also fell short of expectations. Time and again Salman's films start to blur into one another—romance, drama, catchy music and a generous display of his chiselled torso. The formula started to feel tired. His peers Aamir and Shah Rukh were working on *Lagaan* and *Devdas* at this time, both of which turned out to be superhits at the box office and garnered international acclaim.

Work was hardly Salman's focus in those years. It was the push and pull of his love life that kept him busy. Reports began to flood in about how Salman was turning into an obsessive partner. As Anupama Chopra writes in her book *King of Bollywood*, 'For two years, Aishwarya and Salman had conducted a tempestuous affair in a fishbowl (there were rumours of parental disapproval, physical abuse, intimidation), and by the time *Devdas* was shot, the relationship had disintegrated into an unpleasant, incoherent mess. Salman had become a real-life Devdas, simultaneously self-destructing and attempting to salvage his romance. He was as much a part of the *Devdas* shoot as the crew. Salman would spend nights lying intoxicated on the floor of Aishwarya's trailer. One night, Shah Rukh and Aishwarya were doing a romantic scene that required Shah Rukh to extricate a thorn from her foot. Salman was on the set, and he volunteered to demonstrate how this should be done. Shah Rukh agreed and as Salman did the shot, Bhansali rolled the cameras. It was a poignant moment: a spent, tragic lover enacting his own life for film. Aishwarya cried. It was the last time the two were captured on film together.'[5]

> 'He did not know how to handle the media during the initial years. He is a normal boy who was not aware of his responsibilities as a superstar. He did not realize that he can't lead a normal life. Everything he does would be looked at through a magnifying glass and become news.'

The tempestuous fights between the couple began making it to the tabloids. Aishwarya's family disapproved of her relationship with Salman because of his past relationships. According to news reports, Aishwarya defied her parents and moved into her own apartment in Lokhandwala. One night in November 2001, Salman reportedly arrived at her seventeenth-floor residence, furious. Witnesses claimed he banged on her door relentlessly for hours, with some even alleging he threatened to jump off the building if she didn't let him in. Salman's rage was so intense that the neighbours stayed silent, too afraid to interfere or alert the authorities. The incident stretched past 3 a.m., by which time his hands were bloodied from pounding on the door. Eventually, Aishwarya allowed him in. Speculations abounded about what had provoked the episode. Some sources said that Salman had come to demand a commitment, possibly marriage, from Aishwarya. But her career was on a sharp upward trajectory at the time and she was reportedly not prepared to make that leap.[6]

Salman even admitted to the incident in an interview in 2002. He said, 'The incident is true, but it was overhyped by the media. I have a relationship with Aishwarya. If you do not fight in a relationship, it means you do not love each other. Why would I squabble with a person who is a stranger to me? Such things happen between us only because we love each other. Now, even the police have barred me from entering that building.'[7]

Aishwarya's father, Krishnaraj Rai, reported the incident to the police. Salman confessed during the interview that Aishwarya was not returning his expression of love, and that was what had caused him to grow violent. 'Her parents are very nice people. They are orthodox like my family. They have heard about my past affairs and they didn't like me in the life of their daughter. It is my fault, not theirs. I should have understood it earlier. They never stopped me from meeting with Aishwarya, despite the fact that I treated them badly. Aishwarya did not like my behaviour towards them, just as I would not appreciate anybody misbehaving with my father. Aishwarya's father is completely justified in complaining against me. I have no grudge against him.'[8]

This episode marked the beginning of the end for their relationship. What had long simmered behind closed doors now erupted into full public view. Just as tensions reached a boiling point, a phone call from Salman's ex, Somy Ali, became the last straw in their relationship. According to *Stardust*, Somy Ali reached out to Salman for help with her father's surgery. Salman agreed and quietly flew to the US without informing Aishwarya. When she eventually discovered the reason behind his sudden trip, she was livid. Though he once again convinced her to give their relationship another chance, the fragile peace was short-lived.

The strain of this relationship affected Aishwarya's career too. Salman created a major disruption on the sets of *Chalte Chalte*, where Aishwarya was shooting with Shah Rukh. The outburst led to the shoot being halted. Haroon Mirza, who was director Aziz Mirza's associate, said in a news report, 'See, nobody likes disruptions on the sets. Yes, Salman did call up the next day and apologize. He's decent enough to do that. But right now things have stalled for another 8–10 days.' Both Salman and

Aishwarya later apologized to Shah Rukh, but the incident made Shah Rukh eventually replace Aishwarya with Rani Mukerji.[9]

Later, in a shocking interview with a leading daily in September 2002, Aishwarya opened up about her break-up, alleging that Salman still pursued her relentlessly and even harmed himself when she refused to answer his calls. Aishwarya had initially denied rumours of abuse, but after her break-up with Salman, she opened up about what had really happened. She revealed that Salman would call her constantly, say hurtful things and even hurt himself when she wouldn't respond. She said he was possessive and suspected her of having affairs with her co-stars. In later interviews, Aishwarya admitted she had put up with a lot, including verbal and emotional abuse and infidelity. In another interview to *The Indian Express*, she made it clear that it was all over. 'I stood by him, enduring his alcoholic misbehaviour in its worst phases and in turn, I was at the receiving end of his abuse (verbal, physical and emotional), infidelity and indignity. That is why, like any other self-respecting woman, I ended my relationship with him.'[10]

But it was an interview in *Bombay Times* that was the first time she outed him publicly. She said, 'Salman and I broke up last March, but he isn't able to come to terms with it. After we broke up, he would call me and talk rubbish. He also suspected me of having affairs with my co-stars. I was linked up with everyone, from Abhishek Bachchan to Shah Rukh Khan. There were times when Salman got physical with me, luckily without leaving any marks. And I would go to work as if nothing had happened.' In that same interview, she alleged that Salman was cheating on her. Finally, she sealed the fate of their relationship with a statement that probably devastated him. 'The story of Salman Khan was a nightmare in my life. I am thankful that it is over now.'[11]

The reason this interview later became significant was because it appeared on 27 September 2002, the morning before Salman's infamous hit-and-run accident, the most serious controversy in his life. In the early hours of a Saturday morning, Salman was accused of driving his car over a group of people sleeping on the pavement outside American Express Bakery near Hill Road in Bandra, Mumbai. The accident claimed the life of a man named Nurullah Khan and left three others seriously injured, who were immediately taken to Bhabha Hospital. At the time, Salman was reportedly returning home from the JW Marriott Hotel in Juhu. He wasn't alone. He was accompanied by his bodyguard Ravindra Patil, assigned by Mumbai Police due to previous threats against him, and singer Kamaal Khan.

Salman was arrested later that day, marking the beginning of a long legal battle that spanned over a decade, until 2015. He was initially held at the Arthur Road jail and was later moved to the one in Thane due to security concerns.

When I bring this incident up with any Salman fan, the reactions are interesting. It's almost as if they are waiting to defend him. And at the same time they possess the general awareness that this is an act that can hardly be defended. They meekly start with 'but he is a nice guy', and somewhere down the line, lose their way.

Isn't our attraction tainted when the object of our affections probably has blood on their hands? But in public consciousness there exists two distinct impressions of Salman—the kind man who helps everyone and the star who cannot be forgiven. Depending on which news is on prime time, the conversation on Salman shifts. The interesting part is that both these ideas of Salman are true.

Mumbai-based housewife Abida Meher tells me, 'Look, I won't deny that the hit-and-run case shook me. I had loved him since his first film! It forced me to question the kind of person Salman might be off-screen. But here's the thing—I've grown up on his films and I have loved him from the first time I saw him. I remember watching *Maine Pyar Kiya* as a kid and feeling like that kind of love was possible. And then later, as I grew up, I've danced to "Dhinka Chika" at weddings with my cousins, cried during *Tere Naam* and felt pure joy watching *Bajrangi Bhaijaan*. These are not just movies that star him—they are also my own memories of the person I was. They got me through heartbreak, stress, even depression at one point. So when people say, "How can you still support him?" I say it's not that I support everything he does, but I do hold on to what his work means to me. I think all of us are complicated, all of us have sides we wouldn't want magnified. I don't see Salman as a saint, but I also don't see him as just the sum of his worst moments. At the end of the day, I separate the man's personal flaws from the meaning his films and actions have had in my life. Maybe that sounds pragmatic, but for me it's a balance I have created. I don't excuse him, but I also don't erase the good he has done or the hope his films continue to give.'

Another Salman fan, Shalini Saha, a software engineer in Noida, gives me a unique perspective. She feels that in some shape and form we find it easy to forgive celebrities because they stir up intimate emotions in us. 'In India, we grow up on stories of flawed heroes. So when it comes to celebrities such as Salman, for instance, people don't necessarily expect perfection. What they look for is emotion. They want to feel that the star has a heart, that he feels their pain, their joys and, most importantly, that he cares. And Salman, somehow, manages to project that flawlessly, even through all his mistakes. For many of us, he's like that problematic older brother in the family. But at the end of the day, you believe he means well. "Bhaiyya who protects the younger sister for her own good" is the vibe he has. So when stories of court cases or controversies come up, a lot of fans instinctively defend him. Some say the media exaggerates, some believe he's being targeted because he's rich and famous, and others see his legal troubles as part of a larger story of personal redemption. All of which is probably true.'

She continues, 'He is a man who's been through fire and still chooses to help. It's also cultural. In India, we believe in second chances. We believe people can change. That's why Salman's charitable work touches people. It feels like a kind of atonement, whether it's intended that way or not. Also, morality in the public eye is often selective. A fan once said to me, "We cheer for politicians with criminal cases. We forgive cricketers who fixed matches. Why single out Salman?" It's not that people don't care about justice—they do. But for many, their emotional bond with Salman outweighs everything else. It's not rational. It's not even always right. In the end, fans don't just love him for who he is but for what he represents—an idea that even those who fall can rise again. In a way, it's not about Salman at all, but about what we choose to believe when the world feels grey.'

And then there is our deep-rooted pull towards 'bad boys'. A housewife in Abu Dhabi, Sreoshi Sinha, tells me, 'I know it sounds strange, but there's something about Salman that makes you root for him even more when the world turns against him. I'm not saying I support everything he's done. But you know what? That raw, unpolished, unpredictable energy is part of what makes him so magnetic. There's always been something dangerously appealing about a man who doesn't play by the rules ... about Salman. There's a reason we're drawn to bad boys—they don't conform. They push back. And somewhere deep inside, we admire that because most of us don't have the courage to do so ourselves. Salman, with all his flaws, gives us that thrill.'

After a short pause, she adds, 'When he walked into court wearing his sunglasses, that trademark swagger intact, the media might've seen a scandal, but a lot of fans saw a fighter, someone who wouldn't crumble even when the world tried to bring him down. That's what people fall in love with. And let's be honest—there's a deeply romantic fantasy at play too. In our movies, the angry, wounded hero always has a soft heart. The one who breaks the rules is also the one who protects, who loves fiercely, who stands by you when no one else will. Salman plays that both on- and off-screen. It's no coincidence that some of his biggest hits happened when his real life was falling apart, such as *Tere Naam*. He was channelling something real, and we felt it. At the end of the day, we don't fall in love with perfection, we fall in love with contradictions. Salman is rough and tender, arrogant and generous, lost and loyal. And loving Salman is intoxicating. He wasn't the clean-cut hero. Sometimes it's the wounded, wild-hearted man who feels the most real. That's why, even at his worst, we couldn't look away. And some of us, quietly, were loving him even more.'

'So when it comes to celebrities such as Salman, for instance, people don't necessarily expect perfection. What they look for is emotion. They want to feel that the star has a heart, that he feels their pain, their joys and, most importantly, that he cares. And Salman, somehow, manages to project that flawlessly, even through all his mistakes. For many of us, he's like that problematic older brother in the family. But at the end of the day, you believe he means well.'

I, as a feminist, find Salman complicated. There are moments when the casual misogyny in some of his films has riled me up. And yet, I can't deny that there is another side to him that tugs at me. I see the wounded man behind the sunglasses, the boy who never seems to grow up; I see a vulnerability that slips through now and then in his films and interviews. There is something reckless and tender about him at the same time, and that's confusing. To me, loving Salman feels like a test of how much contradiction we are willing to live with. And speaking to his female fans underlined that further—it laid bare our own conditioning as women from the patriarchal set-ups and explains so many of our choices.

However, journalists give me another story. They tell me that the Aishwarya episode, especially the allegations of abuse, followed by the hit-and-run case, caused an irreparable fracture in fans' devotion. A senior journalist told me, 'Post the Aishwarya fallout, Salman's image took a visible beating. While Shah Rukh Khan was serenading women in mustard fields and becoming the nation's romantic ideal, Salman was making headlines for allegedly banging on doors, getting violent and being controlling. It gave women the ick. He was no longer the dreamy Prem, but had become a cautionary tale. Brands distanced themselves, film-makers got nervous and the audience, especially the female fans, began questioning him. That era marked the beginning of Salman's transition from lover boy characters to macho, action-heavy roles, because the image of that love had cracked, maybe beyond repair.'

They, in fact, pointed me to a column written by veteran journalist (and later producer) the late Pritish Nandy, who starts his piece with: 'Let me say it upfront. I do not like Salman Khan.' But in his column, Nandy decoded the media's relationship with Salman. He wrote, 'Salman hates the media; the media hates Salman. In this face-off, truth is the first casualty ...' Nandy further argued that celebrities such as Salman are unfairly judged and constantly scrutinized. 'Salman is not a politician. His personal life does not really concern the nation. If he does something wrong, he must be punished like anyone else. If not, he should be left alone. Not hounded all the time with gossip and snide comments.' In a parting word, Nandy said, 'He may be foolish, but he is nowhere near that dark, monstrous creature the media makes him out to be.'[12]

The media did its thing and the fans theirs. Many fans in those years found themselves moving away from Salman. Anusha Patel, thirty-eight, an English professor from Pune, admits that she distanced herself from Salman in those years. 'I used to be a huge Salman Khan fan growing up. I remember cutting out his photos from magazines, watching his movies on VHS, even fighting with friends over who loved him more. But the day I read Aishwarya's interview, where she said he was emotionally abusive, I felt something break inside me. I understand relationships can be messy, but abuse is not "messy"—it's a deliberate crossing of boundaries. And it's so much worse when the person doing it is powerful, because that power protects them. When we don't hold our heroes accountable, we're complicit in the harm they cause.'

But other women see the incident differently. Shraddha Rane, forty-two, who is an event manager in Mangalore, tells me, 'The things that were said about him were disturbing, yes. And I'm not here to justify any kind of abuse. If he did what was alleged, it was wrong. Full stop. But here's what people forget—relationships are incredibly complicated, especially when you're famous. The pressure, the scrutiny, the expectations from the public, it's like living in a fishbowl. What we see is never the full picture. I've worked backstage in the industry, and I can tell you that no relationship in Bollywood is exactly what it looks like. Did this couple fight? Probably … Did it get ugly? It seems like it did. But maybe both were hurting. Maybe both made mistakes. And when someone is that emotionally invested, they act out of fear, insecurity, maybe even desperation. None of that excuses abusive behaviour. But it explains the emotional chaos of high-stakes relationships. I also think we live in a time where nuance is dead. You're either a saint or a sinner. That's not how real people work. I don't defend the violence—I just don't believe we know enough to crucify him forever. And I believe in the possibility of people changing. If we deny that, we deny hope about ourselves too.'

Rane points me to an interview that Salman's brother Sohail angrily gave after Salman and Aishwarya split. He said, 'Did she ever acknowledge the relationship? She never did. That made Salman feel insecure. He wanted to know how much she wanted him. She would never let him be sure of that.'[13]

However, Salman, along with saying he has never hit a woman, went on to say some very unwise things. 'There was a journalist Prabhu Chawla, who asked me this a long time ago, so I just banged the table and he got startled, the table nearly broke. I mean, if I hit somebody, it's obviously a fight, I am going to be angry. I'm going to whack and give it my best shot. I don't think she would've survived it.'[14]

Statements such as this unsettle even his most forgiving fans. His choice of words feel flippant, and that only deepens the discomfort. Another senior journalist I spoke to said, 'The absence of remorse is troubling, but also the casual arrogance with which he brushes off serious accusations makes you very uncomfortable. He has never seen the need to speak with care. Salman often forgets that words matter just as much as actions. And sometimes, the most dangerous thing isn't the rage you act on, but the power you wield when you feel no need to explain it. Why don't you feel accountable?'

And between these contradictory behaviours and blasé public statements lies the contradiction of Salman Khan.

There was an interesting shift that followed this change in public opinion. His choice of films started evolving, almost as if they began feeding into the narrative of control and hyper-masculinity. Most journalists believe *Tere Naam* was a film that prominently reflected a shift in public perception towards Salman.

After *Hum Dil De Chuke Sanam*, work had taken a hit. In 2001, Salman's only release was *Chori Chori Chupke Chupke* directed by Abbas–Mustan. The film was embroiled in controversy when the CBI seized its prints due to links with the underworld don Chhota Shakeel. Producer Nazim Rizvi was arrested for underworld connections, while financier Bharat Shah was booked under the Maharashtra Control of Organised Crime Act (MCOCA). The film did average business at the box office.

Salman's next three films—*Yeh Hai Jalwa*, *Tumko Na Bhool Paayenge* and *Hum Tumhare Hain Sanam*, all released in 2002—performed poorly. The very public break-up with Aishwarya and the two major legal cases against him—the hit-and-run and the blackbuck poaching case—meant that he had to do something for his career to take off again.

Released in August 2003, *Tere Naam* is perhaps Salman's most polarizing film. The tagline, which said 'Unfortunately, a true love story', gave the impression that the love in the film was meant to be a badge of honour. Long before Sandeep Reddy Vanga brought conversations about toxic masculinity to the forefront with *Kabir Singh* (2019) and *Animal* (2023), *Tere Naam* got audiences and critics questioning the glorification of obsessive love. The same debate was repeated with Aanand L. Rai's *Raanjhanaa* (2013), which marked the Bollywood debut of Tamil superstar Dhanush.

How do you realistically depict the mayhem that obsessive love causes without endorsing it? To be fair, Salman's promotional strategy was calling out the film's definition of love. He outright sold the film as a cautionary tale that mustn't be replicated, and the pathetic ending given to his character, Radhe, absolved Salman of harsh criticism.

In the film, Salman plays a volatile, small-town college student who becomes infatuated with Nirjara (played by Bhumika Chawla), the daughter of a temple priest. Radhe lives in one of the countless unremarkable towns scattered across India. Though he has graduated a decade earlier, he still spends his days hanging out outside the college gates with his gang and harassing newcomers.

The interaction between these two characters starts with Nirjara calling Radhe a mawali, but Radhe is smitten with her the moment he sets eyes on her. When she doesn't return his affections, Radhe responds with violence by kidnapping her, tying her to a chair, gagging her and repeatedly threatening both her life and his own. Nirjara begins to see Radhe differently when he rescues her sister from an abusive marriage. Goons with a vendetta attack Radhe, leaving him so badly injured that he loses all sense of reality. Admitted to a mental asylum, he no longer recognizes those he loves, not even Nirjara. The tragic twist left a haunting 'what if?' in the minds of the audience: Could her love have healed him had life given them more time?

Salman's performance was lauded. He navigated Radhe's transformation—from carefree slacker to obsessive lover to broken man—with a depth that resonated with audiences and critics alike.

Tere Naam stood out in a crowd of conventional Bollywood romances. Unlike most love stories that ended in happy reunions, this one bravely concluded with separation and heartbreak. Romantic conflicts had usually revolved around class divides or parental opposition, but *Tere Naam* dared to take a darker turn, with its protagonist suffering a severe brain injury and being institutionalized, never to reunite with his lover.

Salman's portrayal struck a deep chord, especially with audiences in India's heartland. His distinct hairstyle became a cultural moment, with many young men all over India emulating his look. Film critics back then said that Salman's enduring appeal came from how strongly the masses saw themselves in him, more than in any other star.

Radhe begins as a local bully, but Salman's portrayal humanizes him. Radhe longs to be reformed, to marry and to build a better life, and this is what gives the film a strong emotional tug. Nirjara isn't the typical Bollywood heroine either. She is dignified, self-assured and initially rejects Radhe. Yet, over time, her perspective shifts, and she begins to see beyond his rough edges. *Tere Naam* resonated with audiences because it explored obsessive love in a way no mainstream movie had since *Darr* (1993). And while it showed some dangerous ideas that Salman himself was wary of, its conclusion laid bare the tragic end that obsessive love can lead to. When a superstar embodies such roles, the messaging is cultural. The audience absorbs it all. And hence it becomes even more important for the film to show the cost of the character's choices and not dress them up in charisma. With Salman, the challenge is doubled—his natural on-screen magnetism risks making even flawed characters appealing. Which is why films such as *Tere Naam* must take extra care to underline the tragedy, not the glamour.

Directed by Satish Kaushik, based on Tamil director Bala Palanisamy's *Sethu* (1999), the film was written with veteran writer Jainendra Jain. Years later, Satish Kaushik, in an interview, admitted to the parallels between *Tere Naam* and *Kabir Singh*. He said, 'There are quite a few similarities between *Tere Naam* and *Kabir Singh*, especially the way the hero pursues the girl and some other aspects. In fact, you wouldn't believe that while shooting the movie, Salman had told me that it would work with the audience, but we're sending the wrong message to the youth. This isn't the kind of character we should show to the youth as they could get wrongly influenced by it. Salman has always been very conscious that way, in what he shows his fans on-screen. We must ensure that such negative characters or those with shades of grey are not shown winning in the end.'[15]

Salman, during his appearance on *Aap Ki Adalat*, was asked whether he ever got worried about any of the characters he had played, and he spoke about Radhe from *Tere Naam*. He said, '*Mujhe itna dar laga, ki maine socha mai ye nahi karunga* (I thought of quitting). *Aisa first time hua ki maine picture karne se pehle promotion soch liya tha. Maine socha tha ki sabko bolunga ki ye picture zaroor dekhna, but iss character ko kabhi follow mat karna* (I had planned already [to tell] people that please do not follow the character). He is a loser character. *Yeh ek ladki ke piche pagal ho raha hai aur apni zindagi barbad kar diya. Nahi hota, nahi hota, aage badho life me* (Radhe is crazy about a girl and destroys his life. You must move on in life).'[16]

The film could have had a different director, who might have given the film a very different edge. I am talking about Anurag Kashyap—but alas, it wasn't meant to be. Anurag Kashyap, whose brother Abhinav went on to make *Dabangg* with Salman, also had a story about this film. In an interview with YouTuber Samdish Bhatia, Anurag said, 'I was not asked to leave *Tere Naam*, the film ghosted me. Even Satishji didn't know that I was supposed to be a part of it. I was very involved, scripting was done. We were about to start the shoot. I just asked Salman to grow chest hair and he also didn't say anything. It was the producer who reacted.'[17]

The film struck gold at the box office upon its release. The response to *Tere Naam* surpassed all other films released that year—*Gadar: Ek Prem Katha, Lagaan, Kabhi Khushi Kabhie Gham..., Main Prem Ki Diwani Hoon* and *Koi ... Mil Gaya*—reported trade. Trade analyst Taran Adarsh said, 'Considering that Salman received a lot of negative publicity, the kind of opening the film got is mesmerizing. Besides, a Salman film has been released after a long time [the last was *Yeh Hai Jalwa* in July 2002]. *Tere Naam*'s promotion as a "true love story" worked in its favour. The audience, which interpreted it as [former girlfriend] Aishwarya Rai and Salman's love story, came in hordes. Lately, Salman has been more cordial with the media and, this time, it helped him.'[18]

Tere Naam's total worldwide gross of Rs 24.54 crore in 2003 would be equivalent to approximately Rs 88.43 crore today.[19]

But in many aspects, the frenzy around the film and its cultural impact surpassed the figures. In her book *The Three Khans: And the Emergence of New India*,[20] Kaveree Bamzai writes about how in Shopian a Pakistani militant from Jaish-e-Mohammed, just nineteen years old, was reportedly so taken by the film that he bought a pirated copy, adopted Radhe's hairstyle and began frequenting the women's college, hopelessly in love with a local girl. He dreamt of marrying her and taking her back to Pakistan, despite her parents' disapproval. Salman's influence in the Valley was so deep-rooted that Vishal Bhardwaj acknowledged it in his rendition of William Shakespeare's Hamlet, *Haider* (2014), written by Basharat Peer. Salman appears in a scene showing Indian Army soldiers watching his 1994 film *Sangdil Sanam* at Faraz cinema as prisoners are marched past the screen.

The love for this film transcended borders. In Kabul, Afghanistan, the film became a rage. 'Pictures of the film's stars—Salman Khan and Bhumika Chawla—are being used to sell everything from clothing and makeup to food. Music from the film and its movie posters are hot commodities. *Tere Naam*, which means "In Your Name" in Hindi, looks set to surpass the Hollywood blockbuster *Titanic* as the Afghan moviegoing public's favourite. Its characters are becoming Kabul's top fashion icons,' wrote Rahimullah Samander for the Institute for War and Peace Reporting (Kabul). 'Men used to want *Titanic* hairstyles but now the *Tere Naam* style has taken over,' the piece quoted a barber as saying.[21]

According to top radio channels in Afghanistan, nearly 40 per cent of music requests that year were for songs from the film. The demand for both the movie and its soundtrack kept soaring. A distributor reported selling 5,000 copies of the film and another 15,000 of its music, with twenty to thirty copies of the latter selling daily for more than three months. Trousers embroidered with the film's title sold out rapidly and replicas of Salman's iconic black sunglasses were in high demand.

This widespread enthusiasm for Bollywood is rooted in Afghanistan's long-standing love for Indian movies, which persisted even under Taliban rule. Despite film screenings being banned under the regime, pirated

Hindi movies were hot property, and many Afghans, especially those who lived in Pakistan and understood Hindi or Urdu, continued to be smitten with both Salman and this film. No previous film had sparked this kind of fervour.

A twenty-one-year-old Salman fan, Saksham Ahuja, is a bit baffled, though, by the film's popularity. '*Tere Naam* was a movie that wrecked me when I watched it at eighteen—and I wasn't alone. As a teen, I cried for days. Radhe's pain felt so raw, so consuming, it almost made you forget to question anything else. The music haunted you. The love felt tragic and beautiful. But looking back now, it's hard not to flinch. Nirjara barely speaks. She isn't written as a woman with choices, just someone to be longed for, chased and finally mourned. At the time, we didn't think twice about the stalking, the kidnapping, the obsession packaged as love. We were too caught up in the heartbreak. And that's the part that unsettles me the most now—that we cried with Radhe, but we never asked what Nirjara wanted. She wasn't a love interest but a prize. I carry the discomfort. It's guilty nostalgia. I loved it, but, damn, it was messed up. I hope everyone knows now that idolizing Radhe is wrong!'

Over the years, Salman has built an image that makes people approach him with caution. Will he be warm? Dismissive? Will he throw a joke your way or throw you off with a sarcastic jab? Some people are just worried he'll snap. Others hope he won't disappoint. And honestly, most of us are just unsure of what version of Salman we'll get on any given day.

But is that also what keeps him interesting?

My editor, Mayank Shekhar, has a cool line about Salman: '*Actors toh duniya mein har jagah hotey hai* [Actors are everywhere in this world], but this man is showbusiness!' In his opinion, Salman is pretty much the most interesting man to interview, because you never know which version you will meet that day. And that thrill is unmatched. In fact, journalists who haven't been involved in an ego duel with Salman often say they have enjoyed his company.

My own experience has been pretty hilarious every time. It's either been all jokes or all heart. It felt like meeting a different person every time, or perhaps getting acquainted with a whole different side of him in each interview. But there's one thing for sure—there is never a dull moment with him!

Every time talk of a Salman interview would come up, my former colleague, Sonil Dedhia, would look at me and say, 'That's mine, I call dibs because only I can get a great copy from Bhai!' And he did, every single time!

But I've always asked myself the same rookie question: How do you break the ice with Salman? It's stuck with me for as long as I can remember. One of my most memorable interviews with the actor happened back in 2015, when I was a cub reporter. He was sitting outside his vanity van parked at Mehboob Studio, sunbathing shirtless. When he realized I was there to interview him and looked like a meek mouse hoping not to get yelled at, he softened. He has an uncanny sense of who to intimidate and who to give a free pass to. It depends entirely on his mood, though. He was perhaps feeling kind that day. Luckily, I got a free pass. He put on a shirt and asked if he could have some of the mango milkshake I was carrying. He recommended I eat some keema pav at Good Luck Café across the road.

During that interview, he got emotional while talking about the film he considers the most special to him, *Bajrangi Bhaijaan*. He told me about the team's run-in with the Central Board of Film Certification (CBFC) over Om Puri saying 'Jai Sri Ram' during the burqa scene. Much to my surprise, the energy in him shifted as we talked about the movie. He spoke with warmth and depth, and I really enjoyed talking to him. I went back home with a big smile on my face.

This unpredictability, as I said earlier, is probably the most refreshing thing about him. Journalists through the years have been baffled by this man they cannot make sense of. In her column on thirty years of Salman, journalist Anupama Chopra narrated her first meeting with him. She wrote, 'I first met him in the mid-1990s. I was a reporter with *India Today*. He was a massive star post *Hum Aapke Hain Koun...!* but he was largely allergic to the press. It was the "Bad Boy Salman" phase and he didn't really want to speak with any of us. I had requested David Dhawan's wife Lali to set up a meeting. Because she asked, he agreed to see me. We met at a restaurant called Shatranj in suburban Mumbai. It was incredibly awkward. He was more interested in the tiramisu he was wolfing down than the conversation I was hesitantly trying to make. I said we really wanted to do an interview. He said he would do it but only if the magazine donated [Rs] 10 lakh to his favourite charity. His logic was that his face on the cover would sell magazines and therefore we should be willing to pay it forward. I said we didn't pay for interviews. He ordered a second tiramisu and said goodbye.'[22]

Chopra, in the same piece, wrote about how Salman unexpectedly stepped up to promote MAMI (the Mumbai Film Festival). She quoted film critic Roger Ebert to him: 'Of all the arts, movies are the most powerful aid to empathy, and good ones make us into better people.' Salman agreed and attended the closing ceremony. When someone from the festival's jury froze mid-speech upon seeing him, Salman gently said, 'Don't worry, I forget my lines all the time …'

This mercurial star's charm hinges on the fact that he knows how to keep you on your toes. One of my ex-colleagues who writes for *The Times of India* swore off interviewing him after she had a bizarre conversation where Salman kept interrupting questions with monosyllables and long silences. She tells me, 'He doesn't do interviews often, but when he does, it's like he's speaking in riddles. You can never tell if he's serious or joking. How do you make it coherent? Where's the headline, where's the copy? Vibes are not words. He is all vibes. He could only respond in grunts and smirks. It's possible that you could be asking him what the capital of India is and he'd be discussing a pizza place in New York. Sometimes he could be just staring back until the questioner folds. It is impossible to tell if he's being sincere or sarcastic. For journalists, this is chaos. For the audience, it's fun. Go for a Salman interview for the experience—the less you expect, the better!'

But Salman doesn't believe he is erratic. In an old interview he said, 'There is nothing erratic about my nature. It's just that the way you would react, I would react the same way. It's just that people in the limelight, under the media spotlight, would not react that way. They would go back home and plan their reaction. That would be a more dangerous reaction. With me, it's just there, and I forgive and forget very easily.'[23]

It's not just restricted to journalists. On *Koffee with Karan*, when asked if he was a virgin, he famously said that he wanted to save himself for the person he would get married to. He said, 'I've had friends, but not with benefits.' Salman's straight-faced humour didn't land with many, apparently. While talking about it later, Karan Johar said, 'I have travelled the world over and there are people who genuinely came and asked me if he was really a virgin. He was being funny when he said I am saving myself for the wedding night. Salman has a straight face sense of humour. I can't believe there are people who believe it. That is what is scary as you can say anything and people might take you seriously.'[24] But while his humour might have missed the mark, his responses have, as usual, descended into pop-culture moments.

And that's infuriating for many. For instance, in 2019, Salman was slammed for his interview with Curly Tales' Kamya Jani, where he made many off-putting comments to her. However, as Jani explained later on the show *Tere Gully Mein* with Ranveer Allahbadia, 'Salman Khan was not rude to me. He was taunting someone else because he was very tired of giving so many interviews.'[25]

This unpredictability makes Salman a ticking time bomb and thus the reason for the press's tumultuous relationship with him. For every headline that exalts his box office pull, there's another that documents his brazenness. And yet he remains a darling. Why?

'Because he sells. Simple,' says a former magazine editor to me when I called them for a chat. 'Even when we reported on the most serious charges against him, the interest from readers never dipped. If anything, it spiked. People are drawn to him, no matter what he does.'

There's something almost primal about Salman's connection with his audience. He offers them a fantasy. While others present an image—socially woke, globally savvy—Salman doesn't play those games. At the trailer launch of *Sikandar*, he bantered with Rashmika Mandanna about their thirty-one-year age gap on-screen. '*Phir woh bolte hain 31 years ka difference hai heroine aur mujh mein, arrey jab heroine ko problem nahi hai, heroine ke papa ko dikkat nahi hai, tumko kyun dikkat hai bhai? Inki shaadi hogi, bachchi honge, toh unke saath bhi kaam karenge. Mummy ki permission toh mil hi jayega* (Then they say there's a 31-year age gap between me and the heroine. But if the heroine has no problem, and even her father has no issues, why do you have a problem, brother? When she gets married and has a daughter, I will work with her daughter too. Her mother's permission will be sorted),' he said. People were riled up by the statement. Singer Sona Mohapatra wrote on X, 'The "BHAI" of toxic masculinity, patriarchy doesn't realise that #India has changed?'[26]

But Salman doesn't apologize when he doesn't need to, or overexplain, or chase relevance. That refusal to evolve according to trend is, ironically, what makes him so relevant.

During the course of this book's research, I have had a ball deconstructing the unwavering loyalty of an average 'Bhai fan', which borders on worship. They mimic his style and flock to the first-day-first-shows regardless of reviews. They don't care if he is cycling in shorts around Bandra. His persona is casual. His trainer, Rakkesh Uddiyar, told me during our conversation for this book, 'If you meet him in Panvel, he is usually wearing a sleeveless T-shirt or no shirt. When we cycle to Film City or to Panvel, we are in shorts! He is not trying to make a statement—this is who he is.' His long-time stylist Ashley Rebello articulates the thought better. 'In India, everything a star does becomes a statement. Salman was the first person to wear Ed Hardy in India. It became so popular, they had to open stores across the country,' he said.[27]

Some of Hindi cinema's biggest blockbusters sit next to laughable flops. But Salman isn't defined by hits or misses. He is defined by persona. Whether playing Radhe, Chulbul Pandey or Prem, the character becomes a version of him, not the other way round. And audiences come to watch *him*, not the plot.

Salman dresses like a man who has nothing to prove. His wardrobe is equal parts loose shorts, tees, the occasional sleeveless vest, Pathani suits, lots of jeans and big buckle belts. He is unbothered by cameras or commentary. It's not normcore, it's not anti-fashion—it's his general indifference, and that's the point. Salman's off-screen aesthetic is a rejection of any performance. He is too entrenched in his own myth to cater to image-making. He doesn't dress like a star—he dresses like someone who knows he is one, no matter what he's wearing. And for a generation of fans, that deepens their frenzy for him.

His filmography, too, is a curious mix that reflects the same vibe. Some of Hindi cinema's biggest blockbusters sit next to laughable flops. But Salman isn't defined by hits or misses. He is defined by persona. Whether playing Radhe, Chulbul Pandey or Prem, the character becomes a version of him, not the other way round. And audiences come to watch *him*, not the plot.

In his fandom, Salman's imperfections cease to matter. His stardom isn't aspirational in a sanitized sort of way. The last three decades have seen stars rise and fall, the Hindi film hero redefined and reimagined, but Salman remains rooted in his brand of superstardom, which is larger-than-life, very flawed and maddeningly opaque. I remember reading a column in *Mid-day* the week after *Sikandar* 'bombed'. It read: '*Sikandar* is a commercial "disaster"—having already surpassed R100 crore at BO (Bhai's 18th such); quite weighty for a "bomb".'[28]

Pinkvilla journalist Himesh Mankad breaks this down. He says, 'Salman Khan is the biggest mass star of India and with him if you make the right film, the results will be unbelievable. No one has explored the real potential of Salman Khan. *Bajrangi Bhaijaan* sold approximately 3.55 crore tickets, something even our biggest blockbusters struggle with. With Salman, you can aim for the sky.'[29]

With the success of *Tere Naam*, it was certain that Salman, with all his chaos and charisma, controversy and crowd-pulling skills, had a hold over the Indian psyche that was unshakeable. One can question the roles he plays, the interviews he derails, the attitudes he normalizes, the stereotypes he perpetuates, but you can't ignore him.

By the end of 2003, it seemed like things would probably get better for Salman. The dark times were over and so were the dark films, with *Tere Naam* being the last of these. Over the next few years, the audience would be swept up in the myth of a refurbished Salman, who would be belting out hit comedies such as *Mujhse Shaadi Karogi, Maine Pyaar Kyun Kiya* and *No Entry*. He was probably focusing on bringing laughter back into his life and his fans'. I can read that pressing question on your mind and, as a journalist who has been trained in analyzing Bollywood over the last decade, I can tell you that one question you never ask about a Bhai film is: What's the plot? You don't need that when Bhai is doing his iconic dance moves in a towel.

" Tu Superman hai? Spider-Man hai? Abbe tu common man hai. "

Partner, 2007

7

The King of Massy Entertainers

'WHAT is a mass hero?' a film journalist, Annie Moore, from the UK once asked me. We were both queued up in the same virtual waiting room before an interview for a Hollywood film. It was 4.30 a.m. in India, and I had tuned in along with other colleagues from South Asia. Being the only light-skinned person in the room, she struck up a conversation about Bollywood with the rest of us. Earlier that week, she'd watched S.S. Rajamouli's *RRR* and was amazed by its leads. We started talking about how stardom is interpreted so differently in our respective countries. '*RRR* brings new mass heroes into the fold,' someone said. And she looked blankly at the rest of us. Clearly 'mass hero' was something she had never heard before.

Six scribes from India, Pakistan and Bangladesh then took turns to explain what exactly a mass hero was. And guess whom we turned to for being the most accurate example? Salman Khan. A man made for the big screen and a big crowd. The moment he walks into a scene, the music rises to a crescendo, the walk is captured in slow motion, the camera locks in and the audience knows he's the hero they are going to root for. He does the unimaginable: In Salman's case, it's fighting off ten guys without breaking a sweat before gliding into a euphoric dance. More often than not, in India, a mass hero is also the man who stands tall and fights for what's right. There isn't an ounce of realism in the characters, but somehow, in the film and its world, it feels completely right.

Annie couldn't comprehend it, but we asked her to watch the *Dabangg* and the *Tiger* series. She sent us an email many months later that she had watched both but couldn't understand the *Dabangg* series at all. The *Tiger* films, though, were quite 'her jam'. Through 2024, Annie watched Salman's comedies, which she says were her only respite through the gruelling news stories of one war after another as the genocide in Gaza continued to devastate lives.

When the world feels like it's collapsing, laughter becomes a coping mechanism. Maybe Salman understood that earlier than most. By 2003, after enduring what was arguably the worst spell of his adult life, Salman was beginning to find his footing again. He was breaking existing moulds and building new ones, redefining what mainstream cinema expected of its leading men. While his peers were picking up bigger challenges, slipping into iconic roles and making disruptive movies, Salman was working on fighting his own demons. After establishing himself as the gentle romantic ideal through characters such as Prem and later Sameer, and then the tragically gutted hero Radhe, Salman pivoted to broad comedy, probably his respite, too, like Moore's. Films such as *Mujhse Shaadi Karogi* and *Partner* introduced a new kind of mass hero, someone who could make entire theatres erupt into laughter and make them momentarily forget their own demons as they laughed at Salman's antics.

Until then, directors would cast actors such as Johnny Lever to be the comic relief in intense films, but Salman showed that comedy was well within the reach of a mass hero too. It was something very few except Govinda have been able to ace. And Salman showed his fans that he could too!

In doing so, Salman expanded the acting range of the mass hero. It was a focused effort on proving that spectacle could also come with silliness, and that laughter, too, was a form of heroism.

His partner-in-crime was the ever-dependable David Dhawan, with whom he had already delivered a few hits. Salman brought into Dhawan's storytelling a different kind of energy—more physical and more macho. Both *Mujhse Shaadi Karogi* and *Partner* were bona fide crowd pullers because they mixed Salman's star power with Dhawan's chaotic storytelling style. The result was an unserious, funny, slightly immature but a largely affable and very endearing new Bollywood hero.

Critics of that time often missed how Dhawan's films spoke to the masses. These were not films meant for film festivals or for think pieces in English-language dailies. They were meant for single-screen theatres, small-town crowds and weekend family outings. The humour was broad because it was meant to be understood without subtitles. The plots were predictable because the fun was in watching how the actors played with it.

Salman's acting style fit this format perfectly. He wasn't about craft anyway and didn't overcomplicate his performances. His punchlines were simple, his dancing was flashy and his body language said more than his dialogues sometimes did. And Dhawan used this to its full effect, designing scenes that were all about the energy!

Critics found it easy to write off these films as puerile, but these were the very films that the audience wanted. This was probably the first signs of the gulf between critical acclaim and audience nod for a film!

Many of Dhawan's movies follow a formula, driven by mistaken identities, a love triangle, a meddling friend, a big misunderstanding and an emotional climax that ties it all together. It's formulaic—and tried and tested. And when you add someone like Salman into the mix, it becomes explosive. The slapstick gets funnier. The songs become anthems. The jokes hit harder.

Dhawan, as the director, did not try to tame Salman—he let the actor do what he did best. This trust allowed Salman to play with the frame, breaking the fourth wall, teasing co-actors, improvising lines. That pulled the audience in.

I was told *Mujhse Shaadi Karogi* was a bit of a gamble for Dhawan. This was the start of the multiplex era and movies were categorically being divided into mass movies and multiplex movies back then. Yash Raj Films had pumped in big money into catering to urban crowds, by commissioning films such as *Hum Tum* and *Salaam Namaste*, which might not have been big hits in the heartland but metropolitan cities lapped them up. Dhawan was trying to create a mix of both these sensibilities, and *Mujhse Shaadi Karogi* was the first of its kind in his repertoire. In an interview he said, 'So far I have targeted all my films at the masses. But now I have started looking at what the audiences in the multiplexes want. Admittedly, they look for the same things as audiences in single-screen theatres, only with a little more sophistication. I have given them that. *Maine donon taraf nazar rakh ke* Mujhse Shaadi Karogi *banaya hain* [I have kept both audiences in mind when making *Mujhse Shaadi Karogi*].'[1]

What really made the film shine was the playful banter between its two 'badmaash' leads. Dhawan brought together Salman Khan and Akshay Kumar, and the two seemed to be having the time of their lives. Their comic timing, silly one-upmanship and easy camaraderie gave the film a laid-back charm, as if the shoot was one long picnic. Add Priyanka Chopra to the mix, in one of her early star-making roles, and the chemistry just got better. With veterans such as the late Amrish Puri and the late Kader Khan rounding out the cast, the screen erupted in joyful chaos. It was loud and over the top—and that was the point.

Dhawan's risk of trying to appeal to both single-screen crowds and multiplex audiences paid off. *Mujhse Shaadi Karogi* made everyone feel like they were in on the same inside joke.

But some of these films haven't aged well—some jokes feel outdated and the gender politics in many Salman–Dhawan films are far from progressive. But for a generation of moviegoers, these films were an escape route to unabashed entertainment, freedom and fantasy. These films weren't meant to be lessons, just laughs. And Salman, with his self-awareness, gave those laughs a face.

Critics didn't take to the film easily. *India Today*'s review called it 'partly fun but mostly exhausting'.[2] In *Outlook*, film critic Namrata Joshi wrote, 'Watching *Mujhse Shaadi Karogi* has all to do with one's terribly low expectations …'[3]

Ironically, what critics saw as a lack of depth was actually the whole point. Dhawan's films didn't pretend to be anything else. They wore their commercial intent on their sleeve. They told the audience: Come, laugh, forget your worries, enjoy the ride. And Salman, in all his shirtless glory, drove that home like no one else.

This brand of cinema tapped into the pulse of everyday India, where movies were still a weekly escape, not a moral lecture. With Salman as his lead hero, Dhawan created a template for the mass entertainer that's being copied even today. The real measure of a film's success is that it stays with people—and these films do!

Made on a budget of around Rs 15–19 crore, *Mujhse Shaadi Karogi* went on to earn over Rs 29 crore net domestically and about Rs 40.4 crore gross, and raked in roughly $2.79 million (Rs 12.6 crore) overseas, pushing its total worldwide collection to around Rs 56 crore. Adjusted for inflation, its net box office collection comes to approximately Rs 101 crore. The film's numbers placed it firmly among the top four Bollywood earners of 2004.[4]

This, along with *Tere Naam* and *Baghban*, made it feel like things were looking up for Salman.

While many of his contemporaries were setting their sights on global acclaim, chasing festival prestige or courting crossover roles, Salman stayed firmly rooted in India. It was clear from Salman's choice to do *Baghban* that he wasn't trying to impress Cannes. He was more interested in middle-class families buying tickets for weekend matinees at single-screen theatres, and the millions of fans who saw themselves in the simplicity of his roles.

The greatest edge that Salman has over his contemporaries is that he is always able to put a finger on what makes the common man cheer. That's what makes him a true mass hero. He has the ability to connect across class, language and geography. The real win for an Indian film isn't global recognition, but when it makes sense to both a rickshaw puller in Bareilly and a teenager in Chennai alike. Salman transcended borders with *Tere Naam*, but with *Baghban*, he deepened his roots in India and Indian sentiments. And sometimes the latter leaves an actor with a more powerful legacy.

Legendary film-maker B.R. Chopra, film-maker Ravi Chopra's father, had written the film three decades earlier. Ravi took the original material and had it updated by Dr Achala Nagar, but B.R. Chopra dissuaded him from making the movie. 'Ravi's father discouraged him from making *Baghban*, saying it was outdated. Many believed films like *Avtaar* had already explored similar themes. But Ravi saw it differently—not as a social drama but as a love story between an elderly couple,' Renu, Ravi Chopra's wife, said in an interview last year.[5]

Baghban tells the story of Raj and Pooja Malhotra, an elderly couple who have built a life of love and care around themselves and their four sons. But when Raj retires, the couple realizes that their children have no space for them in their lives. Forced to live apart, the couple faces neglect and heartbreak from the very family they gave everything up for. *Baghban* is about ageing parents and how sometimes family is found in the people who choose you, not the ones you share blood ties with. Salman plays the couple's adopted son Alok, who steps up when they need him the most. When their own children turn away, Alok shows up with the kind of love and respect that speaks louder than words.

> **Dhawan's films didn't pretend to be anything else. They wore their commercial intent on their sleeve. They told the audience: Come, laugh, forget your worries, enjoy the ride. And Salman Khan, in all his shirtless glory, drove that home like no one else.**

Baghban delves into the insecurity of post-retirement life and what it feels like to be left behind by the children you raised. It gently holds up a mirror to families asking what we owe those who gave us everything. That's why the film stayed with people. My father used to joke that he already had his retirement fund stashed away, in case I turned out to be as ungrateful as the kids in *Baghban*. I was twelve when the film was released, and it took me a while to completely understand the complicated parent–child dynamics shown in the film.

But Salman did, and something about the film struck a chord with him, which made him swoop in to rescue the makers in the nick of time.

Senior Chopra's fears were proven right when *Baghban* was completed—no one wanted to release the film. Renu, in an interview, said, 'No distributor wanted to touch the film. They thought it was outdated, especially since Amitji was facing a rough patch in his career, having just made a comeback with *Mohabbatein* and *Kaun Banega Crorepati* (KBC). Then someone suggested approaching Salman Khan for the remaining part. Ravi went to Salman's two-room apartment, where the Khan brothers were casually working out. One by one, they stepped out in shorts, making Ravi feel overdressed. When Salman heard the role, he immediately agreed, saying, "I love this boy, Alok Malhotra. This is exactly how I feel about my parents. I worship them, and I will do this role." He didn't ask about payment; he just wanted to know where to show up for the shoot.'[6]

Salman shot all his scenes in London, and the only request he made was not to start work before 11 a.m. 'He promised he wouldn't leave until everything was done. Every evening, he'd invite us for dinner, and you couldn't tell him what to order. He'd take over and order the entire menu. On the last day, when we tried to clear the bill, we discovered Salman had already paid it,' Renu added.[7]

The greatest edge that Salman has over his contemporaries is that he is always able to put a finger on what makes the common man cheer. That's what makes him a true mass hero. He has the ability to connect across class, language and geography. The real win for an Indian film isn't global recognition, but when it makes sense to both a rickshaw puller in Bareilly and a teenager in Chennai alike.

Salman walked into the film after having delivered *Tere Naam*, which was a huge hit. The role was no more than an extended cameo, but he was sharing screen space with Amitabh Bachchan for the first time. Interestingly, the role of the adopted son was initially offered to Shah Rukh, who declined due to commitments to his own production, *Chalte Chalte*.[8]

When Ravi was asked if Salman's 'bad boy' reputation made him apprehensive, he said, 'No. Salman is a sweetheart. I don't know how he got this reputation. Maybe he has never had a good relationship with the media. I had a great time shooting with him and would love to do another film with him. He has really got a heart of gold. Salman plays an orphan who is brought up by Amitji. I needed someone who looked very decent because he's the good guy in the film. His character is indebted to the man who has raised him. Salman has done a great job.'[9]

Reviewers lauded his restraint, some even saying that he delivered a seasoned performance, despite playing a character that Derek Elley of *Variety* felt was 'uncharacteristically saintly'.[10]

Salman's own father didn't agree with reviewers. Salim felt that instead of coming across as a 'nice man', Salman appeared to be 'looking like a blind man'. In an old conversation with Sooraj Barjatya, Salman recalled, 'I had a problem in *Baghban* as well where my father said, "Why are you looking blind?" I asked "Blind?"'[11] According to Salim, Salman looked 'artificial' in the film.

Baghban was made on a modest budget of around Rs 10 crore but was a solid box office success. Domestically, it earned Rs 31 crore gross. Internationally, it brought in an additional $1.5 million at the time, pushing its total worldwide gross to approximately Rs 43 crore. Adjusted for inflation, that figure would cross Rs 100 crore today. The film enjoyed a silver jubilee run in many theatres.[12]

More than just being a box office success, *Baghban* is a film that found a second life and perhaps even greater popularity on cable television. It registered a TVR (Television Viewership Rating) of 0.7 during one of its reruns, placing it among the top movies aired at the time. Over the years, it became a regular fixture on Hindi movie channels, especially around festivals and family weekends. Ironically, while it's a film about parents and children, it's also one that many families admit they can't watch together, because there are too many uncomfortable truths, too many emotional moments that hit close to home. It is an emotional landmine, sparking self-reflection in living rooms across India. A piece in *The Indian Express* in 2023 even called the film manipulative. The piece read, '*Baghban* is a manipulative propaganda film masquerading as wholesome entertainment. Amitabh Bachchan and Hema Malini as victims of self-inflicted elder abuse, the family drama *Baghban* remains one of the most horrifically ill-conceived movies in recent Bollywood history.'[13]

Many agree; some vehemently disagree. Shambit Roy, an engineer in Arizona, the US, tells me, 'I was about eight when *Baghban* came out. Back then, I thought it was just about parents crying and old-people problems. But now that I'm thirty, I see it for what it truly is. There's something about Salman's character, Alok, that stayed with me. The kind of son we all hope to be, but sometimes forget because the everyday love of parents is something we take for granted until we don't have it any more. I realized this after I lost my father. When first started living in the US, I saw how individualistic society was there. While I was chasing my own dreams, I was reminded that it was my parents who even made it possible for me to do that. That was the core of Alok. It is evident that Salman is the same person too. Also, it takes a superstar to reinforce a strong value system. It is wonderful that he didn't see the film as dated. He saw it as a film that celebrated parents. Our parents sacrifice so much for us. On our worst day, we know we can always fall back on them. But what happens when parents don't feel the same way about us? The film actually perpetuated modern ideas of family, if you think about it. Your family isn't the one you are born into—it's the one you make for yourself. Every time I miss my dad, I watch the film. It makes me value my mother a lot more than I used to when I was younger.'

People who are close to Salman say you can always tell when he is in love. They say it's when he's happiest. There's a softness that slips through—in the way he smiles more, cracks jokes that are gentler ... People around him have often whispered that love changes him. Even if he guards his heart, when he's with someone, you can tell it matters to him.

His life changed again in 2003, when Salman met Katrina Kaif at a party he was hosting at home. It was former supermodel Alison Kanuga who introduced Katrina to Salman at Alvira's birthday party at Salman's apartment. Salman was shirtless, having got out of a shower right then. Seeing him, Katrina burst out laughing. Salman told her that he had just come out of a shower and wasn't aware that guests were waiting for him already. He was immediately drawn to Katrina, and the two ended up spending the whole evening together.[14]

That unexpected meeting soon led to more catch-ups, and within days, Salman began pursuing her. Whenever Katrina finished work early, she would hurry to see Salman, either on his set or at home. They began frequenting cafés in Bandra and taking long walks with Salman's dogs, Myson and Myjaan. Katrina started cherishing the early-morning bike rides they took together.

With her own family based in London, Salman's family quickly became her own. 'They are tremendously wonderful people,' she said in an interview to *People* magazine. Alvira, Salman's sister, became one of her closest friends and most trusted confidantes.[15]

Those who knew Salman at the time often said that Katrina's warmth mellowed him down. He seemed softer, more at ease. In a 2008 interview, Katrina was asked about this change. 'If he has mellowed down, that's wonderful,' she said. 'On occasion, the media can be aggressive and write something hurtful. But at the end of the day, there's no need to be upset. I'm glad that he's more comfortable with the media.'[16]

By then, their chemistry, both on- and off-screen, was being widely written about. Katrina explained their bond with quiet affection. 'Since we've known each other for many years now, there's an equation. He's a very, very special person; you have to give him a lot of leeway, space and understanding. And that's exactly what I do when we work together as well.'[17]

Despite the speculation, Katrina remained guarded. In that same interview, she made it clear that she would never publicly discuss her relationship with Salman.

But in 2011, after years of silence, she finally let the truth slip. 'Salman Khan was my first serious relationship,' she told *Cosmopolitan*. Reflecting on love, she added, 'I think what you learn from relationships is that they are unpredictable. I believe that you cannot control or predict these things. I am also a hopeless romantic. Love should be all about giving and trusting.'[18]

When in 2005, Salman Khan teamed up once again with Dhawan for *Maine Pyaar Kyun Kiya*, his chemistry with Katrina was evident. In the film he plays a flirtatious doctor named Sameer, who finds himself tangled in a web of romantic confusion. He falls for Katrina's character, a sweet and straightforward young woman, only to realize that his heart actually belongs to his caring nurse, played by Sushmita Sen. In the film's cheeky climax, Katrina's character ends up marrying Sohail Khan's character, who as we know is Salman's younger brother.

Off-camera, *Maine Pyaar Kyun Kiya* became something more than just another comedy of errors. It was during this shoot that Salman and Katrina began to spend real time together and got to know each other in a way they hadn't before. She was still relatively new in Bollywood, and he, already a star, was known for mentoring younger actors. Salman helped her out with lines, coached her through scenes and gave her a kind of behind-the-scenes crash course in surviving the industry. Between takes and late-night rehearsals, a connection began to form. By the time filming ended, they were closer than ever before, though they never rushed to make it official to the press.

Good on-screen chemistry isn't just about two good-looking people comfortably sharing a frame. It is about a spark that feels natural and doesn't leave a lot to your imagination. It's rare, and that is what makes it so enjoyable to watch on screen. Some actors just seem to get each other, be it their timing, their reactions, the way they push or steady one another—and suddenly the scene lifts off. Take Shah Rukh and Kajol, for instance. And *Maine Pyaar Kyun Kiya* paved the way for the on-screen power duo of Tiger and Zoya in the *Tiger* series.

It's nearly impossible for actors to speak of the secret sauce behind good on-screen chemistry, but Katrina tried to put it into words in an interview. 'Salman is very unpredictable. He will change it every take. He will throw something else at you so you have to be fluid and that's how our chemistry is when we are on set together. I read him and he reads me and we play off each other. Good chemistry is in the writing. If it's not in the writing then it's not gonna be there. Salman has a very generous heart. We have an incredible equation, a very strong equation, and it's one with a lot of respect and admiration, which is very important,' she said.[19]

Katrina also said that Salman did not talk much on set. He was usually just sitting in a corner and 'chewing on his shirt collar'.

Their fans continue to root for them, even years after their split. Katrina is now married to Vicky Kaushal, but when Salman and Katrina do star together, like in 2023's *Tiger 3*, it still sends fans into a tizzy.

This enduring fascination is not just about nostalgia—there's a spark that still feels alive.

I spoke to media professional Ayesha Vaid, who lives in Melbourne, Australia, and she told me, 'The thing about Salman and Katrina is that they don't just have chemistry, I feel like they fit. They understand each other, both on- and off-screen. Their chemistry isn't just about romance or heat. It's that "I've got your back, you've got mine" kind of bond, and you can feel it in every scene. That is the crux of a good actioner. That's what makes them so compelling as Tiger and Zoya. In most films, the man takes the lead and the woman follows. But with them, it's different. Zoya doesn't play second fiddle to Tiger—she stands right beside him, because she is every bit as competent as him. She's just as sharp, just as strong, just as necessary. And Salman allows that space to Katrina as an actor. There's no ego in it. That balance, that equality is what makes them work. Watching them together feels like watching two people who truly know each other and respect each other. He's wild, she's poised—and, instead of clashing, those opposites lock into place. It's like he brings the storm, and she brings the stillness that holds it. That balance is rare. It's what makes scenes between them feel alive even when nothing big is happening. They don't need explosive love scenes or over-the-top drama. Because at the heart of it, you sense there's a history there. Like they've seen each other at their best and worst, and they still show up. That's what comes through on-screen. They bring a sense of realness.'

This fan frenzy is the result of smart storytelling, which the makers of the *Tiger* series tapped into perfectly. When the duo launched the song 'Swag Se Swagat' from their 2017 film *Tiger Zinda Hai*, their director, Ali Abbas Zafar, said, 'Everyone already knows that both Salman and Katrina have this unspoken sizzling chemistry on-screen.'[20]

The actors themselves have interesting takes on when this chemistry truly began to work. Salman feels the chemistry with Katrina really caught on with the *Tiger* series. 'I liked the characters of Tiger and Zoya very much. I believe the same chemistry wasn't there in the earlier movies that we did together. Though viewers were fond of our on-screen pairing, we didn't have chemistry till the *Tiger* franchise came along. We did a film called *Yuvvraaj* in which there wasn't much chemistry on show.

Thereafter, we did the *Tiger* franchise in which there was a lot of chemistry as our characters were sketched very well. So the chemistry you see is not the Salman–Katrina chemistry, but Tiger and Zoya's chemistry.'[21]

This distinction between real-life camaraderie and character-driven chemistry is affirmed by voices from the industry as well. Trade pundits believe this on-screen jodi clicks. A veteran trade journalist tells me, 'It's the yin-yang energy between them that makes them a crowd puller as a unit. Salman has massive influence over the audience but when paired with Katrina, the power doubles.'

What's perhaps most impressive, though, is how both stars remain deeply committed to maintaining that impact. And the good thing is neither Katrina nor Salman ever allow themselves to be lackadaisical about the audience's love. Katrina addressed this in an interview too. She said, 'The best thing about me and Salman coming together to work is that there's no sense of us taking it for granted. We don't go to the sets thinking, "*dekhte hai* [we'll see]". He knows that I'm going to come after putting 1000% of my time and effort behind finding the character, doing my prep. He has that confidence in me and I know when he comes, he's going to come up with something unique. However well I know him or whatever our equation is, when we come on a set, we both come respecting that this is the producer's and director's place and not a playground. It's not about fun and games but professional territory. We come and we do our scenes and rehearsals. That's how we work well together.'[22]

The primary responsibility of a mass hero isn't simply to entertain. They are said to shape aspiration, identity and behaviour, especially among impressionable minds. That's why their movies lead to so much debate around the message they carry for the larger public. There's always an underlying fear—what if audiences start mimicking not just their style, but also their choices? Salman understands the weight of his stardom. This wisdom comes only after a fair share of mess-ups. After 2000, with the media glare fixed on his personal life and public image, Salman thought it best to not hide behind sanitized characters or preachy scripts. He leaned into the mess he had made. From there on, most of his characters had a shade of grey in them. And it started with *No Entry* (2005).

Salman revisited the role of Prem, a married man who cheats without remorse and eggs his friends on to do the same. The secret to a happy domestic life is to seek thrills outside it, believed this version of Prem. On paper, this is reckless and on many levels problematic. But what made it striking was the lack of pretence. Salman didn't try to soften Prem's flaws or wrap him in moral redemption. He leaned into the contradiction, taking on the role with charm but no apology. It was a bold risk, turning Prem, the paragon of chastity, into someone you couldn't defend. In doing so, Salman was possibly pushing against the idea that heroes had to be spotless. But there was a messier truth here that desi people found incredibly hard to stomach—our stars, whom we consider demigods, are actually just normal people, flawed and sometimes very wrong. For a star who had once embodied the dutiful, romantic ideal, this was a sharp pivot. But maybe that's why it landed. It came from someone who knew how tightly the hero label clung, but still chose to wear its darker shades instead.

But the primary reason Salman did *No Entry* wasn't so much a conscious desire for an image shift but to help out Boney Kapoor from a financially troubling spot. The film was an ensemble comedy, and Boney needed a star to sell the film. Saif Ali Khan was offered the role of Kishen, but he was busy shooting *Kal Ho Naa Ho*, and Anil Kapoor replaced him. When Boney first reached out to Salman, he quoted an unaffordable fee. That was when Anil called Salman directly and asked for a meeting. At that meeting, Anil laid out two roles—Kishen, which would need nearly fifty days of shooting, and Prem, which could be wrapped up in ten. Salman immediately picked the latter. In an interview to *The Caravan* magazine, Anil said, 'Before I could tell him that if he did not do the film it would not happen, I think he sensed it. He was sensitive enough to not make me plead. If he had not said yes, *No Entry* would have never happened.'[23]

In the same interview, Anil also recalled how, when the cast flew to South Africa for the shoot, the team arranged for Salman to stay in a plush hotel suite that reflected his star stature while the rest of the actors were put up in simpler accommodations. When Salman got to know about this, he quietly joined his colleagues in the modest lodging, refusing to stay in a luxury hotel. 'During the making of the film I came to know him more, his attitude, his habits. He was still not the quintessential professional. In the mornings, I would go into his room and not really wake him up, but sit there so that he gets up, because I had a responsibility to the film as the producer. Money was a lot less, it was a sensitive kind of situation. Salman would wake up, order breakfast, have coffee in bed, and I would hang around prodding him, hoping to start the shoot as soon as possible. When Salman finally arrived on set, I would say "You haven't slept all night, you are looking like a wreck." He would tell me, "Fuck off, just look at the shot." [Salman] used to wear his glares, give his shot and sure enough, when I checked the monitor I would say, "This guy is fucking blessed, ya. He's not slept the whole night, but he walks into the frame and translates into magic on stage."'[24]

No Entry is a comedy of errors that thrives on humour derived from infidelity and cover-ups, and celebrates male bonding in meltdown mode. The plot follows the antics of three men—Prem, Kishen and Sunny. It all kicks off with Prem, the Casanova of the group, nudging his more honest friends towards 'a little fun', which inevitably snowballs into a tangle of lies, lingerie and last-minute escapes.

It's obvious that *No Entry* wasn't made for women. It was a film about men and for men, made to make them laugh. A lot. It was a staple 'bro-com', where the chaos showcased male camaraderie as they tried to get away with marital mischief. The film's central trio, Salman's Prem, Anil's Kishen and Fardeen Khan's Sunny, function like schoolboys in adult bodies, navigating a moral maze they have constructed for themselves. And yet, their friendship had easy banter and unspoken loyalty even in its dumbest moments.

Director Anees Bazmee amped up this frenzied male energy, delivering a glossy, fast-paced caper that was part sitcom, part fantasy. The men messed up repeatedly and the world (and the women) just kept absorbing their blows. The settings were lavish, the pacing relentless and the punchlines designed to land best with male audiences who saw themselves in the trio's antics. *No Entry* knew exactly who it was speaking to: the boys on the back bench.

And Salman delivered a Salman. As a review in *India Today* cleverly noted, 'Salman Khan, who makes his entry predictably shirtless and surrounded by bikini beauties, doesn't even pretend to act any more. He plays himself: a Bollywood rock star.'[25]

The film was produced on a budget of Rs 22 crore and went on to become the year's top-grossing title, raking in Rs 74 crore at the box office. It made approximately $2.28 million (around Rs 9.92 crore) overseas, bringing its worldwide gross to Rs 72.03 crore. When adjusted for inflation, that total would land in the Rs 150–200 crore range today, marking it as a blockbuster by mid-2000s standards.[26]

Toronto-based writer Mahesh Sharma says that on most of his weekends with his friends, they watch *No Entry*. There is no better film to unwind with, he says, adding, 'We have the PlayStation set up on one end of our hall and the movie plays in the background, and it's the best way to let off steam. It works because it's funny, but also because it taps into a very specific kind of male friendship. This ride-or-die kind of buddy comedy works for us. The film lets the guys be silly, confused and even selfish, but it never lets their bond break. That's what makes it perfect for a boys' night. It is a completely unhinged film, but underneath all the chaos is this sense of loyalty that you'll do anything for your bro. It's white noise, yes, but also a strangely tender kind of friendship we don't always talk about but recognize instantly as men.'

Mahesh's wife, Shruti Doshi, is a grudging witness to this. She tells me, 'I've watched *No Entry* more times than I'd like, mostly because the men in my life—my husband, my brother, my father—love it. And I get it, Anil Kapoor is genuinely hilarious. But as a woman, it's also deeply frustrating. The whole premise revolves around men cheating, lying and manipulating the women around them, and yet it's all played for laughs. There's this underlying message that male infidelity is harmless fun—a phase, a joke, something to be forgiven because "boys will be boys". And that's hard to ignore. Still, I think what makes the film palatable is that it doesn't try to preach or justify the behaviour of these men—it just tips over into absurdity. So when Mahesh laughs, I roll my eyes. It's comfort cinema for men, like *Sex and the City* or *Emily in Paris* or *Bridgerton* is for us.'

A review in *The Austin Chronicle* beautifully summed up Shruti's thoughts on this film: 'Bazmee has crafted a relatively smart and snarky war of the sexes minus the sex but with plenty of juicily hammy performances and enough outrageous one-liners, sight gags and mistaken-identity yuks to make even the most xenophobic anti subtitler stifle at least a dozen smirks.'[27]

But right before he did this completely slapstick, chaotic comedy, he did one of Bollywood's most tenderly made films, *Phir Milenge*, in 2004, where he played an HIV-positive character. It was the first time and probably the only time any mainstream mass hero had even considered taking up such a taboo role. A year before Onir's *My Brother…Nikhil* (2005) gave Indian cinema its most quietly devastating portrayal of an HIV-positive protagonist and one of the first queer love stories, *Phir Milenge* attempted to start that conversation. Directed by Revathy, the acclaimed actor who had starred opposite Salman in *Love* (1991), the film was inspired by Hollywood's *Philadelphia* (1993) and tackled workplace discrimination faced by an HIV-positive woman, played by Shilpa Shetty Kundra.

Salman played Rohit Manchanda, a popular guitarist and ex-flame of Shilpa's character, Tamanna Sahni. Rohit re-enters her life during a brief campus reunion, but shortly after is diagnosed with HIV—a revelation that changes the course of Tamanna's life. As the story unfolds, Rohit's illness progresses, and he tragically succumbs to AIDS in the film's climax, which was a bold narrative choice, especially for a star of Salman's stature.

And Salman did the film for free.

In a video posted by the film's producer Shailendra Singh, he said, 'Salman Khan charged Re 1 for the movie and in the climax he actually dies. We had to create awareness on the topic of AIDS for the whole of India, particularly the youth. I ultimately realized that cinema is a mirror of society and is also the ultimate heartbeat of every Indian. *Us waqt aur ab bhi sabse bada youth icon Bollywood me*—Salman Khan (Even then and today Salman Khan is the biggest youth icon of Bollywood). But imagine asking Salman Khan to do a movie revolving around the cause of AIDS when he is actually the Rambo, Terminator and the Superman of India.'[28]

There was barely any convincing needed. Shilpa in an interview said that it happened over an informal chat while the two were shooting for a film in Rajasthan. 'No one was interested in *Phir Milenge* because it was woman-centric and was not an entertaining film. I generally told him about it and he said, "I'll do it." I said, "Are you serious?" and he replied, "Ya. It's such a nice subject. Why wouldn't I do it?" It was as casual and bizarre as that.'[29]

Now that's the other thing about being a mass hero—his presence draws eyeballs, opens up wallets and creates a kind of visibility that no marketing budget can buy. When Salman backs a project, it gets made and viewed. We are a country where the stakes of stardom are incredibly high. And somehow, that generation of actors, Salman especially, understood the power of their stardom. They knew that a well-timed film could raise awareness or simply start a conversation that could break down centuries of taboo.

Salman, for all his image as a brawny box office titan, was sharply aware of the ecosystem he inhabited and sustained. He knew that his mere involvement could give a small film the traction it needed. And that's one of the reasons he launched his own production house. Usually stars move to production to own the stories they tell, to design the nature of the movies they do and mostly to have greater autonomy on the films they feature in. But Salman operated from the heart, like he always does. *Chillar Party* (2012) was a low-budget children's film starring a motley crew of vibrant kids, written by Vijay Maurya, who later also wrote *Gully Boy* (2019) for Zoya Akhtar. The film was the debut of one of India's most-sought-after directors, Nitesh Tiwari, who later went on to direct *Dangal* (2016) and is now working on the Ranbir Kapoor–starrer *Ramayana*.

Chillar Party, a heartwarming film, might have slipped through the cracks without big backing. After the film was completed (and had even won the National Award for Best Children's Film), it struggled to find commercial buyers or distributors willing to invest in a theatrical release. Children's films, especially those without animation or major stars, were seen as unviable at the time. That's when Salman stepped in.

Impressed by the film after a private screening, Salman decided to present and co-produce it under his newly launched banner, Being Human Productions. With his name attached to it, the film secured wider distribution and marketing support, and went from being a 'festival film' to getting a proper theatrical release. He actively promoted the film, attended press conferences and even danced with the child actors at events. Salman even showed the film to politician Ambika Soni. He said, 'I asked if she could make the film tax-free. The purpose is not to make more money but to have more people see the film. The proceeds ultimately go to the Being Human Foundation. She assured us that she would speak to every CM. The money which I make through production will go to charity.'[30]

Salman stayed deeply invested in its cast, especially the young actor Irfan Khan, a street kid who played a key role in the film. Knowing Irfan's financial struggles, Salman ensured his earnings were used to help build a home for his family. He continues to check in on the children's studies and well-being. Unlike many producers who move on, Salman stuck around. An NDTV report noted, 'This is a refreshing change from the plight of the other slum kids who played pivotal roles in renowned films like Mira Nair's *Salaam Bombay!* and Danny Boyle's *Slumdog Millionaire*, and have vanished from the scene.'[31]

Now that's the other thing about being a mass hero—his presence draws eyeballs, opens up wallets and creates a kind of visibility that no marketing budget can buy. When Salman backs a project, it gets made and viewed.

It is one of the pivotal learnings of this business that a mass hero's responsibility goes beyond personal success. It means occasionally stepping into films that feed the industry's conscience, even when the opportunity to fatten coffers is limited. That balance, between box office clout and social responsibility, is perhaps what made that era of stardom feel both massy and meaningful. And that is why, perhaps, we won't have a new line of superstars the way we did in the 1990s.

As mentioned earlier, Govinda once said that the only time Salman ever reached on time was when someone needed help.

The actor may have been referring to the rough patch in his own film career when Salman had stepped in to support him. Govinda's home production, *Ssukh* (2005), had failed at the box office, and during this lull, the actor had shifted focus to politics. In 2004, he joined the Indian National Congress and successfully contested the Mumbai North Lok Sabha seat, defeating BJP veteran Ram Naik. However, the honeymoon with politics didn't last. Disillusionment soon followed. Recognizing Govinda's talent and wanting to help revive his career, Salman began recommending his name to film-makers. This support led to Govinda's first major comeback film, *Bhagam Bhag* (2006), directed by Priyadarshan. But it was *Partner* (2007) that proved to be the real game-changer. The film was inspired by the Hollywood hit *Hitch* (2005), starring Will Smith, Kevin James and Eva Mendes. In *Partner*, Salman, taking on the role of Will Smith, plays a suave 'love guru' who coaches Govinda on how to win over the love of his life, Priya, played by Katrina Kaif. Sohail Khan produced the film.[32]

By 2006, Govinda was actively working to move away from his political persona. Eager to return to the big screen, he reached out to long-time collaborator David Dhawan and expressed his desire to stage a comeback in films. 'David said no film will sell just in my name. They also needed to take a star,' Govinda said in an interview in 2019.[33]

For Salman, the chance to act alongside Govinda was both a dream come true and an intimidating challenge. 'It's a story of love and adulation with Govinda. How much comedy can you do when you work with him? I was petrified to come on-screen with Govinda for the first 17 years of my life,' Salman said in a throwback interview.[34]

Govinda had long earned a reputation for being difficult on set, often arriving late and occasionally throwing tantrums. However, after spending nearly five years away from the limelight, he turned over a new leaf with this film. He was eager to prove he had changed. And Salman, too, stepped up to match Govinda's level of expertise. In an interview, composer Sajid Khan, one half of the Sajid–Wajid music composer duo, shared a memorable behind-the-scenes story from the making of *Partner*. For both Sajid and his late brother Wajid, the film was a dream project because of the range of music they could showcase in the film. They had previously done *Mujhse Shadi Karogi*, *Hello Brother* and *Pyaar Kiya To Darna Kya*, but this film had all its songs scored by them. What truly stood out was Salman's unexpected commitment to his dance routines. Known for his relaxed, easy-going style, Salman pulled out all the stops, motivated by the fact that he was sharing the screen with Govinda, who in the 1990s was the undisputed dance legend of Bollywood. Sajid said, 'Salman Bhai said Govinda is a very good dancer. He said he'll have to practise a lot. If you watch the songs of *Partner*, you'll notice Salman is dancing more perfectly than Govinda. Even though Salman Bhai usually doesn't do that much—he would just move on the beat—because Govinda was there, he practised too much.'[35]

The choreographers of the film ratified this. Bosco Martis, who choreographed the songs along with Ceasar, said in an interview, 'The difference between Salman and Govinda as dancers is that Govinda is technically perfect; Salman is the guy with lots of attitude and style. The beauty of working in this movie was the combination of these two things together. On one side you have imperfection, but you have such a great looking guy who has a fabulous body. There is also Govinda—even a layman who identifies with him. ... Salman was naughty on the sets; he would come and tell us, "Make sure Govinda dances properly because I am a super dancer." Everybody would burst out in laughter! Salman and Govinda are very good friends. Their bonding was fabulous. They never did something that would make the other look bad. They would do things that would compliment each other.'[36]

This real-life camaraderie really made the film click. Much of *Partner*'s buzz revolved around the Salman–Govinda pairing. But the women in the film more than held their own. Katrina, effortlessly glamorous but also surprisingly sharp with her comic timing, proved that she could do more than just look good on-screen. Lara Dutta brought confidence to her role, anchoring some of the film's more chaotic moments with a touch of maturity.

Bengaluru-based finance analyst Shishir Kurien says his peer group finds his love for this film strange. 'I am considered to be a man of numbers and pretty serious by nature. But at a party, someone once played the songs of *Partner* and I ended up showing them my fun side. That party disbanded at 8 a.m. the morning after. We rounded it up with watching the film and a final round of beers. *Partner* may seem like a breezy comedy on the surface, but it's actually a fascinating case study on how Bollywood negotiates stardom. You have Salman, a massive star, willingly adjusting his screen space to complement Govinda, whose comic instincts are unmatched in Bollywood. The film is also a testament to David Dhawan's ability to update his own formula, in which he retained the exaggerated energy of his earlier comedies but polished it just enough to appeal to a 2000s multiplex audience. *Partner* is one of the more telling movies in the Salman Khan filmography, not because it centres on him, but precisely because it doesn't. What makes Salman unique among Bollywood's mass heroes is his comfort with not being the focal point of the narrative. In *Partner*, he plays the suave relationship coach, but it's Govinda who gets the punchlines, the character arc and, arguably, the louder applause in the end. Salman's performance is self-effacing, allowing Govinda's comic brilliance to take centre stage. This isn't just star courtesy—it's a calculated instinct born of his understanding of mass cinema. He knows that the film wins when everyone shines. We are obsessed with Salman's almost intimidating star power, but for me this movie stands out because it showcases a hero who uplifts the entire frame of the film by stepping back,' he says.

For Kurien, the film isn't about its women at all. He tells me, 'I am a little undecided on how politically correct it is to say this, but this film is not about its women at all. Their comic timing is great, but that's not the reason the film was made. This was a movie made to service bros like me, who want some time away from the world to laugh. The women are simply eye candy—they are pretty, funny and unserious. Honestly, films such as *Partner* really catered to our innocence, where a movie could simply be a movie. You notice how business was thriving then? Because we could see a movie as a movie, have a good time watching it and go home. Now we have started intellectualizing everything, which has been the downfall of cinema. This is why the comedy of the Salman–Govinda–David Dhawan era has become obsolete now. We outrage too much and laugh too little! Just watch, experience and judge less!'

Perhaps Kurien is right, because the movie's mad concoction worked. It earned approximately Rs 138 crore worldwide (around Rs 61 crore net in India), but was made on a modest budget of about Rs 28 crore. When adjusted for inflation, its earning of Rs 100 crore gross in 2007 would be worth roughly Rs 200 crore today.[37]

His fans are accurate in assessing the paradox of Salman's stardom. While it is built on mass appeal, he often uses his space to amplify others—from Govinda's comeback to Katrina's launch to backing co-stars and friends or even a small film that would never have reached a wide audience otherwise. It's this instinct, to know when to lead, when to support and when to simply enjoy a scene, that defines Salman as a man of the masses. It is one thing to perform for the audience and a whole other thing to perform with them, know their pulse, know what makes for a win—both at the box office and in people's hearts.

" **Jis race se mujhe nikaalne ki baat kar rahe hai yeh bewakoof, woh nahi jaante hai uss race ka sikandar main hoon.** "

Race 3, 2018

8

A Bad Spell

I HAVE often wondered if superstars know when a film is going to flop. Going purely by the theory that they are pretty much the smartest people in the business, there's bound to be a voice in their head that tells them: This won't land. Since as far back as 1992, Salman had this sharpened gut feeling about his own work. During an episode of *Bigg Boss*, Ayushmann Khurrana asked if there was ever a film he realized would flop right from the first day of shooting. To everyone's surprise, Salman named *Suryavanshi*, a film that was released in 1992. He mentioned that there were several such films in his career, but admitted, 'On the first day of the shoot of this film itself, I knew that this film would prove to be a flop.'[1]

Then the next obvious question to ask is: Why would an actor do such a film? Salman is very clear that he does not regret doing any of his films. He said in an interview, 'There are different reasons for doing different films. But the most important reason is the script. You feel the script is outstanding and positive, and there is heroism in it—heroism not in action, but heroism in romance, drama, for a cause. It can be anything ...

and you're either laughing or wiping your tears off [when you come out of the theatre]. Any of these reactions is heroism.'[2]

But quite often, when the idea of a hero and what it means changes, it takes effort for even the most seasoned actors to decide what to do next. Salman starred in films such as *Tumko Na Bhool Paayenge*, *Yeh Hai Jalwa*, *Phir Milenge*, *Dil Ne Jise Apna Kahaa*, *Kyon Ki…*, *Shaadi Karke Phas Gaya Yaar*, *Baabul*, *Jaan-E-Mann*, *Salaam-e-Ishq*, *Marigold*, *God Tussi Great Ho*, *Heroes*, *Yuvvraaj*, *Main Aurr Mrs Khanna* and *London Dreams*, which were all box office duds. He had a sporadic hit here and there, but largely the period failed to spin the Salman magic on-screen. What was going wrong? As my friend film-maker Sanjay Gupta always says, 'Every film has its own destiny. We all set out to make the next *Sholay*. The intent is always honest!' Sometimes that honesty pays off—but often it doesn't.

The first big flop was *Salaam-e-Ishq*, released in January 2007. Fashioned as a desi version of *Love Actually* (2003), this Nikkhil Advani directorial failed to spin any magic at the box office, despite having a host of stars, from Salman Khan, Anil Kapoor and Priyanka Chopra to John Abraham and Vidya Balan. Film critic Sukanya Varma wrote, 'Salman Khan's services are surprisingly underused. He plays the kind of lover boy that made stars out of Biswajeet and Joy Mukherjee. Besides pronouncing his name with a funny twang and parading in fancy blazers, Sallu doesn't get to do anything substantial.'[3] The film was declared a disaster after a lifetime run of Rs 52 crore.[4] The only thing that fans remember of the film is the iconic song 'Tainu Leke'. With Salman at his charming best and full of swagger, dancing in a sherwani in the streets of London, the song has stayed on people's minds. But what many don't know is that it almost didn't get shot because Salman refused to show up for a morning shoot. In an interview, Advani spoke about how he devised ploys to get his leading man to come on set. He said, 'We kept Salman awake for the whole night because he said that I can't come at 5 in the morning. "Either sit with me and I will go to sleep straight at 10 AM!" So we stayed awake, took him, shot, finished shooting and then he went to sleep. For me, it has always been about finishing the day quickly.'[5]

Homemaker Raashi Singh says that the song played during her husband's entry at her wedding. 'My husband trained for six months to get Salman's steps right. I love that song. I had always dreamt that my groom would dance on this at the baraat, and I had it my way! Since I can't marry Salman Khan, this is the closest I am going to get to my eternal romantic dream!' she says.

Salaam-e-Ishq had songs that stayed on people's lips even when the film was forgotten. But the most polarizing flop of that phase of Salman's career was *Jaan-E-Mann*, which brought back Salman and Akshay after their Dhawan-esque escapades, along with Preity Zinta this time. Helmed by Shirish Kunder—who Manoj Bajpayee tells me is a genius waiting for that one big film that will prove to the world what he is made of—the film performed dismally. Trade insiders blamed that on its clash with Shah Rukh's *Don* (2006). Rahul Desai, in a column in Film Companion, called *Jaan-E-Mann* ahead of its time, but reviewers back then were far from pleased with it. A 2006 review read, 'First of all, let me say that *Jaan-E-Mann* is one of the most bizarre movies I have ever seen. The very first scene introduces Salman Khan and Anupam Kher, who plays a short person (that's the politically correct term now). In the next 30 minutes, we get to see a Broadway musical, harem girls, singing dwarfs and a qawwali number. First-time director Shirish Kunder has thrown every visual gimmick he has ever seen into *Jaan-E-Mann* and the results, more often than not, jar your sensibilities.'[6]

The film had Salman play Suhaan Kapoor, a washed-up actor who is hit with a hefty divorce settlement by his ex-wife Piya (Preity Zinta). When her nerdy college admirer Agastya Rao (Akshay Kumar) turns up looking for her, cash-strapped Suhaan schemes to set Piya up with Agastya so he won't have to pay alimony. But his matchmaking plan backfires, and the love triangle inevitably loops back on itself. The film made about Rs 45 crore and didn't do well, but years later, it acquired a cult status. When *La La Land* (2016) was released, the film found a new surge of love. Shirish tweeted then, '#14YearsOfJaanEMann - my first film as a Director. Heavily criticized when released. Started getting some love after ten years when La La Land released. Hoping history will be kinder.'[7]

Akshay even got envious of his co-star. In an interview to *Hindustan Times*, he admitted, 'I did try to cut Salman's role but he is too good in the film, which made it difficult for me to play an editor. Salman Khan is at his best in *Jaan-E-Mann*.'[8]

Salman's fans take this flop personally. Businessman Bhushan Makhija, based in New Zealand, tells me, 'We don't deserve experimentative films. When people tell me Salman is mediocre, he can't act and that he has only three expressions, I tell them that they don't deserve better from him. When he tries something fresh, we never appreciate him. *Jaan-E-Mann* proves that. It takes smarts as a superstar to free-fall, and Salman always free-falls without fear and takes bets on young, first-time makers! I am glad he does only massy stuff now. If the audience doesn't care, why should he?'

For a man of the masses, a certain amount of reimagination is a must. After years and years of playing versions of the same man, what's new can be both daunting and challenging. But courage in such situations is not always rewarded.

Marigold was him shaking things up and taking a step towards Hollywood. Shah Rukh has famously said how he has never entertained the idea of working in Hollywood because there's no place for him there. But Salman was happy to give it a shot. Directed by Willard Carroll and marking the Bollywood debut of American actress Ali Larter, *Marigold* was a cross-cultural experiment. The film is the story of an American actress who flies to Mumbai for a movie that eventually gets cancelled. But she finds herself a gig in a Bollywood musical and falls in love with Prem, the choreographer. Baradwaj Rangan, who is usually not considered harsh with his words and critiques with sensitivity, wrote in his reviews, 'A sleepy Salman Khan falls for an American in a dreadful romance that gets almost nothing right.'[9] Though it may be argued that this film didn't stand a chance because it was released a week before *Chak De! India* (2007), the film itself had a weak script and was panned unanimously.

Carroll, who directed *Playing by Heart* (1998) starring Sean Connery and Angelina Jolie, made a comeback in the director's chair with this film. He quit movies after the film tanked.

The New York Times panned the film, saying, 'It doesn't really have Bollywood's antic, anything-goes quality, and Mr Carroll's script lacks punch and dimension.'[10]

This time, even his fans were unimpressed. Home chef and culinary expert Careem Hooseini, based in San Francisco, says, 'There is always a weight to Salman's screen presence, but in this film he felt fatigued. The glint in the eyes was gone, replaced by a sense of going through the motions. And his audience noticed it. You can charm your way through mediocrity only so many times.'

But the biggest shock was *Yuvvraaj*, helmed by Subhash Ghai, co-starring Katrina Kaif, and with a soundtrack by A.R. Rahman. Within a day of its release, the trade knew this film had bombed. *The Economic Times* reported that *Yuvvraaj* was in the league of big-budget flops, given that it was mounted on Rs 50 crore. 'There were a lot of expectations from this film but it hasn't lived up to them at all. The usual weekend audience has come to watch the film but it hasn't pulled any extra audiences to the theatres. Even though the film has big stars and was marketed well, it hasn't struck a chord with the audiences,' said Inox Cinemas vice-president (distribution and programming) Utpal Acharya.[11]

Salman hates having a flop to his name. But not why you think. Many years later, he explained in an interview, 'I just don't want my films to flop because that would mean my thinking is going wrong and that would be the worst thing. I don't care about the Rs 200–300 (crore club). I don't want to be a part of this number game. I am there (in that bracket) but it is not like I want to break that record. I want to make a good film. As long as my films run and make decent money, I am happy.'[12]

But at that time his instincts were going wrong, one after another. Meanwhile, younger stars and other contemporaries were posing a formidable challenge to his star power. Hrithik Roshan had already proven his mettle with *Kaho Naa... Pyaar Hai*, but it was in this period—the mid-2000s—that Hrithik was truly redefining what brute physicality could look like. *Dhoom 2* (2006) made him the aspirational face of male sex appeal and action—all of which, until then, was Salman's bastion. Hrithik danced better, looked sleeker and carried the kind of polish that appealed to an emerging urban India.

Then there were the Khans, his peers. Shah Rukh wasn't just a romantic icon any more. Between 2005 and 2010, he was backing socially and politically conscious cinema. *Chak De! India* brought nationalism without jingoism to the forefront, while *My Name Is Khan* (2010) dared to speak directly to post-9/11 Islamophobia with a rare tenderness and empathy. Shah Rukh had his finger firmly on the cultural pulse of an evolving India. And then there was Aamir, who, since the start of the millennium, was laser-focused on changing the template of commercial Hindi films. He invested one too many years in the magnum opus *Mangal Pandey* (2005). The grand historical epic underperformed at the box office but showcased his ambition. And then he delivered *Rang De Basanti* (2006), a film that spoke to a whole generation's sense of disillusionment, followed by *Taare Zameen Par* (2007), for which he turned director and left us all teary-eyed.

Even Akshay Kumar, who had long floated in and out of genres without any clear direction, found a groove. With *Mujhse Shaadi Karogi* (2004), *Garam Masala* (2005), *Bhool Bhulaiyaa* (2007) and *Singh Is Kinng* (2008), he proved his comic timing was just as entertaining for the masses as his action sequences on-screen.

In contrast, Salman seemed stuck. His choices felt adrift, tone-deaf even. His choices weren't bad, but they were just not working. The audience had changed and cinema was no longer just about heroism—it was about context. About how that heroism fit into the world outside the theatre. In that shifting space, Salman was still playing catch-up, still living off the inertia of an older image. The stardom remained, but his relevance started to dim.

And this his fans could feel. Housewife Deepika Bisht from Almora tells me that she had gone to watch *Hello* (2008), inspired by Chetan Bhagat's bestselling novel *One Night @ the Call Centre*, and was appalled at how badly it was made. 'I remember being really excited because I'd loved the book. I thought Salman would add that extra spark to the film. But it was just … awful. It was like no one in it cared. The dialogues were boring, the acting was flat and even Salman looked like he didn't want to be there. I came out of the theatre embarrassed that I'd dragged my friends along. That was the first time I genuinely questioned if I could keep defending him. There's a kind of fatigue that comes from watching a beloved actor serve you the same dish again and again, even when it has lost all its flavour. You still show up, out of habit or loyalty or a flicker of old love, but your heart isn't in it any more. You leave the theatre a little emptier each time. Most of his films of that time feel like shadows of something brighter you once knew. There was a time when seeing Salman on-screen meant excitement. That slow-motion entry shot, the slight tilt of the head, the effortless mischief … But somewhere in the mid-2000s, it all started to blur. The dance moves looked recycled. As fans we can tell when our man doesn't want to act any more, because you watch him fulfil a contract.'

Salman's superstar power has always come from instinct, from what his gut tells him will connect with the masses, and it was disorienting for his fans to see him get it wrong, again and again. And yet, Salman kept at it. There was something strangely moving about that too. Even when the applause grew faint, the roles didn't land and the box office turned its back, Salman kept showing up. Not always with the best script, or the best director, or the best judgement, but with that same stubborn belief that maybe that time it would work.

Many years later, when he was asked, Salman explained why he doesn't take a pause after a spell of bad movies. He said, 'Most of the films being made aren't good, and that includes my own. It's simple, if a film is good, it will run. If it's bad, it won't. There's no doubt that if terrible films are made, they will flop. It's the star's job to bring audiences to the theatres. A true star is the one who attracts crowds just by appearing on the poster. If the films don't do well, the accountability lies with the star.'[13]

And that's the thing about a fall—it's not always sudden. Sometimes it's slow and drawn out. Sometimes the star doesn't crash but just drifts away, floating lower with each film, never quite hitting the ground but never really rising either. Salman was drifting. And we, the audience, were wondering, each time, if this was the film that would lift him up again. Wondering if our hero would ever reinvent himself or just keep feeding us warmed-over versions of a myth that no longer thrilled.

But there is one potent risk Salman took in those years that has endured. And that was his decision to open himself up to television. It's been close to seventeen years now, and Salman continues to host one of India's most popular shows, *Bigg Boss*. His tryst with TV began with

10 Ka Dum. 'In 2008, when it came to me, I had a very negative image in public. And I was indeed scared to project my original personality. But then I made my debut, and from then on I have realized that it is the most powerful medium. So I asked my father whether I should do it because there will be the [connection with the] common man. I was scared of being "me". He told me, "Who do you want to be then? If people accept you, it is good. If not, you will need to change yourself." That's when I decided to do this show.'[14]

The show did well and changed the course of Salman's on-screen presence. When he did *10 Ka Dum*, his public image changed completely as per industry insiders. Before that, he predominantly had the image of a bad boy. But the fact that he is a very generous man, who really takes care of the people around him, came to the fore with this show.

Salman is truly at his best when he is unfiltered. Any journalist who has ever interviewed him can attest to that. In my last interview with him, he sang a song mid-conversation. When I looked puzzled, he let out the heartiest laugh. The innocence that we as journalists very rarely get to see now began airing on TV. And people loved what they saw.

In her book *The Three Khans: And the Emergence of New India*, Kaveree Bamzai quotes the show's director, Siddhartha Basu. 'It was a hot day. He was sitting out in the sun. The food was laid out. And I remember Salman taking me aside and asking me: "Do I have to read?" He didn't like reading, so the teleprompter was of no use. And he didn't like to memorize dialogues. Wireless prompts had just come in and we would prompt him line by line, until he would just take off, and then it would be difficult to bring him back to earth. His strength was that he

'There was a time when seeing Salman on-screen meant excitement. That slow-motion entry shot, the slight tilt of the head, the effortless mischief … But somewhere in the mid-2000s, it all started to blur. The dance moves looked recycled. As fans we can tell when our man doesn't want to act any more, because you watch him fulfil a contract.'

connected with ordinary people, in a batty, entertaining way. ... In his place was a teddy bear with rippling muscles.'

Salman was his playful self—dancing, cracking jokes and entertaining the celebrity guests. And he effortlessly made fun of himself. In an episode, cricketers Yuvraj Singh and Harbhajan Singh named Katrina Kaif as their favourite actress, and Salman fired back with a cheeky, '*Bahar niklo tum dono* [Get out, both of you].'[15]

Salman has a knack for walking the line between entertaining and irreverent without ever losing his audience. *10 Ka Dum* was the Indian adaptation of the 2007 American game show *Power of 10*, originally hosted by Drew Carey on CBS. The premise is simple: Contestants don't need encyclopaedic knowledge, just instincts. They are asked to estimate public opinion in percentages across five rounds with increasing value—starting at Rs 10,000 and climbing through Rs 1 lakh, Rs 10 lakh and Rs 1 crore, all the way up to a Rs 10 crore jackpot.

In an early review, Sukanya Varma wrote, 'Of course, he's Salman Khan at the end of the day, and so you get the famously mercurial star shift his body language, accent and reflexes from time to time. His quips range from cheeky—"*Aloo aur Indians har jagah hain* (Indians and potatoes are to be found everywhere)"—to cheesy—"*Mere father ne ek saand paida kiya hai. Log apni apni guy bachayein* (My father has produced a bull. All you people out there, save your cows)." ... If you are a die-hard Salman fan, *10 Ka Dum* is a God-sent opportunity to hang out with the star every weekend.'[16]

My own aunt, Tapashri Sarkar, who passed away in 2018, was a huge Salman fan and prided herself on never missing an episode of the show. When that ended, she moved on to *Bigg Boss* and never missed an episode

Salman is truly at his best when he is unfiltered. Any journalist who has ever interviewed him can attest to that. In my last interview with him, he sang a song mid-conversation. When I looked puzzled, he let out the heartiest laugh. The innocence that we as journalists rarely get to see now began airing on TV. And people loved what they saw.

of that. When I was younger, I'd asked her what about Salman she thinks works on TV. She had given me an answer I never forgot. 'There is a gap between superstars and the audience. Be it Mr Bachchan or Shah Rukh, there is an obvious hierarchy. That blurs when Salman hosts, which is what makes him so powerful on television,' she said.

Movie production executive Monica Shah, another die-hard Salman fan who has never missed a single episode of any of the shows he has hosted, delves into the magic of watching the actor on the small screen. She tells me, 'Watching Salman on television feels strangely intimate. He doesn't stick to a script. He talks like someone who could be in your living room, teasing you, laughing with you, maybe even scolding you a bit. With other stars, you're aware of their stardom. With Salman, you're aware of *him*. His ability to be completely himself, flaws and all, is what makes him impossible to look away from. There's an honesty that makes you forget that there's a screen between you and him. Other stars host with polish. Salman hosts with pulse. He is more natural at this than he is in his movies.'

Now there are certain battlelines between Salman fans. His TV fans claim they aren't anything like his movie fans—both exist in wholly different worlds and are different demographics. Itanagar-based housewife Liana Rai tells me, 'Fans of Salman's TV persona don't feel the need to watch his films. I have watched fewer than ten movies of him but haven't missed any of his TV appearances—be it *10 Ka Dum* or *Bigg Boss*. Salman's anchoring skills are effortless and smooth. I dream of going to his show someday. He is comfort TV. For many of us, especially those watching from smaller towns or middle-class homes, he brings the glamour of Bollywood, but leaves the arrogance at the door.'

And it is that very quality that landed Salman the host's seat on *Bigg Boss* in 2010. After Amitabh Bachchan helmed Season 3 in 2009, the makers approached Salman, who agreed to come on board. And *Bigg Boss* exploded. From October 2010, with Salman fronting it, the show became a cultural fixture. And for millions watching every week, it wasn't simply the star Salman we know from the cinema halls—he had become the storyteller, the judge, the big brother, the provocateur and, sometimes, the therapist.

The Season 4 opener registered an impressive 3.6 TRP, with the grand finale hitting 6.7. Salman's Weekend Ka Vaar appearances routinely dominate viewership charts, and even as the format faces competition today, *Bigg Boss 18* topped reality show rankings last year. Salman and the creators of the series have been able to garner ratings that make it one of Indian television's most bankable properties. This year, too, *Bigg Boss* is recording over 8 million views per episode, which only increases over the weekends.[17]

I know several fans of the series, both in my family and circle of friends, but probably the most die-hard fan I know is my friend Momin Ali Munshi from Lahore, Pakistan. For those who are reading this book in the Middle East and Pakistan, you'll know his entertainment channel Galaxy Lollywood. He and I became friends on Twitter (now X) many years ago, and he is the biggest follower of *Bigg Boss* that I know. His love for Salman and *Bigg Boss* has been at the heart of most of our interactions.

'Watching Salman on television feels strangely intimate. He doesn't stick to a script. He talks like someone who could be in your living room, teasing you, laughing with you, maybe even scolding you a bit. With other stars, you're aware of their stardom. With Salman, you're aware of *him*. His ability to be completely himself, flaws and all, is what makes him impossible to look away from. There's an honesty that makes you forget that there's a screen between you and him.'

I remember, sometime in 2021, I woke up to a voice note from him. He was very upset that *Bigg Boss* had gone the OTT way and that he wouldn't be able to catch the season that year. I remember making a few calls to Jio's executives to figure out how he could watch the show. It turned out that the show would eventually move to TV and that he would be able to eventually catch it. For many years it used to be our routine that we would get on a call every few months to discuss filmy gossip and chitchat. He was aghast when I once told him that I had never watched a single episode of *Bigg Boss*. 'You are missing TV gold,' he chided. Momin is my favourite *Bigg Boss* encyclopaedia.

In fact, one of my sweetest memories from April 2021, one of the worst Covid months, was when I received a phone call from him one evening. The second wave was at its peak and I had spent the entire day trying to find oxygen leads for a friend in Ranchi, who was in the ICU. After a rather disillusioning week, an inane chat with him on *Bigg Boss* reminded me that perhaps things could again be normal someday. It was a time when everything around us was falling apart and on that day, it was that call from him, rambling about some nonsense on *Bigg Boss*, that made me laugh after what felt like weeks.

Momin's love for the show runs deep. He watches it with the intensity of someone tuning into a family drama, where the host is a slightly exasperated older cousin, who never minces words and drops truth bombs intermittently to keep the family in check. Salman, in his eyes, presides over the madness with his signature mix of stern dad energy and cheeky elder-brother charm.

Over the years, I've seen Momin track every season and episode. If a contestant crosses a line, Momin has opinions. If Salman delivers a burn, Momin has it screenshotted for his weekly chat with his amma. I know Salman's presence on TV does a lot for so many of us, but to Momin, Salman is a screen god. *Bigg Boss* and Salman, he says, give the audience something to hold on to, like comfort-viewing should. When I asked him what about the show works for him, so much so that he has stayed a loyal viewer for nineteen seasons now, he tells me, 'Anything about Salman Khan is incomplete without mentioning *Bigg Boss*. I've been following it since its very first season, back when Arshad Warsi used to host it on Sony. Over the years, Arshad, Shilpa Shetty and even Amitabh Bachchan have brought their own charm to it, but it was Salman who gave the show its distinct identity in India. The fact that he has been hosting the show for sixteen seasons is a testament to him being the show's lifeline. His presence, his witty commentary, the way he handles conflicts, even moments when we may not agree with him, are what make *Bigg Boss* what it is. I'm glad that this year Salman is back in full form, because the last season felt a little low, maybe due to personal tensions, but this time it is the OG Salman we all love.'

When people talk about *Bigg Boss*, they rarely talk about the format. The locked house, the cameras, the daily squabbles—all of it is borrowed from the franchise *Big Brother*. What makes it uniquely Indian and what keeps it relevant even after fifteen seasons is Salman. His presence has turned the show from just another reality contest into an ongoing pop culture ritual.

At its core, *Bigg Boss* works because it feels like an often-replicated social experiment. Put a group of celebrities in a house, cut them off from the outside world and wait for the pressure cooker to whistle. Viewers see the full spectrum—fights over chores, alliances in the kitchen, tears at ousting nominations. It mirrors the friction in so many Indian households. But without Salman on the weekends, it would just be surveillance footage with occasional drama. His presence is what gives the chaos shape, which is why the other formats have not met with the same success as the Indian version of the show.

Salman's stern words land harder than any in-house punishment. His '*janta sab dekhti hai* [the audience sees everything]' is a direct nod to the viewers, reinforcing their power as judge and jury. Contestants know that if Salman is disappointed with them, they have probably lost the plot with the viewers too.

Sugandha Kanji, a housewife from Nagpur, tells me, 'Salman mediates the show's drama. He positions himself as a disciplinarian, and sometimes even a protective father figure. When housemates mocked Elli AvrRam's Hindi-speaking skills in Season 7, it was Salman who set the boundaries of the house. And he does it again and again, every season, ensuring the drama never spirals into something the show can't recover from. Some people have called him biased, but he is the one watching the whole footage—we are only watching the edited one-hour episode that is aired on TV. Salman is the audience's representative inside the house, the bridge between our living room and that house in the reality show.'

Salman acts as the moral check on contestants who tend to be nasty to the other contestants, and his tirades are pretty epic to watch. It's like a family drama at home when everyone gets together—some to fight, some to watch, some to fuel the fire. The grudges and grievances spill out as the evening proceeds. Fans tell me it is an addiction to watch Salman's unpredictability play out on TV. My friend, Bhanu Yadav, who is a

Bengaluru-based techie, tells me, 'There was this bizarre episode when a visibly calm Salman enters the house, walks straight to the bedroom and makes Rakhi Sawant's bed. He wraps up her blanket, arranges items lying on it and cleans it. Another contestant, Nikki Tamboli, was asked to do it and she had refused, because Rakhi had not moved her luggage from the bedroom that week. In response, Rakhi had said she wouldn't clean the utensils. Now, on the face of it, this is such a petty fight, but the seriousness with which Salman did it and the fact that he was really mad about it made it seem like it was part of our house. This is why *Bigg Boss* works. It's heightened drama that might have been happening in our own homes. And it is hard to believe when I say it, but watching *Bigg Boss* is so comforting for a single man living away from family. This is all the home drama I am going to get until I start a family of my own. I rarely miss an episode of Weekend Ka Vaar—but watching Salman is such a blast!'

The contestants have just as much fun as Salman. For many he is the elder brother they love, and for others he is the empathetic friend they bond with. He has cried on the show, thrown a fit, been enraged and, through it all, has made his way into people's hearts. Everyone remembers how he couldn't help shed a tear when Rahul Dev was eliminated. Rahul had signed up for the show to raise money for his son's schooling, and his exit made Salman very emotional. When Manu Punjabi's mother passed away mid-show, his words were like balm for the bereaved man. In the same season, when another contestant, Priyanka Jagga, made a personal attack on Manu Punjabi, mocking his late mother, Salman lashed out, 'I would request Colors TV never to get her back, ever, on this show. Not only on this show but on this channel. If she ever comes on this channel, I will never work with Colors ever again.'[18]

Neither has anyone forgotten how Salman called out Pratik Sehajpal's behaviour. He told him, without mincing words, 'You are a bully. You do not know the line. *Kisne haq diya hai below the belt maarne ka? Main tumpe jokes banau toh? Do second ke andar ro doge. Shukar karo mai tumhare saath ghar mai nahi hu. Main tumhara haal kya karta tum soch lo, tum bheekh maangte ki mujhe iss ghar se nikaalo* (Who gave you the right to hit below the belt? Should I start cracking jokes about you? You will start crying in two seconds. You should be glad I am not in the house with you. You would be begging to get out of the house).'[19]

In recent years, it's his warm bond with Shehnaaz Gill that has stuck with the audience. Her childlike persona made her Salman's and the audience's favourite. Salman encouraged her, teased her and often defended her when the other housemates dismissed her as immature. Salman continued to look out for Shehnaaz after the show. He offered her a role in his 2023 film *Kisi Ka Bhai Kisi Ki Jaan*, helping her mark her big Bollywood debut. Talking about her bond with Salman, she said, 'From him, I've learnt to keep moving ahead. He has told me that I can go really far in life if I work hard. He motivates me a lot.'[20] When she lost her rumoured partner Siddharth Shukla, whom she met on *Bigg Boss*, to a sudden heart attack, it was Salman who held her through her grief. Netizens were quick to even speculate that there was romance between them. That led Salman to clear the air. Talking about it to Rajat Sharma on *Aap Ki Adalat*, he said, 'I told her to move on. *Sid ab iss duniya mein nahi rahe* (Sid is not in this world any more). I am sure he will also want Shehnaaz to move on. *Ye nahi ki unki shaadi hojaye, bachche hojaye* (That doesn't mean she should get married or have kids). *Abhi nahi, bohot time hai.* But to get out of that Sidnaaz, *woh bohot hi heavy tha uske upar aur woh toot rahi thi bechari bachchi* (Marriage and kids can happen later. But, it was a piece of advice for her to get out of the "Sidnaaz phase". It was very difficult and she was breaking down. So, I told her to move on).'[21]

Many contestants go on to forge lifelong friendships with him. And many just derive laughs from their time on set. Cyrus Broacha, who was on the second season of *Bigg Boss OTT* (2023), narrated a hilarious incident. 'It was the first eviction, and Salman was giving a serious lecture to someone. I was so tired that I started nodding off. Suddenly, Salman noticed and began laughing; he had never seen a contestant fall asleep while he was talking! Usually, everyone else is all "Salman Bhai", and there I was, napping.'[22]

Of course, they go back a long way, which explains how he escaped this without a reprimand. Cyrus had been entrusted with interviewing Salman during his MTV days for his film *Yuvvraaj*, but Cyrus, who was completely hungover from the night before, wasn't in any shape to do so. Salman's secretary called at 9 a.m. for the interview, and Cyrus said, 'I had to stop at Lucky Biryani to vomit. The only person who got what I was going through was Salman, and there was no judgment from him.'[23]

Bigg Boss usually launches around September and runs through the festive season. Salman brings his own traditions into it—Eid wishes, Diwali jokes, New Year celebrations. It makes the show feel less like a set in Lonavala and more like an extension of the viewer's living room. Families watch festivals unfold with Salman at the centre. Many of those who are stuck working during the festivities watch *Bigg Boss* rather religiously. Why? The answer is simply that it's the most entertaining thing on television.

Constable Barkha Kumari (name changed) from Mohali says, 'Imagine working during the festive season when everyone in front of me is having a gala time with their families. On those days *Bigg Boss* is a great watch. When I return home after an odd-hour shift, there is a recorded episode for me to watch while I eat dinner. The whole family is usually asleep by then. I get very little time with them on bad days, and on those days *Bigg Boss* is my family. Some of my workdays include just tending to paperwork, which is both solitary and somewhat dull. *Bigg Boss* is the tadka I need for a good night's sleep.'

She quotes an episode from the latest season, when a housemate was snapped at for wasting food. Salman reprimanded them, saying, 'Do you know the conditions in Uttarakhand, Himachal Pradesh and now in Punjab? *Baad pe baad, landslides, tabahi machi hui hai. Yeh jo farmers humare liye khaana banate hain, unke pass anaaj nahi hai khaane ke liye, ghar nahi hai rehne ke liye* (Flood after flood, landslides, there is devastation everywhere. These farmers who grow food for us don't even have grain for themselves, or homes to live in).'[24] Barkha tells us, 'When a celebrity shames privileged people, it works wonders. The next day we saw more people walking in to help the local authorities. Salman is one of those men who walk the talk, and so his followers hear his appeal and make the change!'

When Salman's friend, Baba Siddique, was assassinated by Lawrence Bishnoi's henchmen in October 2024, he opened up about his grief on the show. The Mumbai Crime Branch was of the belief that Baba's close ties with Salman was possibly the primary motive behind the killing. Salman had been on the Bishnoi gang's radar since the blackbuck poaching case. Baba Siddique's murder was meant as a warning to those who stood by him, whether through personal, emotional or financial crisis.[25]

While on air on *Bigg Boss*, Salman said, '*Aaj ki meri yeh feeling hai ki mujhe aaj yahan pe aana hi nahi chahiye tha. … But yeh ek commitment hai, toh isliye main yahan pe aaya hoon. Ek mera kaam hai, kaam karne aaya hoon. Mujhe kisi se na milna, mujhe aap logo se bhi nahi milna* (Today I've a feeling that I shouldn't have come here. I didn't want to come here. But this is a commitment so I have come here. This is my work, so I have come here. I don't want to meet anyone, I don't want to meet even you guys). But I'm bound to do this.'[26]

In that episode, Salman got into a verbal spat with contestant Arfeen Khan and at one point exasperatedly said, '*Yaar, qasam khuda ki* (I swear), what all I am going through in my life, and I have to come and handle this.'[27]

Salman is so committed to the show that barely a week after the tragedy, he was on set shooting. He was protected by an entourage of sixty people. The tightened security was because of a message sent to Mumbai Traffic Police demanding Rs 5 crore from Salman to settle the long-running feud. The warning also said that if the actor failed to pay, his fate could be worse than that of Baba Siddique. But he still showed up every day last season. And much to everyone's surprise, returned for a brand-new season this year as well.

Perhaps even he knows that without him, *Bigg Boss* would lose both its TRPs and its audience. But Salman has come close to quitting the show many times. After *Bigg Boss 13*, the actor was sure he didn't want to return. In one of the most unforgettable clashes on the show, Sidharth Shukla called Rashami Desai Asim Riaz's naukrani (servant). Rashami confronted him. The clash escalated when they threw hot tea at each other and other contestants got involved. On the following Weekend Ka Vaar, Salman was livid and reportedly told the producers he might quit hosting because he didn't want to deal with such conduct.[28]

But for Salman, this show, which he has been doing for fifteen years now, has almost become like a habit. During an interview, he said, 'Yeah, a part of me wants to cut that part and throw it out and the other part wants to keep it. And the latter is haavi on [impinges on] the part that wants to throw it out. I like it. It gets stressful, but I learn a lot. And I get to know where the country is going, what is happening to values, morals, scruples and principles. We see it right there, with celebrities. The beauty is once they are out of the house, they are not like that at all. It's not as if they are giving performances, the house makes them like that.'[29]

Earlier this year, there was again a strong buzz that Salman wouldn't return for the new season. Given the security threats he experienced last year, and his fatigue with hosting the show, it was a serious possibility. But what is *Bigg Boss* without Salman? And the makers are well aware of this. We don't know how, but they were able to convince him to return. There's a good chance you'll be reading this book while watching *Bigg Boss* on the side.

Around 2008, the popular sentiment was that Salman was outshining Shah Rukh on the small screen. The latter had started hosting *Kya Aap Paanchvi Pass Se Tez Hain?* around the same time that Salman kicked off *10 Ka Dum*. Now this, for me, is probably the toughest part of writing this book, because I am a huge Shah Rukh fan. And I have always enjoyed watching Salman. In my head, there's never been a debate or a choice to make, until 2008, when the battle lines were drawn between the two fandoms following a spat between the superstars.

This book isn't a tell-all and its purpose isn't to reaffirm the million floating theories about what happened on the night of Katrina Kaif's birthday in July 2008 at Olive Bar and Kitchen, Bombay. But here's the version of the story I have gathered over the years. Apparently ever since *Chalte Chalte*, Salman's and Shah Rukh's relationship had been frayed and, that night, after the two actors said several unkind things to each other, they almost came to blows. Shah Rukh's wife Gauri had to intervene, and it took Karan Johar and Aamir Khan to physically pull them apart to stop the face-off from escalating.

What followed were public admissions by both the actors that their friendship was over. In an interview to journalist Harneet Singh, Salman said, 'Have you ever known me to speak about anybody? Whatever happened is between me and Shah Rukh. It's personal.' When Singh asked if Shah Rukh was his friend, the actor replied, 'Not any more. I'm not going to deny that there are issues between us. I'm a primitive man born in today's time. I can't fake anything. If there is a problem then I'm not going to deny it. We've had problems before also but this time I don't think we can sort them out. We are two different people. Our values and way of thinking are different. I don't think we can be friends. I think it's better to declare that than put on a fake facade of being friends and back-biting each other.'[30] Singh asked whether the spat was because of professional rivalry centred on reviews of their respective shows *Kya Aap Paanchvi Pass Se Tez Hain?* and *10 Ka Dum*, and Salman cleared the air: 'No, I don't think it's because my show is doing better. I don't think he's that insecure. The reason for the fight is personal.'[31]

If you were in school or college then, you'll remember the arguments between the two fan factions in your hostel rooms and Facebook pages. Suddenly you couldn't be a fan of both. You had to pick a side. Mumbai-based corporate communications professional Piyush Bhutada, who is a friend and a Shah Rukh fan, remembers the shift vividly. 'We were always rooting for both. Like, you could love *Hum Aapke Hain Koun..!* and still cry when watching *Kal Ho Naa Ho*. But when the two actors had that showdown, if you happened to be a Shah Rukh fan, you were suddenly labelled anti-Salman. It became almost cultural, like Coke versus Pepsi. You couldn't like both. I regret missing so many of Bhai's films, because we swore not to watch them,' he told me.

Salman fans recall it as a moment when fan loyalty was at its peak. 'It was like a mini civil war,' said Bidisha Nayak, a nurse from Cuttack, laughing. 'Even if you liked Shah Rukh, you couldn't say it out loud in front of Salman fans without getting into a fight. It really was personal. Lines were drawn, camps were formed. We didn't watch their movies and they didn't watch ours. And honestly, if anyone dared bring up Shah Rukh in our circles, they'd be met with instant takedowns. I am not proud of this, but my group has a story. This one guy who was in our tuition class came wearing an SRK fan group T-shirt. The poor fellow thought it would be harmless. By the end of the day, someone had scribbled "*Bhai ka fan hoon* [I am a Bhai fan]" on the back with permanent marker. We hated him and called him names.'

A few months after the fallout, Shah Rukh said to the press, 'I think like a father, while Salman thinks like a child! There is not much common between us, we think differently, we speak differently. We have spent a good time together. But with time, that fact has gotten blurred. We are happy in our worlds. If we come together it is good. If we don't it's even better. We are not friends.'[32]

The anger eventually fizzled out, as is common with friends who have known each other a very long time. Five years later, at the late Baba Siddique's iftar party, the duo made up. On 17 April 2013, Siddique orchestrated a truce when he seated Shah Rukh right next to Salim Khan, Salman's father. That left little room for avoidance. When Salman and Shah Rukh eventually came face to face, they exchanged a hug that was caught on camera. It was the first public thaw in their five-year-long cold war. After their reconciliation, Siddique downplayed his part as peacemaker, saying, 'They both wanted it ... Allah shows the way. I had no role to play.'[33]

But the fan wars continued to get ugly for many years after that. Reviewers critiquing Salman's films were called names on X. His fans would tweet to me, '*Ghar aake marunga tujhe* [I will come to your house and beat you up].' They would hurl expletives at reviewers and go after other fan clubs, especially Shah Rukh's.

It got so bad that Salman had to tweet to make sure the fan groups stopped bullying each other. He wrote a series of tweets, 'Messed up fighting over your (favourite) heroes with each other. Make this journey beautiful, didn't sign up for this ugly Twitter war and (I am) not a part of it. Continue it and I will be off Twitter. Came here to spread love, share some thoughts and have fun with fans, not for them to insult my fraternity. I see a lot of love and respect and am happy to be here but then there are a lot of die hard fans who are going wrong in their competitive thought process. Don't want them to fight or turn nasty, ugly, abusive.'[34]

That infamous fight was a crucial turning point in Salman's life. Until then Salman's career was fraying. His films weren't faring well, even though his TV gig was flourishing. But he was nowhere close to his contemporaries. It's like the engine was rusty. But the rage from that fight kickstarted something inside him.

A day after that fight, Salman said something that turned out to be far-sighted. In her book *The Three Khans: And the Emergence of New India,* Kaveree Bamzai writes, 'Over a three-hour conversation, Salman vowed to a close friend how he would show Shah Rukh his place in the industry. "He thinks I am an ass. You wait, I will finish him." Words spoken in anger but somewhat prophetic, given that Shah Rukh has always known he may be a bigger star globally but Salman is beloved as the eternal "bhai" in the domestic market.'

Just the very next year, Salman starred in the remake of Mahesh Babu–starrer *Pokiri*, which was renamed *Wanted* for the Bollywood market. If rumours are to be believed, the film was originally to star Shah Rukh. The film ushered in an unbelievably golden period of Salman's career, which put him above all his peers. Aamir might be a star, Shah Rukh a superstar, but with that one film, Salman became an unbeatable box office force for the whole of the next decade. As Shah Rukh once tweeted, 'Salman bhai is … woh kya kehte hain aaj kal … young log … haan … GOAT. (greatest of all time) *[sic]*.'[35]

" Zindagi mein teen cheez kabhi underestimate nahi karna—I, me and myself. "

Ready, 2010

9

The Sultan of Bollywood

'**L**OVE me, love me, love me
Your mamma says you love me
Papa says you love me
Then love me, baby, love me ...'

I looked at Adarsh, who works part-time at a car wash, making me coffee while singing this song, at his kholi in the Chaar Bangla chawl, Mumbai. He seemed upbeat. We had spent the past hour reviewing his cassette collection of Salman movies. Of nearly a hundred movies he has starred in, Adarsh owns the audio cassettes and VCDs of eighty of them. 'This is my jaydaad [property],' he told me after he finished singing and wiped the dust off *Wanted*'s audio cassette cover. In an age where digital rights shift every few months, streamers drop films without explanation and movies are reworked with AI by studios and fans alike, Adarsh tells me physical possession is very important to him. 'The past few years I have been getting the feeling that they want to erase our superstars. There is an unusual amount of hatred for them, be it Shah Rukh Bhai or Salman Bhai. *Shah Rukh Bhai ke bachchi ki film ko kitna bura bhala bola* [They trashed Shah Rukh Bhai's daughter's film so badly]. Slowly we fans have realized that if we want to protect our favourite stars, we have to be more active with preservation. *And inhe rehne do social media pe* [Let them be on social media]. Nothing beats physical copies of things. We are planning to set up a library with cassettes and CDs of Bhaijaan's films. They want to turn Bhai into metadata. I won't let them.'

Adarsh started out as a collector. Now he sees himself as a gatekeeper. 'I am a protector of Bhai's aura, which can't be manufactured. There'll never be another star like Salman. No one will ever walk into a frame and own it the way he does. It's his presence. You feel it,' he tells me.

Adarsh has heard the younger generation compare the latest film *Saiyaara* to Bhai's *Tere Naam*, and hasn't taken kindly to it. He laughed bitterly and said, '*Saiyaara*? Those Instagram reels boiled my blood. Not because Bhai can't be replaced. *Of course, duniya ki reet hai* [It's the way of the world]. But you can only compare an apple with an apple. How do you compare an apple with grapes? Do the reel makers even know what the Bhai frenzy is like? People throw coins at the screen during the title card. They cry when he cries because they can't bear to see him hurt. *Aap banao narratives social media pe* [You spin your narratives on social media], but don't tell me that the era of his superstardom is over. They have been saying that about him since *Wanted*. And Salman keeps coming back. That's Bhai for you!'

And with that Adarsh took me back in time to 2009. It had been two years since Salman's last hit, *Partner*. A trade piece from that time is worded with wonder and reads, 'After half a dozen flop films over nearly two years, Bollywood actor Salman Khan has finally tasted commercial success with his latest action flick, *Wanted*, emerging top grosser this weekend, generating around Rs 17–19 crore in domestic box office collections.'[1]

In 2007, producer Boney Kapoor saw a gap in the market and wanted to make a movie with a little bit of everything—romance, comedy, drama and action. 'I decided that I would make it and decided to make it with only Salman Khan,' Boney said during his appearance on the dance reality show *Jhalak Dikhhla Jaa*.[2]

His team had managed to procure the rights of the Telugu film *Pokiri*, which starred Mahesh Babu in the lead role. The original film, made in

2006 by Puri Jagannadh, was a major blockbuster earning over Rs 70 crore upon its release. Boney knew if he were to pull this off, he would need Salman's stardom. He tried for a long time to bring him on board, offered the film to him twice, but couldn't get dates.

'I went to him and said, Salman, I'll never come after this. If you don't like this film, I will never even attempt to offer you another film. You just come and watch this film. So he came at 12 in the night to watch it. And when the movie ended, he left without saying anything, went near the car and just showed me a "thumbs up" and I knew he was on board. And after that, it was "Jalwa hi Jalwa" *(laughs)*,' Boney recounted.[3]

The experience of watching a commercial masala film today feels hollow without the visceral energy of claps, whistles and one-liners, and this energy can be traced back to *Wanted*. No one anticipated that a remake about an undercover cop posing as a gangster, who works overtime to dismantle two notorious crime syndicates in Mumbai, would leave such a lasting impact, but it did— and how.

> 'The past few years I have been getting the feeling that they want to erase our superstars. There is an unusual amount of hatred for superstars, be it Shah Rukh Bhai or Salman Bhai ... Slowly we fans have realized that if we want to protect our favourite stars, we have to be more active with preservation.'

The film was also the reintroduction of Prakash Raj in Bollywood, who had starred in *Shakti: The Power* (2002) and *Khakee* (2004), but hadn't quite left a mark. 'Prakash Raj was on standby as we were trying to cast an actor from Mumbai. However, we couldn't find one. Also, he was a part of the original film and thus it made sense to cast him,' Boney said.[4] After that film, the actor became quite a regular in Hindi movies, most notably in *Dabangg* and Ajay Devgn's *Singham* (2011), which are two of Bollywood's most loved franchises in recent years.

As someone who has worked with Salman, Prakash Raj talks of his superstar colleague fondly. In an interview with the The Lallantop, he said, 'I don't look at him as an actor, I look at him as a pranky kid. He will never get old. He has no filter. I have done two films with him, I like his company. *Wo kisi se darta nahi hai* (He is not scared of anybody).'[5] Maybe on that level, the two—known to not mince words and speak their minds—bond well.

To make sure the villain opposite the hero held just as much weight in the narrative, a spine-chilling entry for Prakash Raj was shot as an afterthought. The team realized they needed the villain to have an impact just as hard-hitting as Salman. 'The intro scene of Prakash Raj was shot much later, in Thailand. This is because we realized we needed a powerful scene to introduce his character as Hindi cinema audiences were not aware of him,' Boney said in an interview.[6]

The film was to originally star Ileana D'Cruz, who was in the original film as well, but she declined as the shoot dates coincided with her board exams. The makers tried to get Genelia too, but eventually went with Ayesha Takia. Boney explained in an interview why it was important for them to get a fresh face. 'There is this crucial scene in the second half after Salman fights the goons in the train. This is where the girl says, "I don't know if you are a good or a bad person, but the fact is that I love you." We needed someone who was in awe of Salman and hence, looked for a new face.'[7]

The film marked the Bollywood directorial debut of dancing maverick Prabhu Deva. Known primarily for his dance, he made a mark with action with this film. He made Salman do his own stunts and choreographed it to perfection, along with action directors Rajesh Kannan and Fefsi Vijayan. During the film's release, Prabhu Deva in an interview said, '[Salman] is a person who doesn't react to anything. He's very cool, composed and mature. He is never hyper. I like him for this attitude. The only time he was excited was when he wanted to dance. He told me, "Prabhu, break my bones but make me dance." When people told him that he would get difficult dance steps, he was cool with it. He said he would dance better than me. And he did. He worked very hard. Since we know an actor's capability, I gave him simple steps. But he worked very hard to do a good job. The USP of the film is Salman Bhai's energy. He has done all the action scenes himself. He hasn't used a body double.'[8]

The songs were an immediate hit with the audience. The twelve tracks scored by Sajid–Wajid, of which five were remixes, had the duo's trademark high-energy vibe. Be it 'Love Me Love Me' or 'Jalwa', each song turned out to be a crowd puller.

Even the reviewers lapped this one up. Considered to be a tough nut to crack, film critic Raja Sen gave the film his rare half-rave. 'Salman sleepwalks through so many mediocre projects that it's genuinely refreshing to see him have a ball with this one, throwing himself into both dance thrusts and clever kills with abandon. This isn't a film about acting, perish the thought, but one built around the star and Salman visibly preens in the wolf-whistles-to-be. He's straight out of a really tawdry comic book, but there's no mistaking he's a superhero. He's the goddamned Sal Man!'[9]

Wanted opened across 1,400 screens in India and recorded a strong first-day collection of Rs 5.1 crore, followed by a solid first weekend total of Rs 15.57 crore. By the end of its first week, the film had earned Rs 33.63 crore, eventually reaching a worldwide gross of Rs 93.23 crore.[10]

The film caused mayhem at the box office, some even attributing Salman's resurgence as an action hero to this film. Manoj Desai, executive director of G7 Multiplex in Mumbai, popularly called the Gaiety Galaxy cinema complex, told me, '*Wanted* has got the film industry and the single-screen cinemas out of the ICU. The response in Gaiety Galaxy was unbelievable.'

Salman fan Suyash Dhingra, a shop owner in Dadar, says, 'The one scene that changed everything was the moment it's revealed that he's actually a cop. Until then, he was just this sharp-tongued gangster. But when that twist hit, the theatre erupted. I still remember this woman sitting next to me with her boyfriend. She couldn't contain herself and literally started jumping up and down in her seat. The energy was so electric that day. There were whistles and uproarious clapping. We were also seeing Vinod Khannaji on-screen after so long. I watched the first-day matinee show at Chitra. I'll never forget the deafening sound of the audience cheering. That kind of mania hadn't been seen in a long time. So many single-screens had to bring out their "Housefull" boards from storage after years. I watched it four times over that weekend. I remember Komal Nahta sir saying that the film was doing well because it was a long weekend, but it ran for about five weeks after that and I watched it once every week.'

The frenzy was maniacal. Salman was to participate in a friendly football match at the Mohammedan Sporting Club grounds in Kolkata after its release. He was to lead the 'Most Wanted XI' team, which featured local footballers, against the 'Md Sporting XI'. But the crowd went berserk to the point that the match had to be cancelled. An *India Today* report read, 'A friendly football match, in which Bollywood actor Salman Khan was scheduled to play, was cancelled on Saturday after the star was mobbed by an unruly crowd at a local football club ground here. As soon as Khan entered Md Sporting Club grounds, a huge crowd lunged towards him, forcing the organizers to cancel the event which was organized to promote his latest release *Wanted*.'[11]

Producers believe the film could have done more if it weren't given an A-rating certificate by the CBFC. The film contained action and violence, but nothing excessively graphic or disturbing. The trade believes that if *Wanted* had secured a U/A certification, it could have earned 25–40 per cent more at the box office.

'No one in Bollywood history had so effectively commercialized their off-screen persona. While others had crafted enduring on-screen identities—the brooding Angry Young Man of Amitabh Bachchan, or Shah Rukh Khan's romantic hero with arms flung wide—this man had done something entirely different. He had discarded plot and character arcs, stormed into [the] frame on sheer charisma and turned even incoherent or barely there narratives into box office gold.'

But numbers aside, *Wanted* established a never-before-seen kind of mania for Salman. Film-maker Samreen Farooqui and co-director Shabani Hassanwalia of the documentary *Being Bhaijaan* (2014) said in an interview to *Hindustan Times*, 'In a darkened single-screen theatre in Meerut, the audience watched as Radhe (Khan), the hero of *Wanted*, was bashed up by the villain. The men in the audience "took off their shirts en masse and roared". A friend who witnessed this scene described it almost as a pagan ritual. When Salman tore his own shirt off on-screen, the crowd screamed "Bhaijaan, Bhaijaan".'[12]

It was this incident that prompted Farooqui to dig deeper and try to make sense of Salman's appeal in a movie, which eventually took the shape of the documentary. 'No one in Bollywood history had so effectively commercialized their off-screen persona. While others had crafted enduring on-screen identities—the brooding Angry Young Man of Amitabh Bachchan, or Shah Rukh Khan's romantic hero with arms flung wide—this man had done something entirely different. He had discarded plot and character arcs, stormed into [the] frame on sheer charisma, and turned even incoherent or barely there narratives into box office gold— whether it was a film with practically no storyline (*Ready*) or one where the storyline defied logic (*Bodyguard*),' the piece about the documentary read.[13]

The mass hysteria kick-started by *Wanted* also marked the beginning of Bhai's second life, where the definition of the hero changed. It wasn't about screenwriting logic—it was about screen presence. Stardom that couldn't be explained but only felt, something incomprehensible to Hollywood or to any other cinema-viewing audience in the world. In India, the hero became the story—and Salman led the way!

A man like Salman, who has built an entire career purely on a fan base, knows what his audience wants, and that instinct is his biggest virtue. He jokes about his lack of craft often and says he has exactly three expressions to deliver, but as a man whose craft isn't his forte, his ability to read the people of this diverse country is what keeps him ruling for decades!

As film-maker Anurag Kashyap said in an interview, 'Stars like Salman Khan, they cannot ignore their fan base. Even when they are experimenting or playing around, they think a lot because if their fan bases get upset, they react very strongly.'[14]

Kabir Khan, who made *Bajrangi Bhaijaan* and *Ek Tha Tiger*, also admitted this. 'Salman knows exactly what his audience wants. Sometimes I had to step back and let that instinct take the lead.'[15]

Which explains why after a hit like *Wanted*, Salman starred in *Main Aurr Mrs Khanna*. In an interview to *The Telegraph*, Salman explained, 'In real life I have always tried to be a normal guy. Try to be like just about everybody else. But because I am in the movies, the image is taken to a different level altogether … it's colossal, it's humungous, it's gigantic. So when somebody like that plays a normal man, it's not accepted. I tried that in *Dil Ne Jise Apna Kahaa*, I tried that in *Jaan-E-Mann* and now in *Main Aurr Mrs Khanna*. All these films, when you watch them later on TV or on DVD, you say: "What a beautiful film! I wonder why it didn't work!" It didn't work because you didn't go to the theatres to see it. Now, you have a film like *Wanted* … you want to go out, make it an event and watch it with all your friends. Have a blast, scream, shout … be entertained!'[16]

And like I said, Salman knew. He said in the same interview, 'Like my own nephew and niece walked out of the theatre while watching *Main Aurr Mrs Khanna*, and I and Sohail realized that this is the biggest disaster we have made. Nirvan and Arhaan said, "It's very boring … we are going!" And they have their Papa and Chacha in the film! *Wanted*—they watched it four times. Then we thought the women audience would come and watch the film (*Main Aurr …*) … The Monday audience, like what Anil Kapoor used to have, when the women would take their husbands to watch his films after the weekend! But even that didn't happen. I guess, husbands don't listen to their wives any more (*laughs out loud*)!'

Superstars, particularly those as enduring as Salman, eventually shape a mythology around themselves. It is a persona so powerful that it begins to dictate the kind of films they can do. While this mould can be restrictive, it's also what keeps the machinery of stardom running. Salman has dabbled in different genres—he started out as a romantic hero, then moved to drama with Bhansali, tried comedy with Dhawan and played the action hero on and off, but *Wanted* marked a palpable shift. It created a newer, harder-to-break image of the invincible, morally upright yet ungovernable hero. Post-*Wanted*, every project had to live up to that benchmark of Salman-ness. The films had to serve the myth, to build upon it, to reflect it back to a fan base that was looking for its icon in yet another form of heroic victory.

His next two films—*London Dreams* and *Veer*—didn't live up to the new myth promised to his fans. They'd obviously been conceptualized before *Wanted* and released shortly after it. These films couldn't weave in the energy Salman had brought to *Wanted*.

As a young intern at *The Times of India* Kolkata newsroom in 2009, I remember having elaborate discussions with colleagues on the smoking balcony of the SN Banerjee Road office. Let me recount some of these conversations. The late Sumit Sen, fondly remembered as Sumitda by us, former resident editor of *TOI* Kolkata, felt that through the 2000s, Hindi cinema had moved towards urban romances and films that catered mostly to multiplex audiences. But a huge chunk of the single-screen audience, especially in small towns, still craved the unapologetic larger-than-life hero. These were people who had grown up on Amitabh Bachchan's image of the Angry Young Man and Sunny Deol's righteous rage in *Damini* (1993), and they weren't being served at all. *Wanted* reminded them what it felt like to watch a hero you could cheer for, because he could bend the world to his will.

Salman, post-*Wanted*, thus became aspirational. His on-screen invincibility worked like an opioid for the masses. Before *Wanted*, film-makers often tried to slot Salman into time-tested formulas (*London Dreams* was a rock-band melodrama and *Veer* a historical epic). Post-*Wanted*, producers realized the safer bet with him was to reverse-engineer. Start with 'Salman the phenomenon' and build a world that serves him.

If you look closely at *Dabangg*, it wasn't a character study of a cop but a festival of Salman traits: the mischievous name, Robin Hood Pandey; the moral rebellion of serving justice but mocking the system; the dance style, which looked both ridiculous and cool, a dare to the audience to try it; and the romantic track 'Tere Mast Mast Do Nain' played as cheeky seduction, but not like the saccharine love Yash Raj Films served.

Wanted was a switch for Salman too; he unabashedly leaned into playing 'Salman'. It was him acknowledging his public image, the bad boy with a golden heart, the man with enemies but also unmatched loyalty for his own people.

In *Dabangg*, Chulbul Pandey mirrored Salman's own paradoxes— lawman and outlaw, charmer and fighter, loner and family man. The audience saw a folk-tale version of Salman himself—and ever since, every time a director has reinterpreted the myth of the superstar in a film that merits his stardom, it has worked wonders! I will get to my favourites

Bajrangi Bhaijaan, the *Tiger* series and *Sultan* in a couple of pages, but it's essential to go back to where and how it started.

The return of macho heroism really roared back with *Dabangg*. But it wasn't the old-school, unshaded masculinity of a muscleman glaring into the camera—it was something far more playful. For years before *Dabangg*, Bollywood had been chasing multiplex sophistication, softening its heroes, sanding off their rough edges. Chulbul put the rough edges back. He bent the law without apology, yet somehow made you believe he was on the right side of it all.

In *Dabangg*, macho returned as a kind of folk theatre. The fight scenes were exaggerated, almost to the point of parody. But Salman inhabited Chulbul Pandey with easy authority—the way he cocked his hip while firing a gun, the casual flipping of his sunglasses before they landed perfectly in place, the unhurried smirk before delivering a punchline, it all worked.

It was a redefinition of masculine power for the 2010s. Chulbul had wit, swagger and a dash of irreverence that made him less policeman and more vigilante. This was macho that could wink at you and still make you feel safe. After *Dabangg*, that became the template, not just for Salman, but for an entire wave of Hindi masala cinema trying to bottle that same vibe.

Salman admitted that he made a conscious effort to bring the macho back to the Bollywood hero. 'I had started missing the macho hero. When my father (Salim Khan) used to write, the heroes used to be strong and central to the story. I would go to the theatre and clap and whistle when I saw the hero on-screen. The macho hero seems to have vanished. Today's generation is missing the macho man and I wanted to bring him back on-screen. I wanted to make sure people remember the hero when they leave the theatre. That's why I am doing such films,' he said in an interview.[17]

What *Dabangg* really did was position Salman as the natural heir to India's biggest mass hero—Rajinikanth. And that's not a crown to wear lightly. I'm writing this a week before Rajini sir's, aka Thalaiva's, latest film, *Coolie*, is up for release, and the trade is already buzzing about an opening-day figure north of Rs 80 crore. Rajinikanth is seventy-four years old, and there's not the faintest sign of him slowing down. His dream run is still on. As trade analyst Girish Wankhede told me, '*Coolie* doesn't need word of mouth to work—it will work regardless!'

Similarly, when *Dabangg* hit the screens, Salman created an aura so potent that the trade started whispering about him in the same breath as Rajinikanth. The comparison wasn't about copying style or mannerisms—Salman himself has laughed off the idea of 'becoming Rajini'—but about occupying that rarefied space where the hero is larger than the film.

Dabangg had the same grammar of mass cinema that has helped Rajinikanth rule for decades. For the first time in years, Bollywood had a hero whose presence could bend a film entirely around himself.

Trade analysts could see it. Single-screens could feel it. The audience celebrated his films like they were a festival and Salman the deity. The trade had begun to believe that in north India, Salman could command the kind of fever pitch that Rajinikanth did in the south.

A column in *The Guardian* was probably the first to draw parallels between *Dabangg* and *Robot* (2010), and said,

It was a redefinition of masculine power for the 2010s. Chulbul Pandey had wit, swagger and a dash of irreverence that made him less policeman and more vigilante. This was macho that could wink at you and still make you feel safe. After *Dabangg*, that became the template, not just for Salman, but for an entire wave of Hindi masala cinema trying to bottle that same vibe.

'*Dabangg* is a pure pastiche of classic 1980s Bollywood, with OTT dialogue, outrageous fight scenes, chaste romance, rural politics and thumping songs. The lead character, Chulbul "Robin Hood" Pandey, is a corrupt policeman with a heart of gold, the body of a Greek god and the most ironic pencil moustache east of Williamsburg. India lapped it up: the folk in the villages loved the story of a gleefully corrupt cop who nonetheless stands up for what is right; urban India fell for the nudge-nudge-wink-wink cheesiness of it all. Less than a month later came the Tamil film *Endhiran [sic]*, starring Rajinikanth. Now 60, Rajinikanth is that rare star who doesn't mind appearing in public as the ageing, balding man he really is. His fans couldn't care less, so long as his on-screen persona continues to be what playwright and columnist Anuvab Pal calls a mix of "Clint Eastwood, Sylvester Stallone, Arnold Schwarzenegger, Charles Bronson and the A-Team, but bigger" ... *Dabangg* and *Robot* are the culmination of a decade of change in Indian films.'[18]

To be seen in the same light as Rajinikanth can be daunting for any star. Salman, though emotional about the comparisons, said, 'Rajnikanth is in a different league. I can never get close to him. I don't want to be anyone. I just want to be Salman Khan.'[19]

There is an interesting story behind how a small-budget, dark gangster drama that was to originally star Randeep Hooda and Arbaaz Khan ended up becoming one of the past decade's most loved franchises. Yes, *Dabangg*. Abhinav Kashyap, the director of the film, in an interview to Bollywood Hungama said he was relieved at not being known as Anurag Kashyap's brother. In the interview, he recounted how the film reached Salman. 'I was approaching people after I had my script almost ready. I was meeting a lot of people when I saw *Jaane Tu... Ya Jaane Na*. I loved the cameo by Arbaaz and Sohail. I thought they were outrageously funny. One of my friends happened to know Arbaaz and he set up a meeting with him because I wanted to cast him for one of the roles in *Dabangg*. I got twenty minutes from Arbaaz and he said, "This is a brilliant script." He called me the same evening and told me that he wanted to turn producer but that he wasn't being able to find the perfect script. He also asked me, "Would you mind if I produce the film too?" I said, "I would love it."'[20]

But in its earliest form, *Dabangg* was far from the masala entertainer it turned out to be. It was first conceived as a much grittier story, with its protagonist Chulbul Pandey written as 'out and out negative'. Salman, in an interview, said, 'It was a very dark film, a small film to be made under Rs 2 crore. At that point of time, it had Randeep Hooda and Arbaaz. So Arbaaz said he has been approached for this and it's a good one so just hear it. Then six–eight months passed before I finally heard it. I think

UTV was supposed to do it. I liked the feel of the film but Chulbul was out and out negative.'[21]

It was Salman who nudged the project towards its more crowd-pleasing avatar. He suggested several changes to Arbaaz and Abhinav about how Chulbul Pandey would be—his naughtiness, his unpredictability, the comic-book treatment. The fun and flavour can be attributed greatly to Salman. The director-producer duo incorporated them and thus from a small-budget indie film, it became the kind of story that merits the presence of a superstar. 'That film didn't have any action, certainly not at this scale. There were no songs and we never got to know who killed the mother ... We started working on it and Abhinav agreed to all those changes. He did a very good job with the first one.'[22]

For Abhinav, the rewriting process was relentless. He wrote nearly fourteen drafts while making the film, and eventually some fine-tuning suggestions came from Salim Khan. 'I wrote 14 drafts because every time I gave a narration to a friend, to my star cast, or even to my brother Anurag, they all made suggestions. All of them asked questions. My softboard in the office had scores of questions pinned up. And I incorporated all those changes in my final draft. I believe that if a script has to deliver, then it has to answer the various questions that people who hear the script ask. Even at the editing table, changes were made and the suggestions that Salman gave were incorporated. I'm grateful to Salim Khan saab for his suggestions, too. I didn't write *Dabangg* with Salman in mind. But in hindsight, I don't see any other actor being able to play Chulbul Pandey. He fits the role to the "T",' the director said.[23]

The film's story was hardly novel—it was its telling that was fresh. Set in Lalganj, *Dabangg* tells the tale of a quirky local cop Chulbul Pandey, who'll rough up a criminal, crack a joke and dance at a wedding all in the same day. His badge gives him power. At home, things are messier, with a stepfather who has never warmed up to him and a half-brother always looking over his shoulder. Then comes Rajjo, a girl who can match him word for word, and steals his heart. The story has a menacing baddie, Chedi Singh, a politician who's as dangerous as he is slippery. Between love, family drama and a rivalry that turns lethal, Chulbul must settle scores and protect the people he loves.

The film became the launch vehicle of Shatrughan Sinha's daughter Sonakshi, who was a design student and not looking for a career in the movies. On season 5 of Kareena Kapoor Khan's podcast *What Women Want*, Sonakshi recalled, 'Salman Khan and Arbaaz Khan saw me at Amrita Arora's wedding. They told me they were writing something and thought I'd be perfect for the role. I never took them seriously. Then, they came to my house to narrate the script. My whole family sat and listened. They nodded, shook hands and left. The next thing I knew, I was on the *Dabangg* set. It felt like an arranged marriage. But once I reached the set, I realized I wanted to do this, and I've been doing it ever since.'[24]

Sonakshi says the film trained her for a life in the movies. 'Whatever I have learnt about acting is from Salman, he taught me well ...'[25]

And given that in the past few years, she has delivered *Dahaad* and *Heeramandi*, both in 2023, with equal finesse, she clearly is making Salman proud!

What was refreshing about her character, Rajjo, was the sass. She wasn't the typical demure woman who'd nod in agreement with the men around her—she'd tell Chulbul off every time he deserved it. In a romantic moment, Chulbul tells her, 'If I try to dominate you, give it back to me. *Biwi ho humari, koi ghulam nahi* [You are my wife, not my slave] ...'

That set the tone of their relationship, which endeared many to them as a couple. 'Rajjo has her own voice and is quite dabangg in her own way. That is how she holds her own before Chulbul,' Sonakshi added.[26]

It's interesting that one of the film's most iconic dialogues belongs to her: *Thappad se darr nahi lagta, saab, pyaar se lagta hai* [A slap doesn't scare me, love does]. In a later interview in 2019, she said how the line has stuck over the years. 'Rajjo is in my blood, I can play Rajjo in my sleep too ... The *"thappad se darr nahin lagta ..."* dialogue worked a lot for me. Till today, people ask me to say it. It is great for a heroine to have a dialogue that has become iconic.'[27]

Dabangg brought on-screen the bravado of the police force. This was the first film in a very long time where the cop was fronting the drama and moving it along. The cops were no longer background characters chasing the hero or the villain. As an *India Today* opinion piece explained, 'Hindi film cops were never the same after Salman Khan came to the big screen as Chulbul Pandey. Not just the portrayal of a police officer, Salman also changed the way we look at khaki ... Salman's swag and handling of khaki gave birth to a new species of cops in Hindi cinema. It also triggered the Rohit Shetty cop universe. Think *Singham*, the 2011 release starring Ajay Devgn in the lead.'[28]

Dev Anand had once said that a Hindi film hero cannot be a cop. 'How can a hero be a policeman? He can't sing and dance, he can't wear fashionable clothes.' Referring to *Dabangg* and its success, a *Tribune* piece said, 'Well, Dev saab would be happy to note that the filmy cop has the cinematic licence to do all that and even have his shirt automatically ripped off his back to reveal his rippling muscles. Bollywood has indeed got on with [the] times.'[29]

Dabangg is a repository of several cool things that became part of pop culture. For instance, a signature Chulbul Pandey move is casually flipping his sunglasses on to the back of his shirt collar. It became so iconic that it inspired a social media filter for *Dabangg 3* that mirrored the exact gesture. Earlier this year, I attended an event where Salman casually did it on stage while launching a motorsports league and it sent the crowd into a tizzy!

The famous hook step of the title song of *Dabangg* was inspired by real-life people Salman met at a wedding. Music composer Sajid Khan (of the Sajid–Wajid duo) revealed that the inspiration came from an uncle at a relative's wedding. 'Salman, I and a couple of friends had gone for a relative's wedding and that was the first time we all had gone as baaratis, so we were basically dancing on the road with the baarat. A huge crowd gathered, so Mathur uncle tried to make them go away. For that, he started doing a step, where he was twisting his wrists. After that we saw a mamaji and he had a step that he always used to do with his belt. Salman Bhai immediately told him, "*Mamaji, aapka step toh gaya* [Mamaji, your step is now mine]." He merged both the ideas and made it into the famous 'Hud Hud Dabangg' hook step, and Mamaji till date says that Salman has stolen his step,' he said in an interview.[30]

Some of *Dabangg*'s most enduring moments came from its razor-sharp one-liners, but it was Salman who turned them into pop-culture gold. '*Swagat nahi karoge aap humara* [Won't you welcome me]?' in Salman's hands takes on a both naughty and charming vibe.

The deliciously absurd '*Hum tum mein itne ched karenge ... ki confuse ho jaoge ki saans kahan se lein ... aur paadein kahan se* [I'll riddle you with so many holes, you'll be confused about where to breathe from and where to fart from]' works because he delivers it with a mix of deadpan menace and mischievous glee, making it both threatening and hilarious. Even something as straightforward as '*Humara naam humari personality ko shobha deta hai ... Chulbul Pandey* [My name matches my personality ... Chulbul Pandey]' becomes a moment of pure swagger. That kind of line mouthed by someone else might just devolve into sounding completely silly, but with Salman it feels like fact, spunk and irreverence all rolled into one.

There were two things happening for the first time in this film. One, Salman was sporting the first moustache of his career, which he was very unsure about right until the last minute. And two, that he was suddenly becoming a favourite with the rural crowd as well, not just the glamorous urban population he had been catering to. But once again reviewers were lapping up both the look and the performance. Film critic Mayank Shekhar wrote in his review, 'Mr Pandey's a super-hero in the tradition spawned by children's cinema since the '70s (films of Bachchan, Dharmendra, thereafter Mithun, Devgn, Sunny Deol, etc). Where the leading man serves for his audience poetic and vigilante justice. The action is comically balletic, and when there's no humour to complete the masala, standalone jokes play out before the screen. This is that epilogue-film-prologue, super-B movie, with reasonably A-budgets. It'd be a shame to watch this anywhere outside of an old, decrepit single-screen theatre, in the spirit of the loud tribal tradition that Hindi movies have always been: severely light on both the brains and the wallet. Mad stuff! Really.'[31]

Nikhat Kazmi of *The Times of India* wrote, '*Dabangg* is designed as a vehicle to showcase the star charisma of Salman Khan and the actor literally hits the bull's eye. He has a ball on-screen and makes sure you join the party too.'[32]

Anupama Chopra in her review said, 'Chulbul Pandey, co-written by writer-director Abhinav Kashyap and enacted by Salman Khan, is the most thunderously crackling character I've seen in a Bollywood film in months. It's the role of a lifetime and Salman Khan bites into it like a starving man devours a feast. He inhabits it fully, strutting and swaggering and even, spoofing himself.'[33]

The song 'Munni Badnaam Hui' was *Dabangg*'s wild card. Malaika Arora, Arbaaz's then wife, smouldered in the number, the music pounded and Salman entered mid-song with his dancing without a care in the world. Salman wasn't even supposed to be in the song. His entry was scheduled for after the song. But during one of the readings, Salman suggested that he jump in and start dancing to throw the villain off guard. With his gloriously over-the-top moves, he hijacked the whole scene!

Hakim Ali, a weaver from Bangladesh, breaks down *Dabangg*'s success as he sees it. 'There is a duality that lets *Dabangg* be both a tribute to and a satire of the Bollywood masala hero. Many films ignore how strong personal angles can be even in action films, but *Dabangg* grounds Chulbul in a messy, almost theatrical family drama—he has a stepfather who doesn't love him, he loses his mother and there is rivalry with his half-brother. This builds him up as a real person, not just a killing machine! *Dabangg* is a masala film that doesn't apologize for being masala, and packs together action, romance, comedy, tragedy and music. The tonal shifts, from joke to fight sequences to wedding dances to death, mirror the syntax of single-screen cinema from the 1970s and the 1980s, where one film could sell all of it together! Unlike many later masala films, it doesn't feel stitched together—it flows as a complete entertainment experience.'

Ali's theory sounded plausible. It was otherwise impossible to explain why the film became that year's biggest Bollywood hit, earning Rs 192.89 crore gross in India and Rs 29 crore overseas, with a worldwide total of Rs 221.14 crore.[34] Adjusted for inflation in 2025, that worldwide gross would be roughly Rs 590–600 crore today, with the India gross alone coming to about Rs 510–520 crore. Made on a modest budget, *Dabangg* not only dominated commercially, but also redefined the masala entertainer for a new decade, taking Salman's position as a megastar to the next level. There was no looking back after this film!

As mentioned earlier, in the decade prior to his golden run, Salman was going through the lowest phase of his career. In 2007, he was arrested in the blackbuck poaching case and was in jail for a few weeks. Puneet Issar, who directed Salman in *Garv: Pride & Honour* (2004), spoke of the turmoil of the legal battle and the intense media scrutiny. He said in a podcast, 'Obviously, the man (Salman) was disturbed. Ultimately, his family members decided that he should start work and concentrate on it. ... Salim sahab told me to tell Salman to stay busy at work, and this was a collective decision taken by his family. It was the right decision and that's what he did.'[35]

Taking his father's advice seriously, Salman put all his energy into work. In an interview with the *Open* magazine, Salim Khan narrated an incident. 'Once, we were at a wedding in Aziz Mirza's family, and there was this alleged rivalry played up by the media between Shah Rukh and Hrithik (Roshan). I told Shah Rukh that the only actor you must fear is Salman because *jis din Salman serious ho gaya, uss din woh sab ko peechhe chhod dega* (the day Salman gets serious about his career, he will leave all of you behind),' he said.[36]

In Bollywood, becoming serious about work entails a careful image reconstruction. Directors should feel you are a viable asset to invest in and that you will give good returns. Studios should see their money multiply because of you. Given the media perception following his arrests, it seemed to the industry that investing in Salman would be risky. What if he got sentenced mid-production? It would lead to the whole project falling apart. That was a risk film-makers were wary of. Salman needed to put the word out that his sincerity would outrun any worries or any doubts that people might have.

To undergo that very image correction, in an effort to put his energy into his work, in 2009, Salman hired the services of Reshma Shetty, who runs one of Bollywood's most influential celebrity management companies, Matrix. Anyone who knows Reshma will tell you that she is among the sharpest people in the business. Her understanding of image-building and public positioning is unparalleled. There is a no-nonsense style and an undeniable winning streak in her work. When she took over Salman's management, he was marked by inconsistent box office results and a volatile public image. Insiders give Reshma credit for re-engineering Salman's career and giving his superstar status a new spin for the new generation. More than films, she transformed Being Human from being a home-run charity into a globally recognized lifestyle brand, multiplying both its revenue streams and its philanthropic reach.

With her in his corner, Salman began to be perceived as a consummate superstar, with hits such as *Ready* and *Bodyguard* solidifying his status as Bollywood's reliable box office powerhouse. There's an interview that Salman did with *The Economic Times* in 2010 that began with his surprise as to why a newspaper about economic shifts even wanted to speak to an actor. 'As far as business is concerned, I don't understand a damn thing. (But) if you put me on your cover, many more people will buy it. For a simple reason: my fans who don't understand a damn about business either, would pick this up and read it,' he said sassily in the piece.[37]

Such was the mood that the press that was once disdainful of Salman began acknowledging the power of this man who was showing studios why he was worth betting on! When asked in the interview what had changed in him, he candidly said, 'Around three years ago, I saw myself on-screen and said I can do much better. In fact, I've started enjoying my work again and feel the same enthusiasm I had when I began.'

As a piece in *The Caravan* points out, '*Dabangg* was not only a sensational hit in Salman's traditional fan-base, but also captured the imagination of the urban middle-classes, who were prone to deride Salman-starrers as lacking "class" and "taste". Salman Khan described the film as a "sten-gun assault on the polite multiplex crowd" who he hoped would "whistle and dance on the chairs". That is precisely what happened. Reeling under the shock of *Dabangg*'s success, magazines like *Outlook*, *India Today*, *Tehelka* and *Brunch* carried cover stories that tried to understand the star's appeal. The stupendous success of *Bodyguard* the following year confirmed Salman Khan's stature as a hero of both the "masses" and the "classes".'[38]

He had begun reading scripts more carefully, connecting with fresh voices, new film-makers. One of his best discoveries of those years was Kabir Khan, with whom he went on to do some of his most memorable work. Kabir, who had started his career as a cinematographer for the

Discovery Channel, had worked with stalwarts such as Gautam Ghosh. His first film was a documentary on Subhas Chandra Bose's Indian National Army in 1999, on which he later made the Amazon Prime Video series *The Forgotten Army*. Kabir had met Salman with the idea of his first feature film, *Kabul Express* (2006). While that didn't work out, Salman kept Kabir in mind. It was, in fact, he who encouraged Katrina to work in Kabir's next film, *New York* (2009), which was about the aftermath of 9/11. In an interview, Katrina said, 'The person who actually was super encouraging of me to do the film was Salman, because he had met Kabir Khan for his first film, which was *Kabul Express*. He wanted him to be in that movie. I don't know what happened there. Salman had really liked Kabir from that interaction, and he said, "I think this is going to be an incredible film and Kabir is going to be a great film-maker. You should be excited about that film."'[39]

But the biggest rule of scaling up is to always make sure that you keep your foundation strong and give your core audience what they seek. Salman kept making sure his run at the box office continued. In 2011, when Salman starred in Anees Bazmee's *Ready* and the much-loved *Bodyguard*, critics didn't think much of either, but in true Salman style, he said, 'My fans are my real critics. I have become very choosy about my scripts because of them. I don't work for money. Even if I don't get any remuneration, I am fine with it. But I have to respect my fans who pay for their movie tickets and expect to watch good entertaining cinema.'[40]

But his fans were flocking to theatres in larger numbers than usual. *Ready* was a major commercial success, earning a gross of Rs 120.72 crore at the time, which would be roughly equivalent to Rs 220 crore in 2025 after adjusting for inflation. The film had a strong opening with a weekend collection of Rs 42.24 crore (about Rs 77 crore in 2025) and a first-day earning of Rs 13.33 crore (around Rs 24 crore today), playing on 2,300 screens. *Bodyguard* was an even bigger hit and made a lifetime gross at the time of Rs 145 crore, which if adjusted for inflation in 2025 brings it to Rs 265 crore. Salman felt the box office was the result of a good run, but he couldn't help but feel vindicated. In an interview, he said, 'When the time is right, every ball will come and hit your bat, wherever you swing it, and go for a six. The choudharies [gatekeepers] of the film industry have all shut up. Now everyone wants to make films like that. Now they find things like "*Mitti ki kushboo aati hai* (It's a film of the soil)".'[41]

What shifted wasn't Salman's star power or fandom but the way in which his fans kept score. Salman fan Badal Nigam, who is a tuk tuk driver in Colombo, Sri Lanka, gives me an interesting perspective on how the rise of Salman's fandom in the age of the internet changed something very pivotal about Hindi cinema's reviewing system. 'Around the time that Salman's blockbusters *Ready* and *Bodyguard* started dominating, something else also shifted. Suddenly we didn't just talk about whether the film was good or bad, whether the story was good or bad, what the performances were like or whether we had fun. It became about how much money it made, how quickly it made it and what records it broke. This became the biggest change in Salman's fandom back then. I was part of several fan groups, and the money-making ability of his movies became a major point of conversation. It is also possible that this was because of his big fight with Shah Rukh then. Money is always a great indicator of popularity, and fans wanted to show how Salman was bigger than Shah Rukh. I think it started like that. With Twitter blowing up, fans were part of a live, buzzing conversation that spilled out into real life. The numbers became a way of celebrating Salman's charisma at the box office. In some ways, the numbers brought Salman closer to his fans, but it was also important in reflecting how cinema culture was evolving. A new kind of excitement was coming in.'

And nowhere was this new-age Salman mania more visible than in Mumbai's legendary single-screen Gaiety Galaxy. I am told it became popular initially because Salman used to visit his fans there every Eid. It is now an essential Mumbai experience. If you have to witness the paraphernalia around a Salman Khan release, you have to watch his film first-day-first-show at this theatre. Old-timers tell me that he used to walk through the crowd here, triggering wild reactions. Fans would leap up from their seats, tear off their shirts, whistle loudly and dance in pure frenzy.

Manoj Desai, the man behind the iconic theatre, who has seen every shade of Bollywood stardom unfold from his box office window, tells me,

'*Salman Khan aur Gaiety Galaxy ka choli daman ka sambandh hai* [Salman Khan and Gaiety Galaxy are intertwined emotionally].'

When I called him for an interview for this book, he said, 'You know why you and so many like you come every year to my theatre to watch Salman's films first-day-first-show? Because nowhere else in the world will you enjoy his films the way you do here. *Multiplex pe multiplex ban jayenge, but Salman ki picture ka flavour aayega toh single-screen mein hi* [You can build multiplex after multiplex, but you'll get the true flavour of Salman's films only in single-screen theatres]. That's what they are made for! Fancy screens, 4DX, sound systems are all great technology and very impressive, but they can never replace what touches the heart. Salman's films have a beating heart at their core. The real magic lies in the emotions that fill the room and the collective cheer of fans. That's what makes this place special.'

I have often wondered what superstars aspire for once they have everything—box office success, stardom, a fandom that worships the ground they walk on. Adarsh, with his dusty *Wanted* audio cassette and his fierce need to guard Bhai's aura, did give me part of the answer— immortality. The reassurance that your presence cannot be erased. There is a lovely line Salman once told *Forbes*, which I think about a lot: 'My life's ambition was 10 lakh rupees. I crossed it in my second film. So now, wherever it goes, I'm on plus.' For a man who had nothing left to prove commercially, the next frontier wasn't money or even mass hysteria—it was meaning.

The years after this showed us what could happen when India's biggest mass hero began to race towards stories that revealed not just his swagger, but his spine.

" Sultan ko bas ek aadmi hara sakta hai, aur woh hai Sultan khud. "

Sultan, 2016

10

Juggernaut

THERE is a long-standing joke among film reviewers on the eve of every Salman Khan release: 'What's the point of this review?' We have all told each other this at some point or another. Salman Khan films are considered critic-proof. As writer-journalist Gautam Chintamani once wrote, '"Bhai Proof" cinema often meant films that would be panned by the critics but loved by the legions … It was the manner in which *Dabangg* was received by audiences as well as critics across the country that fanned the whole "Salman-is-critic-proof" marvel … For many Hindi film critics, Salman Khan was their version of Rajinikanth and therefore their reviews somewhere celebrated the cult of Salman more than the films or performances. Then *Bajrangi Bhaijaan* happened …'[1]

But before *Bajrangi Bhaijaan* came *Ek Tha Tiger*, which truly elevated what a Salman Khan film could be, especially in the eyes of the critics. I revisited it after the soul-crushing experience of watching the abominable *War 2*, when I came across film-maker Kabir Khan's post about thirteen years of *Ek Tha Tiger*. He wrote on Instagram, 'Tiger… Tiger… Tiger…

Thirteen years ago, *Ek Tha Tiger* with the megastars Salman Khan and Katrina Kaif roared into cinemas with the biggest opening in Indian cinema at that time…What began as the story of two spies caught between duty and love has, over the years, evolved into a sprawling cinematic universe.'[2]

That post led me to track where this multi-spyverse began. Turns out, it began with Salman Khan falling in love. On a Friday evening, with a tub of ice cream, I watched the film again after a decade. The minute it ended, I called a friend. 'I know why we are making such mediocre content these days. We lack the ability to tell an absolutely risky story,' I gushed without even greeting her with the customary 'hello'. All my readers would agree that most part of this year has been spent watching rather mediocre Hindi movies, which just feel dull.

There is no intention to do something unbelievably outrageous. Imagine the starting point of *Ek Tha Tiger*'s narration: What if an Indian spy and a Pakistani spy fall in love and elope even as their respective agencies chase them down in different parts of the world?

Why are we not telling wild, fearless stories? I know the answer and you do too, but I am going to spend the next few pages reminiscing of times when bold wasn't a bad word and cinema wished to make a point.

The beginnings of any franchise is the most fearless form of storytelling. There is no pressure to live up to and a relatively lower fear of failure. So you take the leap of faith without thinking about what happens if you can't match the grandeur of your imagination. Because if you don't, you try again, like all artists do. Better to fail gloriously than to never try at all! And with that sentiment, Tiger was born.

To understand why Tiger became the most memorable spy in Indian pop culture, one needs to understand the chutzpah of two people—Kabir Khan, the director, and Aditya Chopra, the producer. They'd met each other for the first time in 2004, when Kabir was looking for a studio for his film *Kabul Express*, which was the story of two Indian journalists and their Afghan guide forced on a forty-eight-hour journey through war-torn Afghanistan. After that, Kabir and Aditya went on to make *New York*. What started as a documentary about the aftermath of 9/11 became a memorable mainstream political film. The film won love from critics for being able to talk about 9/11 without even using the term 'jihad'.

Emboldened by that success, Kabir wrote *Ek Tha Tiger* and Aditya apparently told him to put his politics front and centre. It helped that *New York*'s commercial success made it one of the most watched films in Pakistan, Syria, Iraq and other countries in the Middle East. When the Syrian ambassador to India ran into the then editor of *The Indian Express,* Shekhar Gupta, at an airport, he said *New York* was a film that 'us Arabs should have made but you have made it'.[3] All of this gave faith to both Kabir and Aditya to play on the front foot.

And thus *Ek Tha Tiger* was conceptualized. Kabir says, 'I ensure that whatever film I make must primarily be enjoyed at face value without going into the politics of it. But when you go into the layers, you'll find a much more profound film underneath.'[4] This, in my experience, is the core of *Ek Tha Tiger*'s success. I have over the years had many conversations with Kabir about whether art can exist without ideology. He believes it can, but should it? That's a larger conversation for later.

As film writer Rahul Desai in his analysis of *Ek Tha Tiger* explains, Kabir took the elements of Salman's stardom to chalk out a character that has larger meaning. And that brilliance is what *Ek Tha Tiger* thrives on. In a column for *The Hollywood Reporter* India, he said, 'Good directors don't worship the superstars they work with, they weaponize this reverence into something sharper. They don't cater to die-hard fans by giving them what they want, they expand the idea of fandom by showing them what's possible. Kabir Khan does this skilfully in *Ek Tha Tiger*, fusing the mythical legend of the actor with the slick machinations of the genre. Much of the plot—particularly the characterization of RAW operative Avinash "Tiger" Singh Rathore—mines and memé-fies Salman Khan's off-screen image.'[5]

Kabir had an advantage with Salman on his side. The budgets became bigger, the canvas larger and the spine stronger than ever before. 'The character Tiger is a legend in the world of intelligence, so you need a persona like Salman's, which is larger than life in real life too,' Kabir said in an interview.[6]

Together they went into every detail of the film, whether it was the scene's backdrop or the spy's background, and married it to Salman's image. And then there were tussles with the superstar, of course.

Kabir admitted, 'Aditya told me, "Kabir, making a film with a big star is a different beast and a different kind of film altogether, and I feel that you can now step up to that." (That's when) We wrote Tiger. I never consciously thought that I would have to do something in a specific way just because Salman was in it. It was just the third film of my career, and here I was dealing with Salman at his peak. It was also his first time working with Yash Raj Films, and we were trying to make it international, so a lot of churning happened. Sometimes I had to pull him down and stop him from going overboard; sometimes he was pulling me up to do more. Some discussions were amicable, and some left one of us sulking.'[7]

Most directors, writers—even my own editor—will tell you that the best work comes from great tussle. Sometimes sulking is a rite of passage for long-term collaboration! Kabir's and Salman's tussle gave way to a director–actor duo with potential for several iconic successes, not just one.

The beauty of *Ek Tha Tiger* is that it makes some big departures from the ordinary. For starters, the lead actress isn't passive while the hero does all the action. For the first time in a Salman action blockbuster, his leading lady levels up to the superstar instead of waiting to be saved. By the next part of the film, she is the one saving him from terrorists! Katrina believes that the power of Zoya comes from the way Kabir writes his women. In his stories, women don't play second fiddle to the men. They stand shoulder to shoulder with them, which shows his value system as a writer. But getting these two together wasn't an easy feat.

For Kabir to approach Salman for this film, especially considering Salman and Katrina had broken up at the time of casting, was incredibly difficult. But he knew Katrina was Zoya and Salman Tiger. Their box office pull together was unimaginable. Moreover, it wasn't a bitter break-up between the two, which made it easy for them to do this film together. In Mashable India's *The Bombay Dream* chat show, Kabir said, 'If there's one actor I'd call family in this industry, it's Katrina. She's extremely close to me, to Mini, to my kids. Katrina was already Zoya when we went to see Salman. This was the stage where they'd broken up, so it wasn't comfortable. I told him I wanted Katrina, and he knew my connection with Katrina. Adi and I were driving back from Galaxy Apartments to Yash Raj, and we were silent. We'd just cast Salman Khan for the first time, and for five or ten minutes he was silent, then he said, "*Yaar bahut badi casting hai* (This is a major casting coup)." Aditya Chopra saying this ... And the next day we announced it.'[8]

The other departure the film makes is its ending, which challenged the long-standing template of cross-border love stories. In *Gadar: Ek Prem Katha* (2001), the couple picks India and harbours hostility for Pakistan. In *Veer-Zaara* (2004), the lovers eventually settle in India. Tiger goes Rumi-esque in his approach, echoing the thought that 'beyond ideas of wrongdoing and rightdoing, there is a field ... I'll meet you there'. Tiger and Zoya reject both nations and decide to make the whole world their home. The next time we meet them in the sequel of this film, *Tiger Zinda Hai*, in 2018, they are living in the picturesque Alps and the film ends in Greece. The third part, *Tiger 3*, starts at their home in Austria. Love is beyond borders and *Ek Tha Tiger* ends with the thought that they will keep running until agencies such as R&AW and ISI no longer need to exist, as Tiger says.

It is also ironic that Shah Rukh had passed on Tiger. It takes me back to the big fight between him and Salman. And also makes one wonder: What makes Salman the perfect Tiger? Though he had no actor in mind, while writing it, Kabir says, 'How many actors in the industry today can you call Tiger and not feel cheesy about it? Salman is the perfect choice. Today, when I look at the film, I find it very difficult to think of someone other than Salman Khan to play the character of Tiger. The way the film stands today I don't think I would have made it without Salman.'[9]

The film had a string of highlights, but the most memorable was the subversive entry sequence of Salman. Tiger's face is revealed in a storm of cigarette butts scattering across the screen in slow motion, after a breathless chase that includes leaping across rooftops and through buildings. In a crucial moment, Salman slides down a massive staircase balancing on a table, guns blazing. The sequence ends with a gorgeous silhouette! Kabir tells me it wasn't even planned. He said in an interview, 'I come from documentary training, so I react a lot to space and situations. We wanted a location which looked fabulous and which had never been used by any other Hollywood action thriller. I read about this one location on the Turkey-Syria border (Mardin). I had seen its photographs and had loved the look of these brown mud houses on a hill. Until we went no one had ever shot there. It was really difficult to access. (During our recce) I saw the hill from a distance and I realized that I'd love to see Tiger come in a silhouette and stand over here before my story starts. It went on to become an iconic shot!'[10]

It became the first Indian film to be shot in Iraq. The production even sent a letter to the Iraqi government requesting help. Upon hearing that it starred Salman, they arranged for additional security for cast and crew, and sanctioned travel by designated choppers for everyone.

In Mardin there's now a café named after Salman Khan, which he would frequent while shooting in Del Mar. In an interview Salman talked about how his association with the café came about. 'We ate there once and I liked the ambience, so we used to hang out there. They wanted to learn different cuisines, and found Indian food interesting. So, I had my chef teach them. The owner was very sweet. He used to chant with this tasbi (a religious beaded chain), which he gave me when I left. I took it on the condition that I would return it the next time we met.'[11]

That iconic entry shot went on to become one of the most loved scenes of Salman's career other than *Maine Pyaar Kiya*'s 'dosti mein no sorry, no thank you' and *Hum Aapke Hain Koun..!*'s 'Bas aapse hi toh hum ye gustaakhi kar sakte hai' dialogues. Another close contender is *Kuch Kuch Hota Hai*'s entry scene.

In an interview to Mashable India last year, Kabir said that he had gone to Gaiety Galaxy to see first-day reactions to the film and saw coins thrown at the screen by the jubilant crowd when that entry scene came on 70 mm for the first time. 'There was a barrage of coins that came quickly at me [standing next to the screen] during the entry scene. That's when you know the crowd has loved a Salman film,' he says.[12]

Salman fan Nayesha Choksy, a business owner based in Auckland, tells me, 'For me, Salman Khan's entry in *Ek Tha Tiger* will always remain his greatest. I've seen him storm the screen in *Wanted* and make us go wild in *Dabangg*, but the way he walks into *Ek Tha Tiger* operates on another level. It's not just an entry, it's an experience—the silence before he appears, the thrill in the air the sheer style of his presence. The theatre went crazy, and yet there was this sophistication in the way he was presented, like a true international spy and still our very own Bhai. That entry gave me goosebumps then, and even today when I rewatch it, I feel the same rush. For me, that's the mark of the best Salman Khan entry ever. Because in the end, the euphoria of cinema is all about having a star who can make you feel that rush, that madness, that magic only movies can bring. And no one delivers that better than Salman.'

Tiger's iconic scarf comes from Kabir himself. He used to wear it while shooting in Afghanistan as a young film-maker. That scarf went on to become an inextricable part of Tiger's identity. And in today's world, it shows a whole different spirit altogether. The Palestinian keffiyeh, a symbol of resistance that became popular under Palestinian leader Yasser Arafat, was recently donned by actor Javier Bardem on the Emmy's red carpet as he announced he wouldn't work with anyone who justified the genocide in Gaza.

Even when Tiger comes to rescue Shah Rukh's Pathaan in his cameo in the film, the scarf makes an entry before Salman does. Kabir says, 'I always wore the scarf when I was shooting in Afghanistan as a rule. Even today, I wear these scarves while I am shooting. I was also wearing it when I was doing the look test for *Ek Tha Tiger*. I realized that something was amiss. This is when I removed my scarf and gave it to Salman. He put it on and there it was! A lot of things happen with your gut instinct.'[13]

In an interview ... Kabir said that he had gone to Gaiety Galaxy to see first-day reactions to *Ek Tha Tiger* and saw coins thrown at the screen by the jubilant crowd when that entry scene came on 70 mm for the first time. 'There was a barrage of coins that came quickly at me [standing next to the screen] during the entry scene. That's when you know the crowd has loved a Salman film.'

Ek Tha Tiger, which was made on a budget of Rs 800 million, remains one of the actor's most loved films. The worldwide gross collection for *Ek Tha Tiger* was Rs 3.3 billion, with the India collection alone amounting to Rs 1.98 billion.[14] In 2025, *Ek Tha Tiger* became the sole Indian film to be showcased at the International Spy Museum in Washington, DC. The film now stands alongside *James Bond*, *Mission Impossible* and *Men in Black* franchises.[15] Talking about it, Kabir wrote on his Instagram,

'A film is never only about how much it earned at the box office. It's more about how long will it continue to capture people's imagination. And in that sense *Ek Tha Tiger* goes on and on. Of course it was one of the biggest box office grossers ever when it released in 2012 but what gives me even more joy is that it's still spoken about with love now in 2025. *Tiger humesha Zinda rahega …*'[16]

Of course, the numbers of this film baffled even his peers. They were amazed at how Salman was pulling off such a massive success. This was Salman's first film to work the kind of numbers overseas that so far only a Shah Rukh and an Aamir film had. The film crossed the $10 million mark, which was his first film to achieve that feat. This put it in sixth place among the all-time top overseas grossers, ahead of *Ra.One* and *Dhoom 2*, with only *3 Idiots*, *My Name Is Khan*, *Don 2*, *Kabhi Alvida Naa Kehna* and *Om Shanti Om* ranking higher. In its first three weeks, the film collected £1.35 million in the UK, A$611,794 in Australia and NZ$223,190 in New Zealand. At that time, it was Salman's biggest international hit.[17]

Aamir Khan, interestingly, said *Ek Tha Tiger* is more than just Salman Khan, probably suggesting how it was Kabir Khan's brilliance and good storytelling that made it the blockbuster it was. When Salman heard it, he quipped, 'More than Salman Khan? He wants to take credit for it? Salman Khan is Salman Khan.'[18]

Fans, of course, see the success of the film as completely borne by Salman. Real estate professional Omar Al-Khafaji, who was born in Iraq but grew up in the UAE, told me that after *Ek Tha Tiger*, Salman starred in an array of hits and that he watched each and every one of them. The plot makes the viewing experience better, but he watched because it was Salman who starred in it. 'All movie successes are about the quality of the film. Salman's success is about Salman. There was the incredibly fun sequel to *Dabangg* that I watched after *Ek Tha Tiger*. The frenzy becomes greater with a good film, sure, but it's not about the film. It is about Salman. I'll never forget this day in Sharjah back in 2007. Salman had come for a store opening. This was also the time when his films weren't doing as well. I remember people were screaming and climbing over each other just to catch a glimpse of him. The DXB Police had to fire tear gas at the crowd to calm it down. I was right there in the middle of it, and it really felt like a rock concert gone wild. That was the moment I realized how unstoppable his stardom was. Films only elevate this, but this is sheer fan craze for Salman Bhai,' he told me.

From Emiratis to South Asians, and even Filipinos, everyone's heart beats for Salman. The reverence for the star runs so deep that even when he was convicted in the hit-and-run case in 2002, retail giant Splash refused to remove him as the brand's ambassador. The CEO, Reza Baig, even announced, 'At Splash we love Salman Khan and we will support him through every up and down. He will continue to be our brand ambassador.'[19]

Omar even jokes that Salman's fandom lacks logic—three years after Salman's hit-and-run case, the UAE invited him to be the face of the Belhasa Driving Center's road safety campaign and was also flown in to inaugurate a 42 million dirham driving complex.[20]

Omar reiterates, 'Give me and my friends an incredibly fun Bhaijaan film and I don't care if there's also a Brad Pitt, a Tom Cruise or an *Avengers* film airing for the last time. We'd choose Bhaijaan's film a million times over!' Omar has a slightly deeper reason for this. 'As an Iraqi, I've witnessed more devastation than I can put into words. I have moved around and I have lived. So you can imagine how many people I have lost in my life. Salman's films mean so much to me because they create another world where justice always prevails and the good guy never loses. Real life isn't that simple, but at least in cinema it can be. I love losing myself in that peak fantasy. It helps me stay alive with the optimism that life deserves. How women love rom-coms and Shah Rukh, we love our Salman Bhai! He validates our sense of being and our beliefs of what being a man entails.'

India has seen some of the greatest superstars in cinema, from Dilip Kumar, Rajesh Khanna and Amitabh Bachchan to Rajinikanth, Shah Rukh Khan and Aamir Khan. Each has either defined an era or set new benchmarks of stardom. Yet, Salman Khan has been a phenomenon in his own right, with a fan following and box office power that make him bigger than them all. The only person who can probably rival this kind of stardom is Rajinikanth.

Salman has delivered the most films in Bollywood's coveted Rs 100 crore club. Nineteen of his releases have crossed the mark, starting with *Dabangg* in 2010, which made Rs 140.22 crore, all the way to *Sikandar* in 2025, which made Rs 110.10 crore. In between came a run of hits—*Ready, Bodyguard, Ek Tha Tiger, Dabangg 2, Jai Ho, Kick, Bajrangi Bhaijaan, Prem Ratan Dhan Payo, Sultan, Tubelight, Tiger Zinda Hai, Race 3, Bharat, Dabangg 3, Kisi Ka Bhai Kisi Ki Jaan* and *Tiger 3*.

But it's more than just the numbers. Every ticket sold is really a reminder of the bond people feel with Salman. It's families going to the theatre together on Eid, fans whistling at his entry and audiences who come back film after film because

'I'll never forget this day in Sharjah back in 2007. Salman had come for a store opening. This was also the time when his films weren't doing as well. I remember people were screaming, climbing over each other, just to catch a glimpse of him. The DXB Police had to fire tear gas at the crowd to calm it down ... It really felt like a rock concert gone wild. That was the moment I realized how unstoppable his stardom was.'

they trust him to give them a good time. And this is over and above the respite he brings distributors with his films. The Rs 100 crore tag may be a record, but what it really measures is the love people have for him—and that love cannot be counted.

The box office is what keeps the wheels of the film industry turning. When a Salman Khan release hits the theatres, the money it generates doesn't just go to him alone. It keeps single-screens alive, reassures distributors and gives producers the courage to back their next project. That ripple effect is what allows smaller films, with no big star or marketing muscle, to even get made. In a way, every Salman hit buys breathing space for the rest of Bollywood.

Of course, Salman doing *Kick* was an all-heart decision. The film marked the directorial debut of his friend and producer Sajid Nadiawala.

The screenplay for *Kick*, the official remake of the 2009 Telugu hit of the same name, was written by Rajat Arora, along with Sajid, Chetan Bhagat and Keith Gomes.

The film stormed the box office, earning more than Rs 232 crore net in India and crossing Rs 402 crore worldwide. It became Salman's first entry into the prestigious Rs 200 crore club and stood out as one of 2014's biggest blockbusters. Even a decade later, *Kick* continues to hold its ground on the list of the top fifty highest-grossing Indian films.[21]

It's also the most fun Salman film, in my opinion. There is a scene early on in the movie where Salman dances to 'Saat Samundar Paar' with abandon, and I remember the film's press preview where journalists got up and joined in the dance seeing him on-screen. He is called Devil in the film, which is short for Devi Lal Singh, which gives it the wicked touch! Add to it some cool lines such as '*Aap Devil ke peeche, Devil aapke peeche* [You are after Devil, Devil is after you]', and it's a classic Salman concoction. There is also the iconic '*Mere baare mein itna mat sochna ... dil mein aata hoon ... samajh mein nahi* [Don't think about me so much ... I can only be felt, not understood]'. As a character says about him in the film, '*Iski zindagi bas ek hi cheez se chalti hai ... Kick* [His life runs on only one thing ... Kick].' Pretty much sums up Salman as well. Which is what explains why *Kick* feels like a show reel of the wildest parts of Salman—larger-than-life, driven by thrill and full of heart. Cinema's greatest joy is just watching a star have fun being himself.

The beauty of *Kick* is also in its casting. It starred Salman alongside Nawazuddin Siddiqui and Randeep Hooda, along with Mithun Chakraborty and Saurabh Sachdev, each bringing their ace game to the table.

Jacqueline Fernandez as the leading lady was a delight to watch. The film was to star Deepika Padukone and be helmed by A.R. Murugadoss, but somewhere through the production process, both the actor and the director moved on to other projects.

The only thing Sajid didn't want for *Kick* was for it to look like *Wanted 2*. So they did everything to set it apart—from inspired casting and crackling music to adding animation to the narrative flow. The highlight of the film, however, were the action sequences. For one of the film's key sequences, Salman was required to dangle from the fortieth floor of the Palace of Culture and Science in Warsaw. To everyone's surprise, he insisted on performing the stunt himself.

He said in an interview, 'When you look at some of the action scenes, you think that a lot of hard work has gone into them, but that's not true. And then some scenes look easy but you had to do a lot of hard work for it. It would be hard work if I had not done these kinds of stunts before, but I have done this kind of stuff before. I have been playing sports, riding cycles all my life, so doing these stunts was not very difficult for me. I have learnt how to jump from a motorcycle, fight and drive at the same time, so it's not difficult. We did not compromise. If a scene required 30 cars being blown off by a bus, there were 30 cars waiting to be blown off. The bus was brought from London to Poland for the shoot. The main hero of this film is the heart of the producer, who never compromised. There are about three to four action teams. I have done my own action scenes. But for shots from different angles, a body double has been used.'[22]

There was also a train sequence, but Salman was cautious to not do it without doubles and technical help, given his experience on the set of *Tere Naam*. In the film, in a similar train scene, a stuntman was supposed to keep watch and pull Salman back to safety at the right time. Only, the stuntman froze. Salman wasn't supposed to look back at the approaching train, so he had no idea how close it had come. But thankfully, at the very last moment, the stuntman yanked Salman out of the way. The train clipped his leg slightly. Later, the stuntman admitted that he had panicked, but when he saw the entire unit watching him, he knew that if he let anything happen to Salman, he'd be finished. So he risked his life and saved him.[23] The entire crew was shaken. Only then did it strike everyone that the same effect could have been done in CGI with no risk at all. So while filming *Kick*, they made sure the train was kept at a safe distance.

When *Kick* finally released on Eid 2014, the atmosphere in both single-screens and multiplexes across the country was electric, like a carnival. Morning shows ran houseful, with long queues outside halls, fans waving Salman banners, draped in tees with his face on them, breaking into dance before and after the show. Tickets sold out days in advance, and in some places people had to wait days just to get one.

The numbers only reflected what was happening on the ground. On its very first day of release, *Kick* generated around Rs 26 crore in India, making it the second-highest non-holiday opener at the time, just behind *Dhoom 3*. The opening weekend closed at a massive Rs 82 crore in three days. Exhibitors everywhere reported extraordinary turnouts, with analysts predicting rightaway that Salman had another all-time blockbuster on his hands.[24]

The first week was all about packed theatres, ticket scalping outside halls and fan frenzies inside, where whistles, claps and chants of 'Bhaijaan' filled the air.

And the critics loved it too. A review by Raja Sen read: *Kick* is Salman's best film in a decade.[25] In his review, film critic Rajeev Masand said, 'It's the most fun you've seen Salman having on-screen lately. The actor, fully aware of his strengths and of what his fans expect from him, is in goofball mode. He dials up the charm, and delivers flashes of amazing spontaneity, making you wish someone wrote a better film for him. *Kick* will no doubt break box office records and earn many, many crores for its makers and for its leading man.'[26] Saurabh Dwivedi, then with *India Today* and now with The Lallantop, said, 'The film is replete with all things about Salman, and it's a complete paisa vasool watch.'[27]

The songs also gave the film an extra 'kick'. 'Jumme Ki Raat' was everywhere, blasting at weddings, parties, even in cars stuck in traffic, with Salman's trademark dance steps becoming an instant craze. Then came 'Hangover', which Salman sang himself, and that made fans love it even more. It felt personal, almost like he was singing straight to them. 'Yaar Naa Miley', with Honey Singh and Jasmine Sandlas, became a club favourite. The zany soundtrack of the film was the driving force behind the film's box office storm.

When *Kick* released, its success in India was almost a given. By then Salman had become a box office guarantee. The film stormed into the Rs 100 crore club within days and eventually closed with over Rs 309 crore domestically.[28] But what truly stood out was the way *Kick* travelled overseas, proving Salman's pull wasn't limited to his home turf.

In its very first weekend abroad, *Kick* collected an impressive Rs $3 million, with strong showings in the US, Canada, the UK,

Australia and the ever-reliable Gulf region. The UAE-GCC circuit alone contributed over $4 million, reaffirming Salman's superstar status among diaspora audiences. The US and Canada together brought in close to $2.5 million, while the UK contributed more than £1.3 million. Even smaller markets such as Australia, New Zealand and Malaysia added to the tally, with Australia fetching over half a million dollars. By the end of its run, *Kick* had earned $11.38 million (Rs 68.28 crore) overseas, making it one of the highest-grossing Hindi films internationally at the time.[29]

In Pakistan, the film shattered records. It beat the opening-day numbers of local blockbuster *Waar* (2013) to set a new all-time record. By the end of its second weekend, *Kick* had collected Rs 7.4 crore there, and eventually closed at over Rs 20 crore. Saleem Ahmad, manager at Bambino cinema in Karachi, told *Gulf News* that the competition for *Kick* was from two big Hollywood movies—*Dawn of the Planet of the Apes* and *Hercules*. He added, '*Kick* will do big business because it is an action thriller with lots of stunts and Salman is a big draw in Pakistan,' he said.[30]

The film even went as far as Poland, where it collected around Rs 8 crore, a rare feat for a Hindi release in that market. It was the overseas numbers that signalled something bigger—Salman Khan wasn't just the box office king at home, he was metamorphosing into a true global star, whose films could light up theatres across continents.

Salman fan Hamza Malik, who was a teacher in Warsaw, Poland, when *Kick* was released, tells me, 'I went to watch the film at a cinema hall with my cousins. We pooled in our fresh Eidi money just to buy tickets and snacks. The hall was jam-packed, and the moment Salman danced to "Jumme Ki Raat", people were whistling and clapping like it was a cricket match. For those three hours, it felt like our whole city was celebrating together. The way the film made you feel alive, escape your everyday routine and cheer with everyone around—it was magical. People tell me it's not good cinema, but the whole point of movies is to help us escape our everyday issues. If this is not great cinema, what is?'

Later, Salman would answer the question with a film that moved the entire critics community to tears. And no one saw it coming.

Veteran screenwriter K.V. Vijayendra Prasad, also the father of director S.S. Rajamouli, had heard the story of a Pakistani couple who had come to India for their daughter's heart surgery because they couldn't afford it in their country. 'The parents were touched by the generosity of the Indians so much that they couldn't stop talking about it. This got me thinking. I decided to work on a story that connected people over the India–Pakistan border,' he said in an interview about what spurred the writing of *Bajrangi Bhaijaan*.[31]

I remember interviewing Pakistani actress Mawra Hocane earlier this year, and we got talking about Salman. She told me over a long phone call, 'We all grew up watching Bollywood films. So for us, from our perspective, your stars and my stars are not any different. Salman Khan is as much our superstar as he is India's. Because we also grew up watching *Hum Dil De Chuke Sanam*. I remember watching *Bajrangi Bhaijaan* while I was in India. I love that movie. It's such a beautiful film. So our emotional connection is not just because of Bollywood. I think it's your emotional connection with art. Because we speak the same language. We emote the same way.'[32] And thus it makes sense why Aamir Khan, who was the first star to be narrated *Bajrangi Bhaijaan*, suggested Salman be brought on for the film. Because there's no bigger star for the two countries and for a story of this nature; because there's no superstar who could have done justice as beautifully to this role as Salman did.

Aamir, in an interview in 2025, said, 'Bajrangi Bhaijaan *mere paas aayi thi. Aur kahaani sunke … ye bhi appreciate karo meri sachhai … kahaani sunke maine Vijayendra* (screenwriter) *ji ko bola "Sir, ismein Salman hona chahiye"* (*Bajrangi Bhaijaan* came to me. And after hearing the story … please also appreciate my honesty … after hearing it, I told Vijayendra ji, "Sir, Salman should be in this").'[33]

When Aamir watched the film at its trial, he had tears in his eyes. Visibly proud of his friend, he said, 'Salman's best performance and best film of his career.'[34]

And that's a unanimous opinion. Everyone, including Salman's father Salim, believes that he outdid himself in the film.

Turns out all the creative squabbles with Kabir laid the foundation for them to create magic together. Kabir tells me, 'The character, the politics of the film, what the story stands for—I knew Salman would connect with it very deeply. He has always felt strongly about such themes. And then, of course, his love for children is well known—he adores kids. So when I narrated the story to him, his reaction was instant and powerful.'

Bajrangi Bhaijaan is nothing like Salman, and yet exactly like him. None of that swagger or mischief he is known for made an appearance in the film. For this one, he stripped his heart and emotions bare. He cried on-screen with a little child in his lap, listening to a qawwali at a dargah, and it was for the first time that we all realized that when Bhaijaan cries, our hearts weep with him. Kabir said, 'During *Tiger*, I had seen how much he (Salman Khan) identified with what Bajrangi stood for. The politics of Salman as a person were very close to what Bajrangi's character stands for. Even though the character was the antithesis of what he was known for, as there was no action, no swashbuckling. It was a sweet, endearing character. And he got it immediately. He even said, "This is a film that not too many people will want to produce. Because they'll expect something else from both of us. So let's produce it ourselves." That's how it became his first home production.'[35]

If *Tiger* was the starting point for Kabir and Salman, here they were trying something unthinkable. In 2014, we could still imagine that an RSS shakha pramukh's son named Pawan Kumar Chaturvedi would take it upon himself to drop home a mute Pakistani girl who had got separated from her mother. Kabir isn't so sure this film can be made today, even though he has a script for a sequel. 'Back then, not a single person found it provocative. So could I make it again today? Maybe. Maybe not,' he said.[36]

And he had an uphill task fighting censors on the movie. But Kabir and Salman held their ground. The CBFC insisted on removing a scene featuring Om Puri's character (who plays a Pakistani maulvi) saying 'Jai Shri Ram'. 'They feared that it might upset Muslim viewers. I asked why and they said that Muslims won't like it,' Kabir recalled. 'I said "Sir, what's my name? I don't mind it at all ..." I have grown up in Delhi where "Jai Shri Ram" was not a political salutation. It was used by everybody and I have been in Old Delhi where "Jai Shri Ram" was like saying "hello" and "goodbye". I fought for it. I stuck to it.'[37] And that's the scene that got people cheering in every single screen in India.

The beating heart of *Bajrangi Bhaijaan* was the young girl, Munni. Over 8,000 kids were tested for the part.[38] Kabir knew that without the right Munni, the film wouldn't reach its full potential. Of the 2,000 auditions Kabir saw, ten were shortlisted from different parts of the country and brought to Mumbai. They did month-long workshops with them. Besides the talent and expressions, it was also crucial that they have the tenacity to last the whole film. 'We were shooting a big movie; the shooting window was more than six–seven months long in different terrains. We finally zeroed in on Harshaali Malhotra, who was pure magic on-screen, and the chemistry with Salman was bang on. I remember the first time I took her to Salman's house in Galaxy. Right from there on, you could see the chemistry between them. Ultimately the magic of *Bajrangi Bhaijaan* is that dynamic between the character of Bajrangi and the little girl Munni.'[39] On her first meeting, she apparently told Salman, '*Aap mujhe aap ki tarah ek superstar bana do na* [Please make me a superstar like you].' Salman was amused, but realized that he had a little diva on his hands!

It was also the first time on a Salman–Kareena set that the real star was a five-year-old. Kareena had walked into the film knowing the limited screen time she would have. But the narration moved her to tears and that was enough to make her want to be part of it. Just like Salman, Kareena doesn't need much convincing if the story resonates with her. And superstars such as them know when to put their might behind stories that need their star power to reach the right audience. In an interview, Kareena said, '*Bajrangi Bhaijaan* is a path-breaking story. I think after a long time, maybe over a decade, Salman has acted in a film where the actual hero of the film is the story. The story is what is going to crack the box office.' She was the first to predict that the film would be a blockbuster. Talking about her beloved co-star, she said, 'He is India's greatest and biggest superstar. And he never takes his success or failure too seriously. And that's what sets him apart from every Bollywood actor.'[40]

The other crucial casting of this film was Nawazuddin Siddiqui. Kabir had stumbled upon the viral YouTube clip of the real Pakistani journalist, Chand Nawab (the one seen fumbling through his PTC at a railway station, getting interrupted by passengers), which had already become an internet sensation by 2008. Like us, he, too, found it hilarious but endearing. When he began shaping the character arc of the small-time reporter who helps Salman's character, he approached Nawazuddin with that reference. Kabir felt he was the only one who could play it without slipping into caricature. After the film, Chand Nawab, who had felt his reputation had been marred due to the clip, became a star not just in Pakistan but also in India. The film's success opened unexpected doors for him, including offers to feature in Pakistani commercials and invites for TV and radio interviews. In Karachi, while *Bajrangi Bhaijaan* continued to play to packed theatres, Chand Nawab became a local celebrity.

What makes *Bajrangi Bhaijaan* so special is how it tugs at your heartstrings in a way very few films in Bollywood history have been able to. At its core is a kindness that can beat the overwhelming fear and politics around us. When an elderly character says, '*Koi toh khuda ka naek banda hoga Hindustan mein, jo humari Shahida ka khayal rakhega* [There must be someone kind enough in India to take care of our Shahida]', Salman makes his entry surrounded by a vaanar sena, in front of a towering Hanuman idol, grooving to the beats of 'Selfie Le Le Re'. Very early on, you know Salman's Pawan is someone who won't give up on a child. Even when he is uncomfortable with her Muslim and later Pakistani identity, he realizes that the human bond with her supersedes every kind of division society imposes on us.

The film appealed to that secular fabric of the country that we are fast losing. Even till a few years ago, religious identity couldn't take precedence over human values. Kabir, in an interview, said, 'We can harp on about progress and development but if the secular fabric of our country gets damaged, then nothing can sustain us. I wanted to discuss the Hindu-Muslim issue and in order to bring it all out in the mainstream consciousness, I needed Salman's superstardom.'[41]

Salman stood like a rock with Kabir. When the Vishwa Hindu Parishad (VHP) warned Kabir Khan that they wouldn't accept the film being called 'Bajrangi Bhaijaan', the duo did not relent.[42] They weren't ready to let someone appropriate Lord Hanuman, also referred to as Bajrang or Bajrangbali, as their own. 'Hanuman doesn't belong to only one community. Bajrangi is a symbol of our ethos. And the way the audience has taken to the film, it proves that he belongs to the entire India,' said Kabir.[43]

Salman backed him every step of the way. He said, 'If they are a religious group then the basic thing they should know is that every religion respects the other person's religion. Every religion preaches only one thing: "to follow your religion and to be respectful and to respect the other person's beliefs and religion." I don't think anyone can protest this.'[44]

Salman was even questioned about glorifying peace between India and Pakistan at a time when terrorist activity and the 2015 attack in Jammu had further strained the relationship between the two countries. But Salman, being the people's hero he is, made it clear that the common people were not their governments. He said, 'In Pakistan, 550 blasts happen every year. They are hurting their own people. Besides one or two elements, people there want peace too. Why should one mess up the rest of the 99.9 per cent people? Things can be handled peacefully, and music, films, cricket, transport are influential mediums. Then why ban them? We need to ban the war between the two countries. If people are expecting a war film in *Bajrangi Bhaijaan*, I would ask them not to watch this film. If you want to see India bashing Pakistan, don't come and see this film. This is a very positive film, like *Ek Tha Tiger*.'[45] Say it again, Bhaijaan. In 2025, say it all over again!

Salman knew it was the biggest film of his career, and he left no stone unturned to give it everything it deserved. From fighting fringe elements to getting maximum screens, he went all the way. And mostly, he did something he rarely does—show us the man he is beneath the tough exterior. In an interview, he said, 'It's the biggest character I have played. I had to put in a lot of hard work. My earlier films like *Kick*, *Dabangg* and *Ready*, to name a few, were all chalta purza (mediocre) characters. *Bajrangi Bhaijaan* will bring back the innocence that I had in *Maine Pyar Kiya*. The audience has three different types of reactions when they come out of the theatre: *mazaa nahi aaya* (didn't like the film), *achi film hai* (it's a nice film) and the third one is—*kya kar diya in logon ne? Ekdum zabardast* (What have they done? It's mind-blowing). People who have seen the rushes of *Bajrangi Bhaijaan* have had the third reaction. This assures us that we have made a good movie and people will watch it again and again. I learnt the lesson of showing the rushes of a film during *Maine Pyar Kiya*. Sooraj (director Sooraj Barjatya) would show the rushes and people would want to see it again. When you see a repeat audience during the rushes, it means that the film has something in it. *Humari zindagi main kabhi kabhi aisa hota hai ki koi chehra baar baar dekhne ka mann karta hai* [There are times in our life when we want to see the same face again and again]... That's the same quality *Bajrangi Bhaijaan* has. I am sure people will come and watch the film again and again.'[46]

He was right. *Bajrangi Bhaijaan* hit theatres in India just a day before Eid. The euphoria of this film is not something you see every day. It's probably the only time I have seen mania of that scale. A hall full of people crying with empathy about an India–Pakistan story is a rare sight!

People went to the theatres to see Bhai bash baddies—they came out misty-eyed and a heart filled with the power of kindness. As Anupama Chopra wrote in her review, '(In a Salman film) I don't expect to find—a coherent, emotionally satisfying script; Salman underplaying his supersized image; a heroine with spunk; drama that actually moves you; and tears! Yes, it happened. I have now cried while watching a Salman Khan film.'[47]

I have often asked myself while watching the film: What am I crying about? I rewatched it while writing this all over again and realized I was crying about the loss of hope, perhaps. For the world we could be, where religion and nationality did not define the borders of our hearts. For the possibility that kindness could travel farther than hate and that naive belief in goodness. In that one movie, I truly believed that Salman could heal centuries of mistrust. In *Bajrangi Bhaijaan*, we see the version of India and Pakistan that feels within reach but remains painfully elusive. Every time Salman breaks down on-screen, every time Munni looks at him with those trusting eyes, we are reminded of the innocence we have let slip away.

And maybe that's why the film lingers. It's the story of all of us who want to live in a world where borders don't fracture families. *Bajrangi Bhaijaan* makes you ache for that better world while reassuring you that it isn't foolish to dream about it. Salman, the man who built his superstardom on unflinching swagger, fight sequences far divorced from reality and sometimes slapstick humour, chose to ignite something so primal in us that it brought us to tears. And in those tears, he reminded us that even the biggest stars are at their most powerful when they lay themselves bare and let love do the heavy lifting.

The film was showered with love everywhere it went. It gained a surprising cult following in China, where everyone pirated copies and watched it on their phones. It became so popular that the makers decided to officially release it in China in 2018. In Turkey too, *Bajrangi Bhaijaan* was released around the same time, and in its opening weekend itself more than 10,000 people flocked to watch the film. In 2019, the film made its way to Japan, released as *Bajurangi ojisan to, chīsana maigo*, which translates to 'Uncle Bajrangi and a Small Lost Child'.

The film made Rs 920 crore worldwide, but the real legacy was how it spread the message of peace between the two nations, which, while cut from the same cloth, have been hostile towards each other for decades. What peace campaigns such as Aman Ki Asha and multiple diplomatic talks couldn't achieve, *Bajrangi Bhaijaan* did in 163 minutes. Veteran Pakistani actor Javed Sheikh, whom we recognize from Indian films such as *Om Shanti Om* and *Tamasha* (2015), and hit Pakistani serials such as *Zindagi Gulzar Hai* (2012), said in an interview, 'Salman is a thorough gentleman, a fantastic human being and a superb actor. People in Pakistan love Salman Khan. Salman and Kabir, people love the film. Hats off to both of you for making such a fantastic film. All over Pakistan, people are talking about *Bajrangi Bhaijaan*.'[48]

After a clash earlier this year, the Instagram pages of beloved Pakistani celebrities disappeared. Among the accounts that went missing was the legacy page of Ustad Nusrat Fateh Ali Khan, a man whose voice belongs to Lahore and Lucknow alike. The hate today reflects the times we live in. Even Faiz Ahmed Faiz's 'Hum Dekhenge' is deemed seditious now. What gets silenced in these bans is art and we risk forgetting that on both sides of the border the heart beats to the same music.

That is why *Bajrangi Bhaijaan*'s inclusion of a qawwali sung in a shrine in Pakistan felt like such a highlight. Kabir and Salman understood the power of the art the two nations share, which is why they used 'Bhar Do Jholi Meri', sung by Adnan Sami, a man of Pakistani origin who later became an Indian citizen. The qawwali itself has an older lineage, written by Purnam Allahabadi and composed by Maqbool Sabri in 1975, carrying with it a devotion that refuses to obey borders.

One of the biggest fans of this film is my friend Sofi Nowak, who is a finance consultant based in Amsterdam. Having grown up in London with several Indian and Pakistani friends around, she is aware of the tense relationship between the two nations. She happened to watch the film with a few South Asian friends in Abu Dhabi. Recalling her experience, she told me over a call, 'There is a scene in the climax when the people of Pakistan break open the gates dividing the two countries. My friends Rishab and Shahid, two burly men, held each other's hands and cried. I have seen them fight like cats and dogs over India–Pakistan cricket matches, but that night, seeing them cry like that about the love their respective countries are capable of, was beautiful. They went to watch the film nine times after that and, each time, there were tears in their eyes. Shahid and Rishab have a complex friendship. They love each other to bits, but every now and then they get into blame games over whose country is better. Cricket unites them, so does cribbing about corruption, which seems common between the two countries—but not in the way cinema does! And *Bajrangi Bhaijaan* makes their hearts beat as one till date. I love the visual of grown men crying. This is the most special thing a movie has ever done for someone in my life.'

Salman was overwhelmed with the response from the other side of the border. A Bollywood fan, Momina Rana, in an interview that year said that it was perhaps the first Indian film in which Pakistan was shown in a positive light. 'The general public in both Pakistan and India is peace-loving and that is why this movie is so widely appreciated here, and must be out there (India) as well. I would love to watch this movie again and again, as such a film is not made every day,' she added.[49]

She was right. It was the last time such a film was made. The next year militants struck an Indian Army base in Uri, Jammu and Kashmir, killing nineteen Indian soldiers. The attack was claimed by the terror outfit Jaish-e-Mohammed. India retaliated, and in the wake of the attack, diplomatic relations between India and Pakistan froze. The first to get struck in the crossfire was cinema, when the Federation of Western India Cine Employees (FWICE) issued a ban on Pakistani films being released in India and their actors working here. Within forty-eight hours, Pakistan's top stars were ousted from India. And things have never been the same since!

In some ways, that was the peak Salman era. The superstar was reigning the box office! Eid belonged to him, his films bulldozing competitors and setting records only he could break with his next. His reach was now stretching from the streets of Kanpur to the cinema halls of the Middle East, the alleys of China to the roads of Japan. What Shah Rukh had done with romance in the 1990s and Aamir with his pathbreaking films in the 2000s, Salman was doing now with the sheer force of his stardom. It was his year.

He became a one-man industry, doing it all, winning it all. And that probably felt like the most perfect time for him to go back to his roots and work with the man he had started his journey with.

On Diwali that year, Salman starred in *Prem Ratan Dhan Payo*, reuniting with Sooraj Barjatya. Playing twins in the film, Salman's standout role was of Prem Dilwale, a Ramlila performer from Ayodhya, whose innocence and goodness defined him. He also played the local prince, Yuvraj Vijay Singh, with flair. The film slightly updated Barjatya's formula—in this world his leading ladies initiated romance while Salman donned an apron and made meals for them!

The grind of a superstar's life needs some soothing every now and then, and working with Sooraj felt exactly like that for Salman. In an interview before its release, Salman said that life hadn't hardened his old friend. Working with him sixteen years later made him realize that he was still the simple young man he had met during the making of *Maine Pyar Kiya*. Salman said, 'As a human being, I think Sooraj Barjatya is on a different plane altogether. He is one of the finest humans that I have ever met. And he has been like this since he was 19. He's the nicest person that you would ever meet. What he says he believes. He will never do anything that he is not convinced of. And he is one of the strongest people that I have ever met! He does not need to raise his voice. He does not need to show any anger. He is so clear in his thinking. And he speaks very little. He listens.'[50]

And the film brought back Salman's most affable avatar, Prem. Salman said, 'Sooraj wrote Prem. I play Prem in the movie. Now does Prem make us? Or did we make Prem? We don't know … There were a lot of people who have named their kids Prem. They did a contest recently, of how many Prems are there. And Jesus Christ, there are lots of Prems! That is what Sooraj Barjatya has done.'[51]

The film had Salman star alongside Sonam Kapoor. How do you star opposite your favourite without being a bundle of nerves? While Sonam had started her career with Salman in Sanjay Leela Bhansali's *Saawariya* (2007), during an interview for *Prem Ratan Dhan Payo* she said, 'I was very nervous. It's not easy working with someone who you've been a huge fan of. Also it's not easy because before Salman, I had never worked with a big star like him before. It's usually been contemporaries. I was nervous but he really made me feel comfortable. The best thing about him professionally is that he is the most hardworking actor that I worked with, he pushes himself and he is extremely talented. He's also very modest. Also, professionally it's easier to work with someone who doesn't judge you in any way. I remember when I was messing up he'd come and tell me really nicely, he has a lot of patience,' she added.[52]

Actor Swara Bhasker played Salman's sister in the film. I remember her telling me during the press meet how she had to shed all her cynicism for a Sooraj Barjatya film. But having Salman on the set helped her. In an interview she said, 'He is India's biggest superstar but he is a very generous person. His spirit of generosity is something I would want to imbibe as a person. On the first day of the shoot, I was very nervous. We shot our last scene first and he saw and understood that I was nervous. He made me feel comfortable … He was sweet to me.'[53]

Prem Ratan Dhan Payo enjoyed one of the biggest festive openings of all time, collecting over Rs 40 crore on its first day and setting a new

Diwali record. Despite mixed reviews, the film sustained well with family audiences and went on to become one of the highest-grossing films of 2015. Globally, its box office crossed Rs 400 crore, cementing it as a blockbuster powered by Salman's reprisal of his much-loved on-screen persona, Prem. But Sooraj didn't think the film was his best. In an interview he said, 'I went to him (Salman Khan) with the first version of *Prem Ratan Dhan Payo*. We are at a stage where we can see through each other. He heard it and said, "Sooraj babu, why are we complicating it?" I reasoned, "Salman bhai, your image is so big." He replied, "*Kaayka* image?" He insisted that we should keep it simple. Yet, I put some action into it as I also wanted to serve his audience *(laughs)*. I tried to play a little safe. Whenever I have played safe, I have always (faltered). I realized I added action just for the sake of (pleasing his audience). I feel I should have not done it.'[54]

'It's the biggest character I have played. I had to put in a lot of hard work. My earlier films like *Kick, Dabangg and Ready,* to name a few, were all chalta purza (mediocre) characters. *Bajrangi Bhaijaan* will bring back the innocence that I had in *Maine Pyar Kiya* ... Humari zindagi main kabhi kabhi aisa hota hai ki koi chehra baar baar dekhne ka mann karta hai ... That's the same quality *Bajrangi Bhaijaan* has. I am sure people will come and watch the film again and again.'

Yes, the film did immensely well, but it also set another standard. For years, Diwali had been Shah Rukh's festival. From *Dil To Pagal Hai* and *Veer-Zaara* to *Om Shanti Om* and *Happy New Year*, he had built a tradition of delivering blockbusters during the season of lights, just as Aamir Khan had reserved Christmas for his releases, and Salman Khan had made Eid his own. But that Diwali, it wasn't Shah Rukh but Salman who lit up the screens. Shah Rukh, instead of occupying his usual holiday slot, held back for a December release with *Dilwale* (2015), while also shooting *Fan* (2016) and *Raees* (2017).

At the same time, Aamir, who had smashed every record the previous Christmas with *PK* (2014), was absent from theatres altogether, undergoing his dramatic transformation for *Dangal* (2016). Salman not only owned Eid with *Bajrangi Bhaijaan* earlier in the year, but also claimed Diwali with *Prem Ratan Dhan Payo*. The calendar that had once been divided neatly among the three Khans now seemed to tilt in Salman's favour. In 2015, he had seized the box office and shut down his critics. What else was left to do? Perhaps show everyone why he was the Sultan of Bollywood?

Few images in modern Indian cinema have been dissected as endlessly as Salman Khan taking his shirt off. What began as a spontaneous, mischievous act in the early 1990s has crystallized into one of Bollywood's most recognizable visuals. It is a moment audiences wait for in every Bhai film. Entire chapters of biographies and studies of his stardom have been devoted to it; many parts of this book, too, circle around to his bare torso. Countless newspaper features and glossy magazine spreads have tried to decode why fans go delirious at the sight of him ripping off his shirt. And in the age of social media, the tradition has only found fresh takers—Instagram is flooded with carousels celebrating 'shirtless Salman through the years', showing a body that has itself become an evolving symbol of popular culture.

With *Sultan* (2016), Ali Abbas Zafar found a way to build that symbol naturally into the story, giving the star's admirers exactly what they wanted. 'I have ensured that he not only takes off his shirt but also pants,' he had said famously in an interview.[55] And despite that, his bare body was not the centre piece of *Sultan*. If Kabir Khan gave Salman an image makeover, Ali Abbas Zafar made him breathe fire. Of course, his leading man was reduced to tears at the thought of wearing a langot [a small loincloth worn by wrestlers] for the role of a wrestler in the 2016 blockbuster. Salman said in an interview, 'The most difficult part was the langot. Now I understand what the actress goes through when they wear [a] swimsuit. When I was told I have to wear a langot, I thought "I can do that". When I reached there, we saw like a 5,000 [person] crowd and I was like "no way I am doing this". While I was walking out of the vanity van, I was in tears ...

I feel violated. I was never ashamed while removing my shirt but this was the most difficult thing and thank God, people got used to it.'[56]

It was because of his ultimate love for movies that he put himself through this grind in *Sultan*. Or perhaps it was his gift to himself for his grand fiftieth.

Zafar says the idea came to him while watching wrestler Sushil Kumar at the London 2012 Olympics. A post-match comment made him see the makings of a great story in an Indian sport. He started with drafting about ten pages in 2012 and took it to producer Aditya Chopra, with whom he had made *Mere Brother Ki Dulhan* in 2011. He even travelled through Haryana to study akhadas and the milieu he wanted to portray so he could make sure the ten-page document was packed with the flavour of the story he wanted to tell.

When producer Aditya Chopra asked Zafar whom he had in mind for the lead, the director had a ready reply: Salman Khan. For him, Sultan's journey mirrored Khan's own, marked by dramatic highs and lows. 'Had he not agreed to do the film, it would not have been made. Actually, there are some movies for which you want a particular actor for the character. So we narrated the story to Salman first and then wrote the script,' Zafar told me on a call.

'Wrestling is not a sport. It's about fighting what lies within …' read the film's announcement teaser. This film also marked Salman's return to Yash Raj Films after *Ek Tha Tiger*. Salman played the titular character of Sultan, a forty-year-old wrestler from Haryana, even as Aamir Khan simultaneously transformed himself for Nitesh Tiwari's *Dangal*, inspired by the real-life story of Mahavir Singh Phogat. Many months later, when Salman watched Aamir's film, he bantered on X, 'My Family saw #Dangal today evening and thought it was a much better film than #Sultan. Love u personally Aamir but hate u professionally!'[57]

Zafar was undeterred by the similarities, because for him *Sultan* was a love story in the garb of a film on wrestling. In one of the early interviews after the film's success, Zafar reflected on the rigour it takes to make good commercial fare. He said, 'When you make a mainstream commercial film you are already dealing with a lot of internal conflict as a film-maker. You need to hold your voice yet cater to the last man standing at the ticket window, from prime multiplexes to small single-screens in villages. You kind of creatively question the intellect of such a wide span of audience. At times you have to use clichés and gimmicks. All universal emotions have been done to death, what new ways can be used to tell the same old story?'[58]

Sultan is the story of a man who rises too quickly, falls hard and then finds the courage to begin afresh. Sultan Ali Khan, a wrestler from Haryana, becomes a national hero but loses his way in the ensuing fame and arrogance, which costs him both the love of his life and his purpose. Years later, overweight and broken, he drags himself into the punishing world of mixed martial arts, a sport he doesn't fully understand, just to redeem himself. What makes the film tick isn't only the fighting sequences/scenes, but the idea of second chances—watching a flawed man stumble, bleed and slowly earn back his dignity. Zafar believed this was the story of Salman too, and Sultan's triumph reflected the actor's own. There is a scene where a heavily pot-bellied Salman stands in front of the mirror, stares at himself in disbelief, devastated at what he has become. He weeps helplessly before picking himself up and going back for one last fight, but by the time it ends, his opponent lies lifeless. '*Maine pehelwani zaroor chhodi hai, par ladna nahi bhula* [I may have given up wrestling, but I haven't forgotten how to fight],' Salman tells his coach, eyes shining with that red-hot intensity we know so well. What follows is a rousing training montage of the character rising, fighting and training to reclaim his position as the Sultan he is!

The real challenge of the film was the brisk age jumps the film took its characters on. Salman, then fifty, took it upon himself to play a character who was thirty for a large part of the film and then forty for the rest. In a later interview, Salman tackled the biggest criticism of age that the film faced. '*Sultan* was painful. I had to lose 18 kilos of muscle. I'm not into diets. I eat *ghar ka khana*. And I don't eat for taste. As soon as I've got my proteins and carbs, I leave the table. So, to lose 18 kilos of muscle was the most difficult thing on the earth. But I've always believed that hard work should be seen on-screen. And that's what I've been doing from *Wanted* to *Sultan*. I don't see myself doing character roles. So what if I'm 51? Stallone is still Rocky and Rambo at 70. Film-making is the most beautiful industry. We sell dreams. Why shouldn't I live mine?'[59]

This was, of course, a far more coherent use of words after he was cited saying that the training made him feel like 'a raped woman', which landed him in hot water.[60] When the National Commission for Women sought the actor's public apology, his father Salim Khan, tweeted, 'Undoubtedly what Salman said is wrong. The intention was not wrong. Nevertheless I apologise on behalf of his family, his fans & his friends.'[61] The matter was finally forgiven and forgotten when people saw the film.

We let too many of Salman's slip-ups pass, don't we? Every fan of his I have interviewed for the book, across age groups, geographical locations and classes, has tried to convince me that this man is too precious to be cancelled. I am guessing if you are reading this, and have got till here, you somewhere are in agreement with that idea.

Sultan was released on the Eid after Salman's fiftieth birthday. Along with being an instant hit with fans, it was also a smooth reminder that superstars didn't get to relax with age. Whether a film soared or sunk, they couldn't afford to go soft, because the weight of expectation never let them. By fifty, Salman was proving that point better than anyone. The old joke that his films required you to 'leave your brain at home' no longer applied. He was bending the masala form to his will, making films that hit the heart as hard as they thrilled the senses. Watching Salman in this phase meant using every part of yourself—your laughter, your tears, your memory and, yes, your mind too.

Zafar said in an interview, '*Sultan* is probably the toughest role he has played—both emotionally and physically. It is a very demanding character. One of the reasons Salman agreed to do *Sultan* was to challenge himself as an actor, to see whether he can pull it off. When I narrated the script to Salim Uncle, the first thing he told Adi (film-maker Aditya Chopra) during dinner was—*Is mein Salman ko bahut mehat karni padegi* [Salman will need to slog for this one].'[62]

In the decade before his reboot, Salman was sleepwalking through his roles, and that was no surprise, but by the mid-2010s one could see how Salman had put himself back together. He had the drive to better his best, stay committed to his characters—from changing his hairstyle and putting on weight to learning Haryanvi, he was willing to do whatever it took to deliver a memorable film. 'There were days he was bruised and battered and he'd say I'm going to shoot. His doctor would call me and say "Don't shoot with him, he is not in a good condition, just give him rest". But Salman wanted to shoot. This is what actors live for. This is the kick. My respect for him as an actor and human being is great,' Zafar said.[63]

The film-maker told me during a chat that he built *Sultan* on a contrast that felt both Indian and global at the same time. On the one hand you had kushti, with its mythological lineage going back to Mahabharata's Bheem and the earthy akhada identity, and on the other you had mixed martial arts, a violent but thrilling international format that spoke to modern audiences. The film's story came out of that clash—a small-town pehelwan trying to hold his own inside a cage that was nothing like the dusty pits of Haryana he had trained in. As someone who grew up on sports dramas, from *Rocky* (1976) and *Raging Bull* (1980) to *Lagaan* and *Jo Jeeta Wohi Sikandar* (1992), his primary motivation was to deliver a high. 'Sports films give you a particular kind of feeling, the underdog climbing a mountain in real time and the same feeling Indians had when Dhoni's six won us the World Cup,' he said. That was the energy he wanted *Sultan* to deliver.[64]

For this film to have the right punch, it needed a leading lady who would evoke the rage and persistence in Sultan that the story needed. If the love story didn't work, the rest of it wouldn't either. Zafar knew that right at the start of the project. The film was to earlier star Deepika Padukone, but after a series of scheduling conflicts, Anushka Sharma stepped in to play the female lead, who came out strong in the film despite it being a Salman show. Sultan's journey is through Aarfa, and thus Zafar needed an actress who would be able to hold her own in front of Salman. While their twenty-three-year age gap was a subject of debate, not once did we feel the chemistry lack.

In *Sultan*, Salman played a Muslim man, but his religious identity was never underlined. In an interview with author and journalist Anna M.M. Vetticad, Zafar said, 'In every film you will see some side of that film-maker as a person, and my understanding of being a Muslim in India is replicated in *Sultan*. The idea of religion not being an overbearing force in the text came effortlessly because it doesn't matter whether Sultan is Hindu, Muslim, Christian, Sikh—the film is not about that. Tomorrow if I'm making a film about that issue then definitely that part would be highlighted, but this story was something else. When a person tells you "Ram Ram", you don't say "Salaam alaikum", you say "Ram Ram". So that was a very conscious idea. I've not had Rooh Afza in every Muslim home I've visited. I've not seen every Muslim wearing kaajal.'[65]

For him, it was a film about a man rising from the ashes after having been beaten to the ground and losing everything—and who better than Salman to portray that? There isn't another Bollywood superstar who has been razed to the ground that many times, and yet Salman is made of something else. And like Sultan, he will always return with unputdownable gusto!

When the film arrived in theatres, it was clear that Salman had another juggernaut on his hands. The film stormed into the record books with an opening that crossed Rs 200 crore in just three days, something no Indian film had managed before that. By the end of its extended first weekend, the figure had already touched the Rs 300 crore mark, setting a new benchmark even in an industry used to Salman's festive dominance. Eventually, the film wrapped up with more than Rs 420 crore in India alone, and close to Rs 600 crore worldwide before its release in China. With the China run added, Sultan went past Rs 620 crore.[66]

What made these numbers remarkable was not just their size but their consistency: In territories as far-flung as the Gulf, the UK, Pakistan and North America (the US and Canada combined), *Sultan* drew packed houses. For weeks, it was second only to *Bajrangi Bhaijaan*, proving that Salman's superstardom was not tied to one genre or formula. If *Bajrangi Bhaijaan* was the tender, cross-border tale that softened his image, *Sultan* was the bruising sports drama that showed him reinventing himself at fifty, with box office thunder to match. And Salman basked in the love he received. 'I learned that my fans should see my hard work, the sweat and blood that I put into my movies, and that they should enjoy my pain. Then only would they invest that love and money into me. It's simple logic. But hard work has to be in the right direction. Otherwise it's pointless. It's like you want to be an actor and are working hard at cooking! You work hard at your craft, at your acting skills, dancing and action, you work hard at meeting the right people and getting the correct script,' he said.[67]

The hard work was softening the toughest of people. An otherwise 'hard to impress' film critic and author Shubhra Gupta wrote in her review, 'Salman Khan cracks and bleeds in his most real performance. It has him breaking free from Bhai-giri bondage by getting his character to crack and bleed. His down-and-out wrestler has foibles, is fallible, is human. Sultan Ali Khan has faults, and is punished for it. Because of which *Sultan* scores, and delivers a solid entertainer with heft.'[68]

Many of his fans believed it was Salman breaking the barriers that had held him back all his life—he was finally free and accepted for who he was.

Shazeb Khan, a construction agent who lives in Muscat, Oman, tells me that he flew down to Mumbai to celebrate Salman's birthday that year with his cousins. He and his boys drove down to cut a cake in front of Galaxy Apartments at midnight. Shazeb told me, 'We as fans have seen him stumble through controversies, court cases, endless headlines that called him finished and useless, called him a man who couldn't act. Every so-called critic had written him off. But standing tall as a fiftysomething, with *Bajrangi Bhaijaan* and *Sultan* behind him, Salman made us proud. We have seen the whole journey—the heartbreaks, the failures—and never stopped believing that he was the Sultan of our hearts. That night, it felt like all of us were

For Ali Abbas Zafar, *Sultan* was a film about a man rising from the ashes after having been beaten to the ground—and who better than Salman to portray that? There isn't another Bollywood superstar who has been razed to the ground that many times, and yet Salman is made of something else. And like Sultan, he will always return with unputdownable gusto!

celebrating too, because his victories were ours. People said he was just muscle and swagger, but in those films he showed heart, vulnerability and soul. And to anyone who still doubts him, buzz off. Because when Salman is in his element, he is untouchable. No one comes close—not in box office collections, not in charisma, not in the way he makes you feel. Salman Khan has it all, and for those of us who have loved him from the start, this feels like the sweetest vindication.'

Like always, Salman partied with his friends at his farmhouse on his grand fiftieth. Not one to shy away from ageing, he was certain of just one thing: He didn't want to lose his childlike glee. He said in an interview, 'I am turning 27. I think 27-year-old is the right age. I have always liked that age. I am not scared about ageing. It is always going to be 27. So what is there to be scared of?'[69]

Sultan was the perfect film to herald in a new decade for Salman. For a long time, everyone around him—his peers, film-makers, trade, the press—had said, not incorrectly, that his success was due to his stardom. But that impression lay dismantled after *Sultan*. The film was Salman's own reflection that a battle was fought as much in the ring as within oneself. At an age when most stars begin to settle or even fade, he chose to bleed, stumble, break his body, rebuild it into the physique of a champion and rise again in front of millions. As Salman says in the film, '*Asli pehelwan ki pehchaan akhade mein nahi, zindagi mein hove hai … taki jab zindagi tumhe patke toh tum phir khade ho … aur aaisa daanv maro ki zindagi chitt ho jaye* [The mark of a true wrestler is not in the pit, it's in life … so every time life throws you down, you get up again … and punch back so hard that life is the one that lies buried in the ground].'

Sultan was never just another sports drama or a box office juggernaut. It was the story of a man reborn from his own ruins, to win back his love—for his wife, the sport he denounced and for himself. With *Sultan*, Salman Khan the myth and the man converged. And that's why every time someone declares he's finished, I smile and say: This is Salman. He'll rise again from the ashes, fists flying, swagger intact, because he knows his fans will always be waiting.

Epilogue

WHILE I was writing this, I saw Salman shrug off talk of legacy on a chat show. He said, 'What have we done? *Shooting pe jatey hai, thodi average, mediocre acting karke ghar chale aatey hai ... Phir wapas koi badi picture mil jati hai toh wapas uss muqam pe pahuch jatey hai* [What have we done? We go for a shoot, do some average, mediocre acting ... and then come back home ... Then if we land a big film again, we go back to that same status all over again].'[1] Unlike great artistes such as Dilip Kumar, whose craft became his legacy, or Amitabh Bachchan, whose ability to shake the system as the Angry Young Man became his legacy, Salman Khan's legacy does not lie in his roles. It springs from the man he is. He is Bhai, who belongs to everyone. His myth is sustained less by the films and more by who he is and what he stands for. His philanthropic persona flows into his star persona. For millions of fans, Salman is not only the muscular hero who defeats villains, but also the older brother who protects and provides. The generosity that many people who know Salman claim to have been witness to softens his image and redeems him to a large extent. To many he is the man with a big heart who helps strugglers and co-stars alike.

Salman represents the fantasy of a flawed but fundamentally good-at-heart, kind brother, who is seen as the protector of the masses.

Where others will be remembered for the characters they played, Salman will be remembered for being Salman. In him, stardom inverts itself—the art seems to be merely incidental.

In one of his most memorable discussions about legacy, Salman said, 'I don't want to be remembered. I just hope that Being Human continues even after our names are gone as actors. Even if they say that some actor started the charitable trust ... [W]e can help as many people as possible ...'[2] Back in 2007, when Salman registered the Being Human—The Salman Khan Foundation, it didn't come out of a corporate brainstorming session, I am told. By then, Salman had already been known for quietly picking up hospital bills or helping out kids who couldn't afford school. His family says it is second nature for him. Having grown up seeing his father Salim and mother Salma always open their doors to people in need, Salman imbibed those values. What changed in 2007 was just the scale of it. Requests had grown, and Salman needed structure. That's how Being Human was born. It was an extension of his own instinct to give back to the world. Salim and Salma have always had an open house policy. Anyone can walk in, have a meal and feel safe in the confines of their home. Talking about it in an early interview, Salman said, 'The concept of Being Human came to me from my parents, who have always been active in charity. But the flip side to charity is that you are not sure that the money you are giving is going to the right person. My parents and even I have been conned several times, and that hurts. I decided to channelize giving. I have made sure that I don't give to individuals. I only give to institutions, which gives me complete accountability of where my money is being spent.'[3]

The foundation began with eye camps and women's health drives. In 2013, he launched the Little Hearts Programme with Fortis Foundation, focused on surgeries for children born with congenital heart defects. By 2015, nearly 850 children had been operated on, their lives rewritten in OTs that most of their families could never have afforded. Singer Palak Muchhal, who funds heart surgeries for underprivileged children through her charity initiative the Palak Muchhal Heart Foundation, with earnings from her concerts, spoke about Salman's help for children with heart disorders. In an interview she said, 'Salman Khan has been one of the biggest supporters I have had in Mumbai. He made me meet so many important people. He introduced me to a lot of people, recommended my name to so many of them, contributed to my mission also, and sponsored 100 surgeries.'[4]

What proved to be a game changer for Being Human was when Salman decided the foundation shouldn't survive on donations alone. The model had to be able to fund itself. Most of Salman's own income, too, is directed at funding the foundation, but that wasn't enough. He wanted fans to feel involved with the work he was doing. That's how the Being Human clothing line took off. The foundation partnered with schools and NGOs to sponsor children, set up career centres and even launched Project Veer, which has since trained thousands of differently abled young people for jobs. Every store was encouraged to hire at least one differently abled staff member. Over time, the brand has grown into something that doesn't need Salman's face on every poster.

But beyond the facts and figures, let's have an honest conversation about Being Human. What made Salman really do it? In his own words, he wanted to make it really difficult for actors to do the bare minimum. Charity for him isn't lip service. He wanted the stars, who benefit incredibly from the love of the masses, to hold themselves to higher standards and work to create palpable change in the lives of the people who love them so much. Salman said, 'Stardom comes every three years and anyone can beat anyone in this. I think till the time fame is there work is there ... till the time work is there money is there, and till that time Being Human is there. My mission is to take Being Human to a different level and I am struggling very hard for it. I have never worked so hard in life. For Being Human we are trying to get things right like CSR, etc. I want to take it to such a level that it becomes difficult for anyone to reach that success or reach the magnitude of a charitable trust. I want all of them to start their own charitable trust and beat me in this, destroy me at what I do with Being Human. I will be happy when they beat me in being human ...'[5]

For many who are disdainful of Salman and his ways—and there are plenty of them—Being Human is seen as a carefully constructed effort to absolve India's biggest superstars of his misdeeds. For Salman's fans, the brand is an extension of what Salman stands for. His fans see it as proof of his large-heartedness.

I have often seen this split in the press, where any act of generosity could be framed either as instinct or as image management. One of the sharpest examples of this came in Meena Iyer's column in *The Times of India* while Salman was being tried in the hit-and-run case. Iyer wrote, 'In 2007, the world noticed how the Bollywood actor—who was always the Khan family's most responsible member and biggest benefactor—opened his arms to embrace outsiders as well. In his new avatar as Robin Hood, he floated an NGO, Being Human, his own brainchild ... Always willing to lend an ear to someone needy, Salman became popular as "bhai" (big brother) and has made an immense contribution to saving ailing children and the downtrodden. It is estimated that in the last eight years since his NGO was floated, Salman has done charity to the tune of approximately Rs 43 crore.'[6]

When I first read the column, the day after Salman was granted bail in the hit-and-run case by the Mumbai sessions court, it unsettled me. Iyer wrote of Salman as a chastened man who had opened his arms wider than ever before, embracing everyone in need, while the question younger journalists were asking was: Isn't this how public memory gets rewritten?

As I spent more years in the industry and met more people, I began to see things differently and understood what Iyer really meant: Salman's generosity wasn't a product of Being Human—rather, the NGO grew out of a quality that had been part of him from the start. One of his co-stars, Ayesha Jhulka, recalled how, after late-night shoots of *Kurbaan* (1991), he would pack leftover food and go feed people long before charity became a formal institution for him. She said, 'I'm very fond of Salman, because he is a great human being. I remember back then, whenever we used to finish the shoot and we were going back home, I would see him packing the food that was left over. He would make an effort to find a beggar, even if it was late at night, (and they were) sleeping on the road, then waking the beggar up. Or somebody was really needy of food, and actually making an effort, stepping out of his car and giving that food.'[7]

Around his farmhouse in Panvel he provides for thousands of struggling families, taking care of their daily needs. On Eid, he sends out help so that even the poorest households can celebrate. Over the years, his reach has stretched far wider—helping fund life-saving surgeries for children, supporting ailing actors with hospital bills, even working to give thalassaemia patients a second chance at life. Perhaps most moving is how he secured the release of more than 400 prisoners who had finished their jail terms but were still languishing behind bars because they couldn't afford to pay their fines. For many families, Salman was the miracle they never imagined would arrive.[8]

My first-hand experience with Being Human happened during Covid. With shoots stalled, the daily wage workers of the film industry were left at the mercy of the biggest studios in town. And it is the only time I remember this dog-eat-dog industry standing together. Every studio, every star donated generously. But on the ground it wasn't so simple. With the layers of middlemen, and the chaos of distributing aid, not every worker saw the money that was promised. It was around that time that Salman's team reached out and took the bank details of over 25,000 workers. One by one, the accounts were verified and money started flowing in, month after month until the situation stabilized.[9]

In the homes of thousands of junior artistes, there was finally some steady income. One of them was Jaano Begum. She told me, 'I have been a junior artiste for more than twenty-five years now. When the pandemic hit, our world changed overnight. We live day to day. In those months, my children would ask me, "*Ammi, khana kab ayega* [Mother, when will we eat]?" And I had no answer. There were days we used fermented rice water because we didn't have enough. The biggest fear was that if someone fell sick, we would not survive. I think word reached Bhaijaan. It felt as if we had an elder brother looking after us when the world had abandoned us. Bhaijaan held us through it all.'

Jaano Begum is one of the many who feel that philanthropy is the foundation on which the aura of Salman Khan is built. The memory of help arriving at the right time because of him makes him invincible to his fans. For those who have lived and felt it, Salman is not an untouchable star but the man who remembered them when the world forgot.

Durgesh Bir, a junior artiste from Madh, told me, 'There is a day of the week when you can walk into Being Human's office with your medical reports requesting for aid. If you are in need, they will help. They will arrange for doctors, and send you to the right people. There are no strong unions here in Bollywood. We are an unorganized industry and most employed here are freelancers and daily wagers. We have little job security and even fewer avenues for help. But if we are in dire need of medical help, Being Human is there for us.'

Every time a Salman film doesn't work, which lately has been quite frequently, I read about trade mourning the loss of their biggest revenue generator and naysayers saying the era of Salman's stardom is over. But Salman can survive films such as *Race 3*, *Radhe*, *Kisi Ka Bhai Kisi Ki Jaan* or even his latest underperformer, *Sikandar*. That's because his legacy does not rest on the mediocrity or the brilliance of scripts.

My friend and photographer Prathamesh Bandekar, who has spent a lifetime shooting celebrities, describes Salman rather cinematically. 'You know Salman is around when an entire sea of people come to say hello. His entry can multiply a crowd from 10 to 100 within seconds. And what's beautiful about him is that he is unfazed by crowds. He is calm even in the most mad crowds. If you notice, people never pounce on him the way they do with other stars. They want to say hello to him. Say "*Salaam Bhai, ghar pe sab theek? Aapke liye dua kartey hai* [We hope all well at home. We pray for your well-being]. Because, for Salman, his fans are like his family, and people think of him as one of their own. He is so casual about who he is that people gravitate to that energy—like a man who knows he rules the jungle!'

It is evident from the fact that a few months after dissing *Sikandar*, people have now huddled up in their living rooms to watch Salman schooling contestants on *Bigg Boss* during the weekend episodes.

But there's a flip side. When folklore begins to overshadow filmography, it can also breed complacency. A star who knows that audiences will forgive bad films no longer feels the urgency to chase excellence.

The irony is that Salman did try to step away from this comfort zone several times, most noticeably with *Tubelight* (2017) in recent years. For the first time in a while, he deviated from playing his 'type'—not the invincible larger-than-life hero but a vulnerable, almost child-like man grappling with faith and loss. It was a role that demanded restraint and innocence. But the audience, conditioned to see him as Bhai, rejected it. *Tubelight* underperformed at the box office and critics dismissed it as Salman's weakest outing in a decade.

That failure seemed to scar him. Rather than persist with experimentation, he retreated to what was safe—formulaic actioners, masala entertainers and films designed to deliver opening-day euphoria even if they collapsed in the days after. Trade observer and Salman fan Mujahir Khan, whom I connected with on X, told me, 'The problem for a megastar such as Salman is that he has an image that is larger than life, which has mass appeal. The youth and the mass audience can never accept Salman in a content-driven role. They see Salman as a "mass hero". That's why when he tried films such as *Tubelight* and *Kyon Ki* ..., they didn't succeed. Which led to him playing the same massy roles again and again.'

If I comment purely as a fan, I suppose the last enjoyable Salman film for me was *Tiger Zinda Hai*, which was back in 2017. On the canvas laid out by Kabir Khan, Ali Abbas Zafar built a grander movie. It starts with one of my favourite Salman entry sequences—him and his son escaping a pack of wild wolves in the Swiss Alps. Salman announces right at the start, '*Shikaar toh sab karte hai, lekin Tiger se behtar shikaar koi nahi karta* [Everybody hunts, but no one hunts better than Tiger].' Much like the first part of the film, *Tiger Zinda Hai* holds on to its messaging of peace and kindness. Tiger, now married to Zoya, goes on a joint mission with Pakistan's ISI to save Indian and Pakistani nurses in Syria. The banter in the film is heartwarming. Kumud Mishra, who plays a R&AW agent, tells fellow officers, '*Agar batware ki line nahin khichi hoti toh Akram aur Sachin ek hi team se kheltey. Aur saare World Cup humare hotey* [If the line of Partition hadn't been drawn, Akram and Sachin would have played for the same team and all the World Cups would have been ours].' The conversation leads to bickering, as is common between Indians and Pakistanis while discussing cricket. Salman as Tiger gets the best line in the film: '*Iss duniya ki shuruvat insaaniyat se hui hai ... aur aaj iss duniya ko sirf ek hi mazhab ki zaroorat hai ... aur woh hai insaaniyat* [This world began with humanity... and today, the only religion this world needs is humanity].' It's almost derived from Salman's own words from 2017: 'My dad is a Muslim, my mother is a Hindu and I call myself insaan [human].'[10]

Director Ali Abbas Zafar says the fans love both the action junkie side of him and the naive optimist he is. He told me, 'When I took on the film, there was a spy who does his duty for his country but falls in love with an enemy. In the second part, he's brought on to a mission, and on that mission he proves that he is very much alive and out there for his country. So the love which the country felt was very much there and while they felt he betrayed the country, he ultimately shows that for him the nation will always come before love. And that is what soldiers and spies are all about. The best part of that film was that it didn't propagate hate—it propagated that humanity is above all. A soldier doesn't fire to kill; he has to fire to save his country. And every bullet that should be fired should, in the end, bring peace. In some way or the other, all these thoughts came together to create a hostage drama and to create a film which is an edge-of-the-seat thriller. Somewhere

Salman as Tiger gets the best line in the film: '*Iss duniya ki shuruvat insaaniyat se hui hai ... aur aaj iss duniya ko sirf ek hi mazhab ki zaroorat hai ... aur woh hai insaaniyat* [This world began with humanity… and today, the only religion this world needs is humanity].' It's almost derived from Salman's own words from 2017: 'My dad is a Muslim, my mother is a Hindu and I call myself *insaan* [human].'

along the way, we need to tell these stories without making them preachy but finding the human element in it. At its heart, the real problem is terrorism, not differences in belief. Two individuals can have completely different philosophies and still sit down to talk and debate and that's healthy. But the moment you turn to violence, to threats, to creating terror, that's where it becomes wrong. And we need to stand firmly against that.'

I tell Zafar why I was drawn to his film so deeply. As someone who has been covering the cultural ties between India and Pakistan since 2014, when Zee Studios launched the Zee Zindagi channel and brought Pakistani dramas into Indian living rooms, the film introduced me to the biggest Salman fan I know.

My special connection with *Tiger Zinda Hai* is because of him. This young man showed me how far someone would go to watch their favourite star on the big screen. In 2018, from a well-known indie film-maker I heard the story of a man in Lahore who had hosted a private screening of *Tiger Zinda Hai*, which was banned in Pakistan.

I spent several hours trying to track him down. Starting with a Facebook message, hitting up common friends, finding his contact through fan clubs, I tried it all. It was well past midnight several days later that I got a reply from him, and we decided to get on a call. My first question to him was, 'Aren't you scared?' He retorted with, 'Aren't you scared calling an unknown Pakistani man at 12.30 a.m.?' We were both petrified. But we both loved Salman more.

Over the next few minutes, he narrated how he had paid a large sum of money to procure the HD print of the film from a distributor in Dubai. He had brought it back to Pakistan to host a movie night for his Amma. Though he never disclosed the exact amount, I gauged it had cost him as much as a new car would have. The fan screening, which was initially to be hosted for the family, was eventually attended by 150 people, including some of their top television stars. When the home theatre couldn't accommodate that many people, they booked a whole theatre and informed fans in the city to drop by for the film as long as they kept it quiet. It was free for everyone. 'My treat on behalf of Bhaijaan,' he told me.

Yes, I had the same question that must have just cropped up in your mind: Why would anyone illegally procure a film and then show it to 150 strangers in a theatre? It was risky and if someone from India, like me, could trace it back to him, the Pakistani authorities definitely could. He laughed when I asked him that. 'You know how much I love Salman Bhai. *Unke liye jaan qurbaan hai* [I would sacrifice my life for him].'

There was no remorse in his voice. The film was called out by the Pakistani censor board for showing the country's law-enforcement agencies in a demeaning light. But this man was just too much in love with the movie to care. '*Masla yeh hai ki humari hukumatein ladti rehti hai, aur sabse pehle picturein rukwati hai* [The problem is that our governments keep fighting and the first thing they stop are the films].'

The film screening was a major hit. Reliving the overwhelming feeling of joy, he told me, 'I wish you were there to see how we were cheering and hooting for Bhai. In the last scene, when a Pakistani soldier waves the Indian flag, we all cried. We endorse the idea of brotherhood that it promotes.'

I wrote a piece about him that appeared the next day. Fan clubs celebrated the unnamed hero's bravado for weeks after that. Salman's father, Salim Khan, told me, 'It's a wonderful gesture. I feel films from India should be allowed to be released in Pakistan, and their films should be allowed to screen here. That will happen only once the situation between the two countries improves.'[11]

In the years that followed, Salman's releases came and went but none of them carried the charge to inspire fans to risk everything just to catch a glimpse of it.

The trouble with Salman's cinema today is not fatigue of the star, but fatigue of the legend. Every enduring superstar in Indian cinema has periodically reinvented the grammar of their stardom, in sync with the times. Salman, however, has allowed his myth to calcify. And now even his fans have begun to notice and call it out. After *Sikandar* didn't fare as well as it should have, for the first time his fans grouped up to go meet him at his home. As per a news report, 'Instead of defending Salman's choices (after *Sikandar*), his huge fan base began voicing their displeasure about it and Salman Khan's recent choice of films. They began making various trends on X (formerly Twitter), hoping that Salman Khan would pay attention to them. And as luck would have it, Salman Khan found out about the fans' woes. A meeting took place yesterday, on April 5, where some fans were able to meet the superstar. Salman was moved by the love and care from his fans. He confessed that from the nascent stage, he felt something was off about *Sikandar* and that it was not the way a big film should be made. However, he promised that he would now do films that would make his fans happy. The fans requested Salman Khan to do films with credible directors like Kabir Khan and Ali Abbas Zafar, who have given blockbusters to Salman in the past and with whom the star has a very good bond. Salman Khan promised to take all these aspects into consideration. The meeting lasted for an hour. It's unprecedented to see a star of this stature meeting the fans in this manner and listening to their woes.'[12]

Today's viewers, especially the younger ones, expect complexity—they consume anti-heroes on OTTs and morally conflicted protagonists in global cinema. Salman, instead of leaning into his own fandom, is doubling down on one-dimensional celebrations of himself.

A fan, Urmi Bose, a homemaker based in Dhanbad, says a solid Salman film can do wonders for an industry standing on shaky ground. 'Salman's inherent honesty is no longer showing in his movies. But if there is a superstar who can still explode, it's Salman Khan. He needs to do films that show us this larger-than-life hero who is vulnerable, ageing or even confronting his own self. But he definitely needs a smarter film-maker who gets this. The audience isn't rejecting Salman—they are rejecting his pattern of repetition that lazy film-makers are trying. And that's exactly why people are even rejecting Bollywood at large nowadays.'

What makes Salman's complacency hit his fans harder is that he was once the most restless of his contemporaries. Unlike many stars who stuck to safe zones, he was always eager to work with new people and try new things. He is the only superstar of his generation who has genuinely diversified and succeeded across every genre. The machinery around him today no longer functions like a creative ecosystem. Films often begin not with a script but with a Salman-sized outline: Bhai as cop, Bhai as spy, Bhai as saviour. And the rest is reverse-engineered. But lamentably, the star who once embraced risk now seems ensconced in safety.

The loyalty for Salman is touching, but it also traps him in amber, denying us the actor who was once fearless. Like Katrina Kaif once said on *Koffee with Karan*, she would love to have Salman's fearlessness. 'He fears nothing and no one,' she said.[13] Have we trapped Salman in fear of failure, or a mould that's reducing him?

'Maybe you're asking the wrong question,' says Hasan Rizvi, a shop owner based in Karachi, who has followed Salman for over two decades.

'Cinema is supposed to surprise you, yes, but with Salman the surprise is irrelevant. We don't buy tickets to see what new thing he'll do, we buy them to feel the same rush again and again. I feel the rush just seeing him on the big screen.'

Isn't that limiting? He shuts me down, saying, 'He will take bigger risks, try newer things, because "*Tiger abhi Zinda hai, yaar*".'

Zafar told me that Salman is pushed by only one thing—the love of the people he works with. 'I feel that Salman Bhai loves to work hard with the people who love him and stand by him—whether it's a good day or a bad day. For him, the motivation has to come from within—from himself, from the film he's doing and from the people he's working with. The kind of hard work he put into *Sultan*, all of it came from him. Neither of us who was making the film inspired him to do something special—it all came from within. And that's why I keep saying he's such a rare phenomenon—when he leans into his craft, he can move a mountain without raising an eyebrow, because that's the kind of charisma he has. As a star and as an actor, I think he's a beautiful performer. In fact, I've felt this not only in *Sultan* but also in *Bharat*. A couple of things going up and down don't decide who you are or the kind of stardom you have. Also, it's not a risk-free business. Every time we set out to make a film, we want it to succeed. Sometimes destiny is with you and you make a blockbuster; sometimes it doesn't happen. But we put in the same hard work every single time. I just feel that what we did for *Sultan* was really special—and it all came from him. And it will happen again and again. This is Salman Khan we are talking about!'

What makes Salman's complacency hit his fans harder is that he was once the most restless of his contemporaries. Unlike many stars who stuck to safe zones, he was always eager to work with new people and try new things. He is the only superstar of his generation who has genuinely diversified and succeeded across every genre.

When I tell Dubai-based banking executive Immy Sheikh this, he retorts with, 'Is the love of fans not enough for him to give his all? Our love should make him want to chase grander things! We watch him because it is almost a habit now. His stardom alone is enough to keep us coming back, but is that enough for him? I miss him restless and raging. I want that spirit back in my Sultan.'

He says his first-day-first-show Bhaijaan ritual remains unaltered regardless of the quality of the films, but he is waiting for fireworks!

To get some female perspective for a thorough dissection of his current phase, I called Chitra Submanyam, book editor and a former journalist. She explains Salman's stardom is detached from his work. She feels his stardom remains unfazed because his duality is exciting to fans and his lack of pretence is the reason they value him more than any other star. Over a call, she tells me, 'My mom rolls her eyes every time Salman comes up in conversation. She finds him very problematic. Maybe that's why I was firmly Team Aamir throughout my teenage years. The first time I really noticed Salman was in *Phir Milenge*. And it struck me because it wasn't coloured by the usual Bhai impressions. He was so mainstream, yet he chose to do a film about AIDS when other stars wouldn't touch the subject. This duality in Salman has always fascinated me. On the one hand, he can do films that are socially interesting or risky, and on the other, he knows exactly how to cater to the masses. There's a strange honesty about him. If the audience wants him to strip on-screen, he'll do it. Unapologetically. If they want a larger-than-life hero, he'll give it to them. He's very blasé, almost like he's saying, "This is who I am—take it or leave it." Most actors try to appear nuanced or cool, but with Salman, what you see is what you get. And somehow, there's nuance in that lack of pretence. Salman always has this twinkle in his eye—even when he's being bad. And yes, he's hot. That whiplash between his flaws and his charm is part of the intrigue. At the end of the day, why do we watch Bollywood films? To be entertained. And Salman never disappoints me on that front. The script might be terrible, the film might collapse, but he is never bad. Even now, I could watch some of his films every single day and feel blown away every time. There aren't many actors I can say that about. When shit hits the fan, I won't put on an Aamir film, but I'll happily rewatch a Salman one. Because he enjoys himself—and isn't that the whole purpose of cinema, to pass on that joy? Yes, he's constantly in the news for the wrong reasons, and yes, there are plenty of contradictions in what we know about him, but that's part of why he's so intriguing. He embodies the messiness of art and the artist. Even when a film is bad—*Race 3* made me groan—I never walked out uncomfortable. A bad film with him is still watchable. And that, for me, is Salman's real charm. He has a hold on people that just doesn't go away.'

Listening to Chitra, I realized she wasn't just talking about Salman the star, but about the role cinema itself plays in our lives. For us, films shape how we dress, how we flirt, how we behave, even how we pray. Alisha Gour, a student in Berlin, tells me, 'We don't look at our stars and think, "Good acting." We look at them and think, "If only my son were like that." Or, "If only I could love like that." In a country where you can be sure of very few things, you can be sure that a Salman film will brighten up your mood. He makes clean films—there is never anything sensational or outrageous in his movies. It's for everyone. He is for everyone. In a country still learning to balance tradition and modernity, Salman reflects in the truest sense what India is all about—a little bit of this and a little bit of that.'

'Most actors try to appear nuanced or cool, but with Salman, what you see is what you get. And somehow, there's nuance in that lack of pretence. Salman always has this twinkle in his eye—even when he's being bad. And yes, he's hot. That whiplash between his flaws and his charm is part of the intrigue. At the end of the day, why do we watch Bollywood films? To be entertained. And Salman never disappoints me on that front.'

With Salman, the line between the man and the star is porous. He feels less like a celebrity and more like someone who has been living alongside us all these years. It's in the way his dialogues make their way into our lives, in how his swag gets picked up by boys in our neighbourhood alleys, in the way his songs make us bond with a fellow Indian in a foreign land, in how his fitness regimen becomes our reason to adopt a healthier lifestyle. He has also seeped into our everyday conversations. '*Zyada Salman mat ban* [Don't act like Salman]' is a fairly common way of trimming down someone's ego. In the West, they call a man handsome; in India we say,

'*Kya Salman lag raha hai* [You look as handsome as Salman].' When someone becomes a little too active in the gym, we tell them, '*Salman jaisi body bana raha hai* [You're building a body like Salman's].' Salman has crossed over from cinema into a common, everyday vocabulary.

In the month we wrapped up this book, Salman was busy shooting his new film, *The Battle of Galwan*. Everyone on social media is hailing the comeback of Bhaijaan. But lately, even he is beginning to acknowledge ageing. In an emotional episode of *Bigg Boss* this year, he said, '*Humare jitne din chale gaye hai, usse aage ke din bohot kam hai! Toh ab hume jitni kam neend aaye, hum jitna kaam kar sake, jitna aur naam kama sake, woh toh karenge hi ab na! Active hone ka bass ek hi ilaaj hai ki active raho* [The number of years we have lived is more than the number of years we have left to live. So now, the less we sleep and the more active we remain, the better for us. We will work more and establish ourselves more! The solution to being active is staying active],' he said.[14]

His words do make you think, don't they? He is a constant in a country that keeps changing too fast and too much, sometimes beyond recognition. We may grow older, our cities may change, our films may fade, but the moment Salman walks on-screen, something in us returns to who we were, to our happy place, in our favourite childhood memories.

We often ask why there isn't a new line of superstars, why today's actors don't seem to belong to the masses the way Salman Khan does. There is a beautiful Julianne Moore line that sums it up: 'The audience doesn't come to see you, they come to see themselves.' That is Salman's secret of success. When people watch him, they don't see a star, they see fragments of themselves—the swaggering youth, the ideal son, the flawed lover, the eternal kind-hearted man. At a recent event in Riyadh, Salman said, 'I was 13 or 14 when I went to see this film called *Enter the Dragon* (1973). When I came out of the theatre, I thought I was Bruce Lee. And I got beaten up! But due to the impact, I realized one thing that when you come out of a theatre, somebody should want a son like you. A mother or a father should want a son like you, a sister should want a brother like you, a girl should want a husband or boyfriend like you. When you come out of a theatre, you should go back home at least 20-25% a better person.

That is the character that is liked.'[15] He knows he isn't on a pedestal but that has never come in the way of him making his way into people's hearts.

Superstars such as him are born out of a very specific alchemy of time and culture. And it takes a rare person to embody it all. Salman arrived at a moment when cinema was still a community experience, when heroes belonged with us, when a dialogue could ripple through the smallest gullies of the country to the largest thoroughfares. That India has changed, and with it the grammar of stardom. Which is why there will never be another Salman Khan. Because the world that made him no longer exists.

But beyond blockbusters, songs or swagger, Salman stands for miracles, be it on the big screen or in real life. In a country still developing, caught between the aspiration to acquire the finesse of the West and the stubborn realities of a nation that is still grappling with basic issues, hope remains India's strongest drug. Salman fills that gap of hope—he offers an escape into an alternate reality where good men defeat bad men after a big fight sequence. Even in this age of OTT and low attention spans, when stars fade quickly, trends change incessantly and the movie industry reinvents itself every day, Salman remains a constant. Because more than a man on a screen, he is a feeling. A feeling that says no matter how difficult life gets, there will always be room for laughter, love and miracles. There will always be the movies!

Acknowledgements

'Bollywood is dying,' I am told quite frequently these days. Every visit to the cinema this year has made me miss the euphoria of Fridays, the chaos of trying to get tickets, the lengthy discussions after a movie and the promise of being swept away by the magic of the 70 mm experience. No one embodies that big-screen feeling quite like Salman Khan. The collective joy of watching him take down the bad guys is unmatched. My friend Raisa often jokes that she has never seen me more alive than when I watched *Tiger Zinda Hai*—screaming, clapping and completely unhinged in the best possible way. And she's probably right.

People often ask me why I chose this beat of journalism. Fourteen years on, I think it's because I'm still that person in the crowd, waiting to shriek at the hero's entry. Nothing makes me happier than cheering in a movie hall. This book is written for people like me—those who will never get over the thrill of first-day-first-shows.

After my editor Bushra Ahmed and I published our last book, we were asked, 'What next?' We had discussed the idea of a Salman Khan fan book earlier as well, but this time we decided to go for it, fully aware of the inevitable hiccups that would come along the way. How do you condense the life of a man as dissected as him into about a few hundred pages? And then there are his fans—colourful, opinionated and gloriously feisty, but much like him, not exactly eager to chat with the press. Coaxing and cajoling them to talk has been the biggest hurdle while writing this book. But thanks to them, I've had a blast. They sent me on a rewatch spree of some of the most eclectic films of our growing-up years, making me laugh harder than I have in a long time.

As we send this to press, I can tell you this has been a challenging project. None of these ambitious experiments would be half as fun without my editor, Bushra, who made sure my rambling (and overwriting) turned into a manuscript. Collaborating with her remains one of the greatest joys of my work life. Thank you to the wonderful people at HarperCollins India—Ujjaini Dasgupta, Shabnam Srivastava, Poulomi Chatterjee, Ananth Padmanabhan, Rahul Dixit and everyone else who helped this see the light of day.

Thank you to my wonderful boss, Mayank Shekhar, and my entire team at *Mid-day*. I wrote this book for the OG Salman fan—my ex-colleague and dear friend Sonil Dedhia. No one loves Salman Khan like he does. Caramel popcorn waits for us, Dedhia.

Thank you to Prathamesh Bandekar, who opened up his father's library of beautiful pictures for us. And thank you, Pradeep Dada—we have missed you every day while working on this.

This book is a gift to my favourite girl, Debanjana, who has always been Team Salman through every high and low. Thank you to my friends Shamik, Rudrani, Tushar, Purvaja, Garvita, Prerona, Pratishtha, Devki, Aastha, Zora, Manav, Kashyap, Raghav, Shadan, Siddhi, Ebrahim and Murtuza. Without them, I'd be an empty person.

But mostly, a big thank you to my mother, who tolerates my angry rants and late-night phone calls, who often says the wrong things but always reminds me to work hard.

Notes

Scan this QR code to access the detailed notes.

About the Author

Mohar Basu is the Chief Correspondent (Entertainment) at *Mid-day*. She has also worked as a film critic at Koimoi.com and reviewed movies for *The Times of India*. Her work focuses on the dynamics of the Hindi film industry. Her stories include coverage of censorship in movies and OTT platforms, a news series on the 2016 ban on Pakistani actors in India and their eventual return with the rebirth of Zee Zindagi in 2020, and in-depth reporting on the systemic culture of sexual harassment in Bollywood, among others. Basu's reporting has contributed to industry changes, such as the creation of safe spaces at casting agencies and talent management companies. In 2024, she was recognized by the Indian Achiever's Club in their '40 under 40' list for her piece on the toxic nature of the Indian paparazzi and the rising tide of vitriol on social media. She has previously authored *Shah Rukh Khan*, published by HarperCollins in 2024.

 HarperCollins *Publishers* India

At HarperCollins India, we believe in telling the best stories and finding the widest readership for our books in every format possible. We started publishing in 1992; a great deal has changed since then, but what has remained constant is the passion with which our authors write their books, the love with which readers receive them, and the sheer joy and excitement that we as publishers feel in being a part of the publishing process.

Over the years, we've had the pleasure of publishing some of the finest writing from the subcontinent and around the world, including several award-winning titles and some of the biggest bestsellers in India's publishing history. But nothing has meant more to us than the fact that millions of people have read the books we published, and that somewhere, a book of ours might have made a difference.

As we look to the future, we go back to that one word— a word which has been a driving force for us all these years.

Read.

Harper Collins

HARPER FICTION

HARPER NON-FICTION

HARPER BUSINESS

HARPERCOLLINS CHILDREN'S BOOKS

HARPER DESIGN

Harper Sport

HARPER PERENNIAL

HARPER VANTAGE

हार्पर हिन्दी

BOOKTOPUS